# Intrusion Detection

## An Introduction to Internet Surveillance, Correlation, Traps, Trace Back, and Response

Edward G. Amoroso
AT&T Laboratories

First Edition

Intrusion.Net Books

# Intrusion Detection: An Introduction to Internet Surveillance, Correlation, Traps, Trace Back, and Response

By Edward G. Amoroso, AT&T Laboratories

 AT&T

Copyright © 1999, by AT&T, Inc. All rights reserved.

Published by Intrusion.Net Books, P.O. Box 78, Sparta, New Jersey 07871
http://www.intrusion.net/

First Edition, First Printing: January, 1999
Second Printing: June, 1999 - Minor Corrections
Printed in the United States of America

ISBN 0-9666700-7-8

```
Publisher's Cataloging-in-Publication
(Provided by Quality Books, Inc.)

Amoroso, Edward, G.
     Intrusion detection : an introduction to Internet
  surveillance, correlation, traps, trace-back, and response
  / Edward G. Amoroso. - 1st ed.
    p. cm.
    Includes bibliographical references and index.
    ISBN: 0-9666700-7-8

    1. Computer networks—Security measures. 2. Internet
  (Computer network)—Security measures. 3. Computer
  security.  I. Title.

  TK5105.59.A47 1999                          005.8

                    QBI98-1073
```

For book ordering and volume discount visit the Intrusion.Net Books Web page at http://www.intrusion.net/, call us at (973) 448-1866, or fax us at (973) 448-1868.

This book is dedicated to the fine and outstanding technical staff on the "C" and "TG" projects at the Information Security Center of AT&T Laboratories.

**About the Author**:

**Dr. Edward Amoroso** is presently the Chief Technical Officer in the Information Security Center at AT&T Laboratories in Florham Park, New Jersey where he is responsible for various Internet security research, development, and engineering projects for commercial, government, international, and AT&T groups. His areas of interest include intrusion detection, Intranet perimeter protection, public key infrastructure (PKI) design, mathematical security policy modeling, firewall and router configuration, and system security engineering. He has been with AT&T since 1985.

In addition to his position at AT&T Laboratories, Ed holds adjunct faculty positions in the graduate computer science department at the Stevens Institute in Hoboken, New Jersey as well as the graduate software engineering department at Monmouth University in West Long Branch, New Jersey. During the past decade, nearly a thousand students have taken his Internet security, introductory cryptography, and intrusion detection courses. Many students have changed their careers to security as a result of their experiences in one of the courses.

Ed's publications include nearly three dozen security research and technical articles for journals, conferences, and magazines. His first book *Fundamentals of Computer Security Technology* (Prentice-Hall, 1994) remains in print and continues to serve as a text for many introductory computer security courses. His second book *PCWeek Intranet and Internet Firewall Strategies*, with Ron Sharp (Ziff-Davis, 1996) also remains in print and has been translated into Dutch, Japanese, and Spanish. Ed's third book on intrusion detection is the result of two years of research and development in this area.

Ed is a frequent lecturer around the world on topics related to system, network, and Internet security. He was recently sworn in as an Internet security consultant to the Social Security Administration and has testified before many committees and panels in Washington and elsewhere. He is a proud, long standing member of the IEEE, ACM, and Internet Society and serves as an advisory editor for *Network Security* (Elsevier Publications).

Ed can be reached by readers at eamoroso@att.com. He looks forward to hearing from you.

# TABLE OF CONTENTS

**Chapter Three: Intrusion Detection Architecture**

**Chapter Four: Models of Intrusion**

**Chapter Eight: Incident Response**

# PREFACE

## HOW DID THIS BOOK COME ABOUT?

I've wanted to write this book for a long time. Back in the late 1980's, I observed with fascination as members of my department at AT&T tried to create a security management service called ComputerWatch. It involved pulling remote audit feeds from various customers and performing analysis, correlation, and processing to determine if security vulnerabilities existed. This service was amazingly ahead of its time. It predates the regular outsourcing of security scanning that is so common in today's networking environments. I still proudly wear my ComputerWatch sweatshirt, although I doubt that many people have any idea what it means.

I remember dreaming of the myriad of possibilities that such a service opened for AT&T customers. And to my surprise, I recently found an old piece of a manuscript (shoved under some product brochures) that I wrote sometime around 1990 or so. It consists of twenty or so pages of thoughts on what might be possible for a security and intrusion processing service. Here is a direct quote from these lost notes:

> If customers would be willing to share an entire feed, then the potential for statistical processing in a centralized operations center would be great. I'll bet this could open new directions in intrusion detection services. We could correlate information, look for known patterns of attack, and maybe even profile behavior across a series of customers.

Since then, of course, intrusion detection has become somewhat stymied in research objectives far removed from any real network service requirements I've ever seen. Most of the reports available focus on trying to increase the statistical likelihood that a needle can be found in a haystack. In fact, the intrusion detection community has become so mired in what it cannot do, that it's forgotten what it *can* do. I find this focus disappointing because real network operations in service environments do not follow this paradigm and I've tried to address such technology shortcomings in my book.

The material for this book is based on a program of intense research and development in intrusion detection performed during the past couple of years at AT&T Laboratories. It is also based on an intrusion detection graduate seminar I teach each year at the Stevens Institute in Hoboken, New Jersey. The presentation of material has evolved through multiple iterations of technical discussion, thought, and presentation with my colleagues and students. I delayed publication until I thought the content was just right. It's taken me almost two full years of work.

I've kept the material in the book largely technical, as opposed to philosophical, legal, or policy-oriented, focusing on methods, algorithms, and architectures for performing intrusion detection in Internet environments. Brief case studies of different products, systems, or organizations are sprinkled liberally throughout the chapters to illustrate the general intrusion detection concepts. Over one hundred different drawings and pictures are also included to depict the various notions presented. Feedback from early reviewers and graduate students has been incorporated into the work—resulting, I believe, in a well-tested and used book. And to those of you who contributed to this, I offer my heartfelt thanks.

It was tempting to include lots of system administrative detail on how existing intrusion detection products are set up and used. For example, when the various intrusion detection vendors became aware of this project, I found myself deluged with boxes of detailed product information and marketing glossies. In fact, it's now apparent that a new industry for commercial intrusion detection systems has emerged and very little general material is available on how such products should be properly configured, operated, installed, and set-up. I reasoned that if I included this sort of material, I could easily produce a seven hundred page book. And the back cover would be pretty enticing as well: "Learn to *set-up*, *install*, and *configure* the XYZ, ABC, and 123 intrusion detection systems! Save hours of time and frustration!" I probably would have sold barrels of books.

In spite of the temptation to include such vendor-oriented system administrative information, I decided against it. You should know that these commercial intrusion detection systems are changing so rapidly—more so, I believe, than most other areas of computing and networking—that detailed descriptions would be out of date before the book was even printed. As an example, the company formerly known as the WheelGroup was purchased by Cisco Systems during the writing of this book. As a result of the purchase, the architecture plans and direction for the NetRanger product have changed dramatically. And they continue to change as I type these words.

By the way, reporting *change* is precisely what the World Wide Web is all about. In fact, for accurate, up-to-date information that may not have a great archival quality, you're advised to use the Web. Information that has been digested and presented in a manner that will hopefully have some shelf life, however, is best inserted into a book. So for those of you who expect to see books go away, I wouldn't hold your breath. I think we'll always have printed words on paper that you can hold in your hands.

I also can't resist mentioning here a review I remember seeing in one of the trade rags for my first book: *Fundamentals of Computer Security Technology* (Prentice-Hall, 1994). The reviewer criticized the book saying it had too much information and not enough quick fixes to problems. My publisher called it an off-hand remark, but I remember taking it as a high complement. In fact, I've tried to follow the same approach again here: *Lots of information and no quick fixes*. I think that's the best way to go.


## WHO IS THIS BOOK WRITTEN FOR?

I think this book will be of interest to anyone that wants to understand more about the topic of intrusion detection. This includes technical managers, system administrators, software engineers, network managers, and security officers. Some knowledge of computing and networking is assumed, but at least three non-technical colleagues of mine have gone through the material and survived. So virtually anyone with an interest in technology, computing,  or networking should enjoy the material.

But I have to warn you. While writing this book, the target audience I had in mind was my graduate student population at the Stevens Institute and Monmouth University. These students are typically full-time MS or Ph.D. track computer scientists or full-time software engineers, system engineers, developers, testers, or managers working in local government or industry labs. In short, they look very much like my colleagues at AT&T Laboratories. So if you are not a computer scientist, system administrator, system engineer, or programmer, then you may have some difficulty with some of the material. If you see something you don't understand, skip that section and read on.

I should mention that a new group of individuals has emerged in the computing community. They refer to themselves as *information warfare* or *information assurance* specialists. Some of these folks have considerable technical depth and they bring a new dimension to the cat and mouse game of network security. Others are so steeped in government policy and politics that they typically don't have time to delve into the technical details of intrusion detection. I suspect many information warriors and information assurance specialists will purchase this book simply because the topic is something they hear about all the time. I hope the book doesn't just sit on their shelf. I think the content inside may be of use to them in their important mission.

I also think law enforcers will find this book of interest. They have a tough job in the new communications environment and most people *really* want them to succeed in their critical job of maintaining law and order. One piece of advise I'd offer is that law enforcers need to learn—along with the rest of us—to differentiate between hackers and crackers. Hackers are focused on exploration and knowledge acquisition. Most of the people I work with learned UNIX by hacking, for example. Crackers, on the other hand, break laws. No one, including the hackers, condones cracking behavior, especially since the Web offers an infinity of resources for knowledge exploration and learning. You no longer have to break into systems to gain access to interesting information.

My further advice is that law enforcers may find that hackers can be one of the most powerful sources of useful guidance, learning, and partnership in the future. And I'm not talking about snitching; I'm talking about real technology sharing. Keep in mind that hackers share with law enforcers a common disdain for anyone breaking the law. This potential and ironic kinship between hackers and law enforcers may characterize the next few decades of law enforcement on the Internet. I hope it happens because it will be good for us all.

## ON RESPONSIBLE AND ETHICAL SURVEILLANCE

During the writing of this book, I became sensitized to the importance of surveillance only by responsible and ethical groups. If this is not the case, then individual liberties and basic privacy considerations will never be properly maintained. Examples of irresponsible or unethical behavior include businesses using surveillance to create marketing dossiers, governments doing illegal monitoring, crackers placing sniffers in backbone networks, or companies doing unfair data collection on their employees.

All of these types of surveillance have societal implications that need to be openly discussed and understood. Let me quote from Whitfield Diffie and Susan Landau in their recent book *Privacy on the Line* (MIT Press, 1998):

> We must consider the sort of world in which we want to live and what effects our actions will, indeed can, have in bringing about such a world. Such consideration depends on awareness of many factors, including technology of cryptography and electronic surveillance, the aims and practices of intelligence and law enforcement, and the history of society's attempts to deal with similar problems over more than a century.

So let me emphasize that the material in this book is intended for the purposes of defensive system design for those who have resources at risk. If you are trying to protect your Intranet or if you are trying to ensure some level of security protection for any of your resources from malicious invasion by crackers, then I think this book can help you.

By the way, please let me know of your experiences. I am very interested in any anecdotes, questions, or comments you might have concerning the application of this material to your real-life intrusion detection applications. And if there is any way in which I can help you with a problem you might have, then I will do my best to do so. You can reach me via email at eamoroso@mail.att.net. You can also use that email address to complain about the inevitable problems you will find in this book. I also expect to post an erratum of errors found by readers at the Intrusion.Net Web site at http://www.intrusion.net. You can also find information about future printings and editions of this book.

## OUTLINE OF THE BOOK

Chapter One provides an overview of the critical issues in intrusion detection. I guess if you had to read only one chapter, this would be the one. And if you are standing with this book at the copy machine, hopefully not infringing too blatantly on AT&T's copyright, then I guess this would be a good chapter to copy. If you are reading these words and happen to be one of my graduate students, then I strongly recommend that you read the other chapters as well. They will be on the midterm.

Chapter Two covers basic methods for intrusion detection. Audit trail analysis and on-the-fly processing techniques are the major areas of focus. Understanding these methods is prerequisite to understanding the rest of the chapters. I spent a lot of time on this chapter. I believe that this will be a major focus in intrusion detection in the future as vast data warehouses are created for security attack mining.

Chapter Three covers a generic architectural schema for intrusion detection. It was hard to come up with something general for this chapter, just as it might be hard to explain a general computer or network system architecture. It is nevertheless required for readers and students to follow the concepts in subsequent chapters. The Common Intrusion Detection Framework (CIDF) is included here.

Chapter Four covers topics related to intrusion and attack modeling. I tried to include some basic semantics for intrusions. As you might expect, if a system is going to detect intrusions, then a proper definition of intrusion is necessary. My original draft of this chapter got all caught up in semantics related to intrusions. It was a big mess. Now that it is completely rewritten, however, I think it's much better.

Chapter Five covers techniques for promoting or tracing identity and anonymity. This was a fun chapter to research and write. It strikes me as being central to the intrusion detection challenge in spite of being ignored by so many researchers.

Chapter Six is on correlation. I was amazed that a problem so important to intrusion detection is so under-examined in the literature. I think the network management community is much further along in correlation tools than the security community. Most of the algorithms in this chapter are high-level, but they provide a start for intrusion detection system designers trying to make sense of this problem. I should also say that during the writing of this chapter, I was reminded how boring statistical analysis textbooks can be. I'm not sure how I ever got through all that stuff in college and graduate school. There is some beauty in the mathematics—you just have to look carefully.

Chapter Seven is on traps and honey pots. This was also a fun chapter to write, and I think many new concepts are introduced here. My graduate students are really into this topic and I have quite a few projects on-going at AT&T Laboratories in this area. I think this is the future of law enforcement on the Internet. I can see some of you grimacing at the thought.

Chapter Eight is on incident response. This topic is usually considered pretty dry. I found it fascinating and I hope this seeped into the presentation. Knowing what to do after an intrusion has been suspected or detected is important. Anyone running a real Internet service knows this and can probably share some pretty scary incident response stories with you.

The Annotated Bibliography contains mostly books and articles with my subjective reviews or comments on the content. When I started this book a year ago, there was much less to read on this topic than there is now (which is a good sign). When I thought some World Wide Web or Internet resource was useful, I shoved the reference into the text or the bibliographic notes at the end of that chapter rather than into the bibliography. This seemed more natural than including a bunch of URLs in the bibliography, although I guess I did include a few in there somewhere.

## ACKNOWLEDGEMENTS

I'd like to start by thanking the students of CS668 at the Stevens Institute. They challenge my lectures, work hard on projects, surf the Net looking for things that are relevant to intrusion detection, and are just a delight to work with. I hope you all get very high paying jobs when you graduate. When I planned the first intrusion detection seminar in 1997, I asked the registrar at Stevens to limit attendance to five. By the second lecture, we had over thirty bodies in the room. In spite of this overwhelming size, I'm glad to have interacted with each and every one of them, and I look forward to the next batch of you. I'd also like to thank the students in my regular Internet security classes at Stevens and at Monmouth University. You've also contributed to my overall appreciation of this topic.

Next, I must thank my colleagues in the Information Security Center at AT&T Laboratories. Your collective experience in security technology and intrusion detection is so extensive that I find it a pleasure to come to work each day. I'm continually amazed at your ability to solve problems in this area and I find myself beaming with pride when your successful work is demonstrated to our customers. My management at AT&T has also been supportive of my various attempts to get books written. They deserve a nod if only for putting up with my incessant whining about one thing or another.

Other friends and colleagues who have offered particularly useful help and insights into intrusion detection over the years include Pat Bastien, Mark Bennett, Susanne Best, Wali Beyah, Dick Brackney, Ike Cole, Tony Cira, Tom Curtis, Steve DeGeorge, Osmund Desouza, Steve Eisen, Corta Etheredge, Davis Flaus, Chuck Flink, Pat Fox, Sunita Gaer, Jim Gleason, Dan Goddard, Eric Gore, Eric Hewins, Kurt Hockenbury, Eugene Kogan, Li Hsu, Tim Hurr, Kevin Kealy, John Kevan, Eugene Kogan, Kevin Kooy, Kim Kotlar, Rick Kwapniewski, Teresa Lunt, Joe Massi, Rich Mayer, Brenda McAnderson, Jean McCarthy, Mary Jane McKeever, Bob Meushaw, Erv Morton, Larry Nelson, Bill Nitsch, Bill Oeschger, Barnaby Page, Joe Pepin, Andrew Peters, Steve Phillips, Ana Pinczuk, Dan Powell, Paul Ramstedt, Marcus Ranum, Brian Rexroad, Burl Ryding, Mike Salicio, Karen Salvo, Sami Saydjari, Fred Schmidt, Steve Schuster, Mark Schwartz, Pete Sell, Phil Sikora, Dave Singel,

Wayne Smith, Duncan Sparrell, Larry Spilman, Anthony Stramaglia, Lee Sutterfield, Dan Teal, Tony Triolo, Pat Wall, and Brien Weissenborn.

Last, but not least, I want to thank my wife Lee for putting up with so many late nights of writing. She never complained—not once. Stephanie (5 years old) and Matthew (3 years old) are the greatest kids in the world and were nice enough to get to bed every night by at least midnight so I could do some writing. And as usual, a long walk with Scrappy inevitably produced more good ideas than weeks in the lab.

E.A.

Andover, New Jersey

eamoroso@att.com

# CHAPTER 1:
## INTRODUCTION TO INTRUSION DETECTION

*Most existing systems have security flaws that render them susceptible to intrusions, penetrations, and other forms of abuse.*

Dorothy Denning

*Even with the best security mechanisms, we must expect that a determined adversary will be able to penetrate our defenses. This is especially true of the potential information warfare adversaries of concern to DoD.*

Teresa Lunt

### WHAT IS INTRUSION DETECTION?

As with most new technologies, intrusion detection has come to mean different things to different people. We have seen the term used, for example, to describe audit trail processing, firewall filtering and logging, router-based access list usage, telephony-based toll fraud detection, operating system probes and monitors, camera surveillance at gates and fences, and even physical surveillance by law enforcers. Each of these perspectives on intrusion detection is essentially accurate, but such disparate definitions make it much more difficult to understand this new security technology for information assurance in computing and networking environments. To illustrate this problem, let's consider the following scenarios:

- You ask your network service provider about an intrusion detection product advertised on their Web site. But the information they send you describes a toll fraud prevention system for a private branch exchange (PBX)—and you don't even have one!
- At a conference, you ask a famous network security researcher about their recent advances in Internet intrusion detection. You are then treated to a complex lecture on the mathematical foundations of statistical processing, Bayesian analysis, and Markovian transitions (whatever *they* are).
- You ask your local network system administrator about how intrusion detection is used in your infrastructure. What you get is a description of how the gateway firewall filters traffic based on internet protocol (IP) address, network service information, and universal resource locator (URL). You will probably also learn that these filtering decisions were made arbitrarily, rather than based on a well-defined security policy.
- You go to a lecture on intrusion detection at a security conference and the speaker talks in general terms about how intrusion detection systems are now being used successfully to catch lots of hackers and crackers doing illegal things. When asked to substantiate this wild claim with some practical examples, the speaker can offer nothing.
- You purchase an intrusion detection system for fifty-thousand bucks and are disappointed to find that most of the really serious attacks that you were worried about for your Intranet about are not addressed by the product. To make matters worse, the

intrusion detection system vendor tells you that while they *are* currently considering some enhanced solutions, nothing should be expected in the near term.

All of these disparate scenarios contribute to a general misunderstanding of intrusion detection in the computing and networking community. Even information available on the Internet may be somewhat misleading. Performing a search for the terms 'intrusion detection' or 'hacker detection', for instance, will uncover a variety of different documents— some helpful, and some not so helpful. Try it.

---

*Search Engines You Probably Already Know About*

If you've been in a cave or in jail for the past few years and have never used a search engine, then some good ones that will help you find information on intrusion detection include the following:

- http://www.altavista.digital.com/  ⇦ very thorough
- http://www.excite.com/
- http://www.hotbot.com/
- http://www.infoseek.com/
- http://www.lycos.com/
- http://www.yahoo.com/  ⇦ well-structured approach

---

In this book, one of our goals is to introduce a common framework for the topic of intrusion detection. This is certainly not a new goal. A group sponsored by the United States Department of Defense Advanced Research Projects Agency (DARPA), for example, is currently trying to create a framework called the Common Intrusion Detection Framework (CIDF) for message interoperability among multiple intrusion detection systems (this is described in Chapter 3). Their effort is particularly encouraging, as it demonstrates the importance of commonality in this emerging discipline of intrusion detection. You should keep both DARPA (nee ARPA) and the CIDF in mind as you work your way through this book. Both are playing an important role in the emergence of intrusion detection as a legitimate discipline.

Since this book is based primarily on a series of graduate school lectures, the focus is inevitably on underlying principles. Our emphasis is on how a basic understanding of such intrusion detection principles provides a means for cutting through all the confusion rendered by vendors, researchers, and managers. In spite of this, however, the technical discussions and examples in the book arise *not* from academia but from practical day-to-day design, development, administration, analysis, integration, and support of real intrusion detection systems in practical network environments. This combination of academic principles with practical experience should provide a treatment suitable for most readers.

We are ready now for the first of several definitions that we will introduce throughout the book:

---

*Definition of Intrusion Detection*

*Intrusion detection* is the <u>process</u> of <u>identifying</u> and <u>responding</u> to <u>malicious activity</u> targeted at <u>computing and networking resources</u>.

---

It is instructive to isolate and examine in turn the underlined words and phrases from the definition shown in the box above. This sounds a bit tedious, but the reader is encouraged to go through this section carefully, as it will help avoid common misunderstandings. Try to think of this sort of thing as the calisthenics that will make you stronger in the topic of intrusion detection (spoken like a typical professor).

*"Process"*. Intrusion detection should be viewed first and foremost as a process—one that involves technology, people, and tools. This is important because processes involve time and interaction between entities, and many of the hard problems in intrusion detection will stem from this inherent interaction. This emphasis on process also illustrates that intrusion detection will never be implemented in a plug-and-play black box solution. People will always be involved in the process.

*"Identifying"*. This identification of an intrusion can be done before, during, or after the target malicious activity proceeds. If the identification is done before the activity proceeds, then the activity might be prevented and any potentially damaged assets might be salvaged. If the identification is done during the occurrence of the malicious activity, then decisions must be made about whether to allow target activity to proceed and whether to create alarms (which might alert the attacker). Finally, if the identification of an intrusion is done after the malicious activity completes, then questions of what damage might have been done and how such actions could have occurred must be addressed.

*"Responding"*. As you might expect, response to an intrusion usually follows identification of the intrusion because you can't respond to something that hasn't been identified (the exception is an environments in which predictive analysis is used to guess that something *might* be happening and to initiate response as a result). Some considerations that must be addressed in the response process include whether the response should terminate service, whether the response is targeted at catching the attacker, and whether the response includes counterattacks, as in an information warfare context.

*"Malicious activity"*. Malicious activity refers to security-relevant actions by people who intend to do harm. Rows and rows of shelves at your local technical bookstore are filled with books that try to provide an understanding of these security-relevant actions.

---

*A Note on Malicious Intent*

If you're new to network security, then think for a moment about the potential danger of malicious behavior. Imagine, for instance, that a system has a one-in-a-million chance of serious failure ("the conditions have to be just right," the reliability report concludes). This is comforting, until you realize that an attacker might *establish* these one-in-a-million conditions. The failure potential is thus very high and depends on the whim of the attacker. (Not very comforting news for the flying public.)

---

For the purposes of intrusion detection, you should keep in mind that bad things can happen to assets whenever vulnerabilities (perhaps better described as errors) are exploited by malicious individuals and groups. Intrusion detection systems are supposed to pick up on this.

*"Computing and networking resources"*. This is a subtle but important point. In truth, the basic principles covered in this text are derived from a variety of sources, many of them having little or nothing to do with computing and networking resources. Furthermore, these principles can be applied to many types of protection systems; for instance, criminal safecrackers and Internet crackers share a kindred spirit not often obvious because they live in such different worlds—unless, of course, they share a jail cell.

The discussions in this book maintain consistency with the above definition, and intrusion detection is presumed to encompass the relevant technology, tools, procedures, and policies used to detect malicious activity in computers and networks. It will also be important to keep in mind that although the target of a malicious intruder may be a computing or networking resource, not all of the actions involved in the intrusion have to involve computers or networks. The implications of this observation are often dramatic.

## WHAT ANALOGIES ARE USEFUL FOR UNDERSTANDING INTRUSION DETECTION SYSTEMS?

We have found in our lecturing on intrusion detection that the following analogies help in an understanding of what intrusion detection systems are supposed to be doing:

- Network managers using tools such as Simple Network Management Protocol (SNMP)-based management tools are comfortable with the notion of getting information from a remote device and pulling it into a common framework for analysis. Intrusion detection systems often follow this paradigm.

- Users of telephony (pretty much everyone) and credit cards (pretty much everyone here, too) are becoming more familiar and comfortable with service providers monitoring usage for the purpose of detecting fraudulent use. For example, if you've never called Malaysia and then suddenly one evening your phone number originates a flood of calls to Malaysia, then your telephony service provider will probably contact you to tell you that you've been cracked. They do this using profiles and algorithms very much like the ones used in intrusion detection systems.

- Sometimes when you're driving down the road, perhaps on your normal commute into work, you notice that something is not normal. Maybe it's the general speed of the vehicles in front of you or maybe it's the traffic pattern. Whatever the reason, we've all experienced this feeling that the traffic is not right, and such a feeling usually serves as an early warning or indicator that an accident is ahead. It also may serve as a indictor that it is a Sunday morning and that the pattern is different because people are not rushing to work.

- In our everyday life, we frequently encounter physical surveillance cameras that are watching our movement. Such physical surveillance cameras provide a particularly useful analogy because so many of us have experienced the welcome feeling when such surveillance exists for our protection in dangerous areas (e.g., a lonely subway platform late at night). At the same time, however, most of us have also experienced the feeling of being self-conscious—or even annoyed—that we are being watched by such surveillance cameras.

This particular analogy of surveillance camera is so useful that we should examine some features of such cameras to illustrate certain key requirements for intrusion detection systems:

*Constant vigilance.* One goal of a surveillance camera is constant and vigilant watchfulness. Without such vigilance, the potential for missing critical information is great. A recent and well-publicized use of surveillance cameras involves working parents who are suspicious of their baby sitters. Obviously, for this type of surveillance to work properly, the camera must be in constant watch for the duration of the baby sitter's involvement with the child. As you will see, the same type of constant vigilance is often, but not always, true for intrusion detection systems.

*Stealth design.* Intrusion detection systems, like good surveillance cameras, often require that they be hidden. In fact, many readers may have already presumed that intrusion detection systems *must* be stealth. We've seen surveillance cameras inserted into smoke detectors, clocks, speakers, telephones, exit signs, emergency lights, and white boards. Intrusion detection systems often, but not always, must be inserted covertly into an unexpected component of some computing environment. (Question: When should an intrusion detection system not be stealth? Answer: Read on.)

---

*Web Site for Budding Spies*

Visit the Web site at http://www.starlink-dss.com/spy.html for an intriguing catalogue of hidden surveillance cameras. Their stuff looks very cool, but you'd better be careful before using them to spy on your babysitter. I believe that a phone call to a knowledgeable attorney would be very prudent before you do anything like this, even if you just want to experiment.

---

*Infrastructure.* The camera analogy also highlights the need for a well-designed infrastructure behind the surveillance system. If, for example, a surveillance camera is capturing images that no one is bothering to examine, then the surveillance may be a waste of time. An application that has received some attention recently on the Internet involves the use of cameras on roadways to detect traffic patterns, enforce toll collection, and monitor traffic law compliance. In California, for example, 180 surveillance cameras in the Oakland area feed an extensive Traffic Operations System infrastructure. Similarly, a so-called Nerve Center is located in San Jose to monitor feeds from 18 cameras located on 40-foot poles throughout the city. What is interesting about the San Jose experience is that the cameras are also being used to detect "suspicious characters." (Hmmm.)

*Adversary belief.* The camera analogy also highlights the importance of making one's adversary believe that the surveillance is *real*. We've all seen, for instance, those dummy cameras in convenience stores and card shops. These unconvincing devices do little to deter crimes by even the most timid thief. Believability, however, requires balance with the potential stealth design of a surveillance system; obviously, if we want an adversary to believe they are being watched, then stealth design may not be desired (by the way, this is the answer to the question posed earlier). Such non-stealth design is an interesting point. In fact, to my knowledge, no intrusion detection vendors currently note the *non*-stealth aspects of their systems. This is especially surprising because most home surveillance and protection systems come with stickers that are considered as valuable to the buyer as the system itself. Here's what the electronic sticker might be: "Warning: This site is protected by XYZ intrusion detection. Go crack someone else."

We have to be careful with our surveillance camera analogy, because intrusion detection systems are obviously much more complex than simple physical surveillance cameras. Intrusion detection systems must deal with intrusive computing actions that can be orders of magnitude more complex than normal human actions. Consider, for example, that human real time activity may involve handfuls of actions in times counted by minutes or hours. Computers, on the other hand, generate many millions of actions in times counted by seconds or even less.

As a result, the algorithms for differentiating between normal and abnormal computing activity can be quite complex. Intrusion detection systems also involve processing and storage requirements that can be significant if the target environment involves great volumes of network or computing capacity. Furthermore, they can require interoperability and plug-compatibility with a variety of different systems that may have nothing to do with intrusion detection.

## WHAT IS THE BASIC CONCEPT IN INTRUSION DETECTION?

The basic intrusion detection concept can be depicted with relative ease. Such straightforward depiction may be misleading however, as we will show throughout the book, because the practical implementation of this basic concept is anything but simple. We've found in our lecturing that the topic of intrusion detection can be introduced by the following picture:

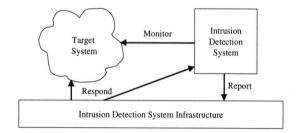

**Figure 1-1**. Simple Depiction of Intrusion Detection Concept

The diagram in Figure 1-1 introduces three critical functions in the basic intrusion detection concept:

*Monitor*. Intrusion detection systems examine and process information about target system activity. Many technical and operational issues arise in this monitoring function including timeliness of detection, confidence in information obtained, and processing power required to keep up with monitored activity. The degree to which these factors are properly handled will determine how successfully the intrusion detection system can detect actual intrusions. Keep this notion of monitoring prominently in mind as you go through the material in this book.

*Report*. Intrusion detection systems report information about monitored systems into a system security and protection infrastructure. This infrastructure can be embedded in the intrusion monitoring component or can be done separately. In either case, the manner in which derived information about an intrusion is processed, stored, protected, shared, and used as the basis for risk mitigation is the most challenging aspect of practical intrusion detection.

*Respond*. The purpose of intrusion detection—ultimately—is to reduce security risk. When risk-related information is made available by the intrusion detection system, an associated response function initiates mitigation activities. Response actions introduce a myriad of factors related to the timeliness and appropriateness of the activities initiated by the intrusion detection system to deal with an incident. As should become evident through the pages of this book, response is an extremely challenging process that requires attention to many technical and non-technical issues.

It's worth mentioning that the simplistic drawing in Figure 1-1 often suggests a rather mundane function for intrusion detection systems—a comment made by more than one of my graduate students. Fortunately, as we will show throughout this book, intrusion detection is one of those rare topics that becomes more fascinating as one considers the topic in more detail. This may explain the growing emphasis on this technology in research and engineering circles.

Furthermore, the depth of interest in this topic of intrusion detection is equally rich in the areas of monitoring, reporting, and response. In fact, we believe that the issues raised in this book merely scratch the surface of interesting and important technical challenges that exist in the emerging field of intrusion detection. The next few years promise to be exciting ones for intrusion detection enthusiasts, particularly as results begin to emerge in environments using the technology to protect real infrastructures.

## SEVEN FUNDAMENTAL ISSUES IN INTRUSION DETECTION

Seven fundamental issues in intrusion detection are proposed and discussed briefly below. We use these seven issues as a framework for the organization of the remaining chapters of this book. In at least a couple of different cases, certain issues actually combine a collection of different concepts together. So this partition into seven classes is somewhat arbitrary. It does offer, however, a useful means for structuring our discussions.

## ISSUE 1: WHAT METHODS ARE USED BY INTRUSION DETECTION SYSTEMS?

Obviously, different intrusion detection systems will employ different methods. This is true in currently available products and should continue in the future. We believe that as intrusion detection becomes a more attractive product option, particularly for major workstation, server, switch, firewall, and router vendors, differentiation of methods will be an important selling and marketing point. This is already happening. Just scan some of the marketing and advertising literature available for intrusion detection products. You will find that some product vendors tout their audit trail processing capability, whereas others tout their on-the-fly processing capability. Different intrusion detection methods are also prevalent in the various research intrusion detection systems that are being reported in the security conferences. Some focus on graph-oriented processing techniques, others focus on statistical correlation, and so on.

In spite of this difference in various products and systems, we *can* identify a collection of common methods that are generally present on a given intrusion detection system. These methods will be examined in detail in Chapter 2. As a preview here, we briefly outline high-level aspects of these methods. Note that these methods are neither mutually exclusive nor mutually dependent. Instead they comprise a collection of security protection strategies that are available to the intrusion detection system designer for use in a given product.

*Audit trail processing.* The method of processing an audit trail may be the most commonly used intrusion detection technique. This was certainly the first application of intrusion detection that emerged in the community and it is likely to remain important in the future. Figure 1-2 depicts a high-level view of the audit trail processing method of intrusion detection.

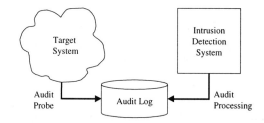

**Figure 1-2**. High-Level Depiction of Audit Trail Processing Method

The idea in audit trail processing is that an existing log is available for parsing and interpretation by an intrusion detection system. This method is typically performed off-line and rarely involves any real-time analysis. Such processing introduces issues of audit trail formats, storage techniques, archival policies, and real time auditing standards. It also raises issues in an intrusion-processing center of the manual processes required by human beings involved in the audit trail processing, particularly for archived data. Unfortunately, the security community has been negligent in the area of developing standard formats and techniques for audit trails.

Note that in current Internet and Intranet environments, audit trail information is readily available from operating systems (e.g., UNIX *syslog*), network systems, routers, firewalls, switches, applications, and other components. As a result, in many environments, the desire to perform intrusion detection via audit trail analysis is great because the data is already being collected. It's worth noting, however, that very few environments exist where audit data is properly collected, stored, and protected. The enormous volume of audit data generated in a typical environment doesn't help matters.

*On-the-fly processing*. This method, sometimes called network intrusion detection, involves the monitoring of traffic so that real-time or near real-time analysis can be done with respect to appropriate detection algorithms. Specified strings of characters are often used in this method as a means for parsing traffic for so-called "dirty words". These dirty words might include '/etc/passwd', '/etc/shadow', or other sequences one might consider suspicious to be passing through an intrusion detection system.

---

*Why is '/etc/passwd' Considered a Dirty Word?*
Suppose that an intrusion detection system exists between two networks in which no valid transactions exist involving password files—the password file on a UNIX system is traditionally located in the /etc directory and is called passwd. In this case, the strings '/etc/shadow' (used to hide passwords) and '/etc/passwd' that define the password files might be interpreted as dirty words if they traverse these networks. On Windows NT, a file called SAM contains passwords and is located in the '\\WINNT\SYSTEM32\CONFIG' directory. So these strings might be worth looking for as well.

---

The on-the-fly method complements audit trail processing in the most effective intrusion detection environments. Both techniques have the capability to detect a given intrusion, but the method of detection will differ in each case as will the information used for processing. Figure 1-3 depicts a high-level view of the on-the-fly processing method.

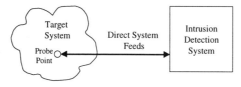

**Figure 1-3**. High-Level Depiction of On-the-Fly Processing Method

One point worth highlighting with respect to the on-the-fly method is that it requires access to network traffic. Packets that pass through the target of the intrusion detection system are typically sniffed and passed to the on-the-fly system for real-time analysis. As more Intranet environments are designed around gateway choke points with routers and firewalls, this often provides the type of network access required. One should expect on-the-fly intrusion detection systems, router processing, and firewall processing methods to be integrated more closely by vendors for this reason. The recent acquisition of the WheelGroup by Cisco Systems would certainly suggest that this might be true for at least one major vendor.

*Profiles of normal behavior.* Profiles of normal behavior are used in intrusion detection to capture expectations about user and system computing and networking activity. This follows the basic paradigm of comparing expectations about behavior with actual observations. The creation of such profiles involves at least the following three basic concerns—it involves much more, but these are the big ones.

- *Estimation of Initial Profiles.* Initial profiling for new users and systems requires estimation of expected behavior. Such estimation is nontrivial and makes profiling vulnerable to malicious teaching approaches by intruders (i.e., by altering initial behavior to set-up an intrusion profile to support a subsequent attack). One way to deal with such initial profiling problems is to maintain a stealth intrusion detection system so that new users are not aware that their behavior is being profiled. This raises all sorts of legal, ethical, and organizational policy issues that may make such a method unacceptable. This initial state problem may become less serious as more empirical evidence emerges for a given monitored environment.

- *Fine-Tuning of Profiles.* Observed user and system behavior provides a basis for fine-tuning existing profiles. Proper fine-tuning is also nontrivial, as it requires attention to statistical concerns about probability of occurrences and regularity of events. In the best case, fine-tuning would be automated, but manual techniques must be developed for this before such automation can be considered trusted. This fine-tuning is also vulnerable to malicious teaching approaches by profiled users or systems.

- *Profiling Using All-Source Information.* Information should be used from any relevant source to more accurately predict expected behavior. These sources do not have to be based on computing or networking information. In fact, some of the most powerful profiling information is derived from sources that are out of band with respect to any computer or network (e.g., personal characteristics and habits).

These intrusion detection system profiling concerns are depicted in the diagram in Figure 1-4.

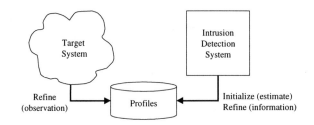

**Figure 1-4**. Intrusion Detection Profiling Method

As we will show in more detail in Chapter 2, the profiling approach is one of the most mature intrusion detection methods available, primarily because it is used extensively in telephony-based service provision environments. Techniques for toll fraud mitigation by service providers, a topic mentioned earlier in the chapter, is an example of a stable application of this method that has been used successfully to mitigate security risk.

*Signatures of abnormal behavior.* The use of abnormal behavioral signatures, also called attack signatures in some security books and research articles, is particularly common in on-the-fly intrusion detection systems. These abnormal behavior signatures generally come in one of two different flavors:

- *Known Attack Descriptions.* Dynamic descriptions of related activity patterns that might constitute a security problem. These descriptions of known attacks are often referred to as attack signatures. Databases of these descriptions are reminiscent of virus databases in virus detection software.
- *Suspicious String Patterns.* Designated character strings (like '/etc/shadow', 'top secret', or 'proprietary') that correspond to traffic content that must be considered suspicious. These are often determined locally by security administrators.

The use of abnormal behavior signatures for intrusion detection is depicted in Figure 1-5.

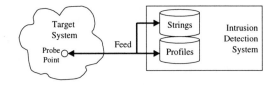

**Figure 1-5**. Abnormal Behavior Signature Method

The greatest challenge in abnormal behavior signatures is that the intrusion detection system must have advance knowledge of the attack to be detected. As any Internet security expert will attest, new attack methods are invented every day, and intrusion detection systems relying solely on this method will always, by definition, be slightly out of date. Users of virus detection software should be familiar with this basic problem. Very few of us have the patience and resolve to ensure that our virus checking software is always up-to-date with the latest viruses. Abnormal behavior signature checking methods will be vulnerable to this as well.

---

*Threats, Vulnerabilities, and Attacks in a Nutshell*

*Security threats* include disclosure, change, blocking, or theft of resources. They are possible because systems have *vulnerabilities*. Intruders exploit vulnerabilities through sequences of actions called *attacks*. Unfortunately, there is an infinity of different attacks and many intrusion detection systems only target a tiny subset of the most common such attacks. This is a *very big* problem for vendors relying on attack databases. The databases will never be completely accurate. By the way, this is why expert system security engineers base their analyses on threats rather than attacks.

---

*Parameter pattern matching.* This method involves the use of day-to-day operational experience as the basis for detecting anomalies. From a logical perspective, this method can be viewed as a special case of the normal profiling method. It is separated out here because the explicit development of user and system security profiles may not be included in the approach. Instead, operators doing normal system and network management activity might, or might not, detect some sort of change in the parameters they typically monitor—hence our use of the pattern matching term for this method. Actually, one of the more attractive characteristics of this method is that the administrators are not specifically targeting security issues. This introduces a more robust environment in which anomalies and patterns might be detected and matched.

Such pattern matching constitutes an especially powerful processing approach because it provides an intrusion detection capability for attacks that might not be predictable. In fact, human operators in a network operations center might detect subtle changes as part of their normal security and network management operations that they can neither explain nor understand. It is these types of unpredictable changes, however, that could lead to detection of a problem. A high-level view of the method is depicted in Figure 1-6.

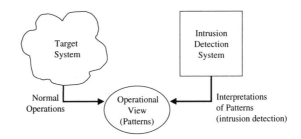

**Figure 1-6**. Pattern Matching Method of Intrusion Detection

Recall from earlier comments that our approach in this chapter is to introduce each of the seven fundamental issues in intrusion detection at a high level. In subsequent chapters, we delve into the technical detail and address more subtle research and development problems and potential solutions for each of the seven issues. Thus, if you have specific questions about any of the material posed in the chapter to this point, or in subsequent sections, remember that later chapters re-address these issues in more technical detail.

## ISSUE 2: HOW ARE INTRUSION DETECTION SYSTEMS ORGANIZED?

A second fundamental issue in intrusion detection involves the identification of basic components in an intrusion detection system and how they are interconnected and organized into a coherent architecture. As was the case in the methods employed by intrusion detection systems, clearly there will be differences between vendors. However, just as we can identify the baseline components and organization of a computer or a network—as any computer sciences graduate student will testify—we can do the same for intrusion detection.

The primary components of a typical intrusion detection system can be organized into a schema not unlike like the one depicted in Figure 1-7.

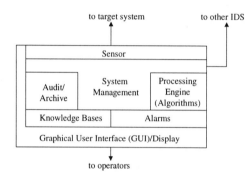

**Figure 1-7.** Intrusion Detection System Component Organization

It should be noted that different systems from different vendors will certainly have unique attributes and components. We introduce this architectural schema as a means for organizing our discussion in a general manner. In Chapter 3, we examine this basic intrusion detection system organization in greater detail with emphasis on the functions and interfaces of each component. In addition, we introduce the generic architectural model being proposed as part of the Common Intrusion Detection Framework (CIDF). The CIDF is an excellent piece of work, even though it introduces more acronyms to an already acronym-flooded discipline. As a preview of the information detailed in Chapter 3, we briefly outline descriptions of each intrusion detection component below.

*Sensor.* This component provides the necessary information about the system targeted for intrusion detection. Sensing components are also sometimes referred to as probes, monitors, feeds, and taps. In the CIDF, they are referred to as Event-Boxes or E-Boxes. It is not uncommon for sensors to be physically remote from the rest of the intrusion detection system.

*System management.* Every intrusion detection system needs some system management function to maintain control over the internal components and to provide a means for communications with other intrusion detection systems. This management can be centralized or distributed in the system architecture. Network management systems based on the Simple Network Management Protocol (SNMP) and the Remote Monitoring (RMON)

Management Information Base (MIB) are becoming more and more common as the basic system management functionality for intrusion detection systems.

*Processing engine (algorithms).* Processing is obviously required for intrusion detection and the associated processing algorithms are generally nontrivial. Clearly, at the highest level, we can characterize intrusion detection processing as consisting of a collection of different goals including reduction of irrelevant data, identification of key intrusion evidence, decision-making about evidence with respect to defined thresholds, mining of intrusion data warehouses for specific patterns or trends, and decision-making about the types of response activities to initiate. Practical concerns such as amounts of available processing power and memory inevitably arise in this area. Incidentally, the CIDF refers to this component as an Analysis-Box or A-Box.

*Knowledge bases.* Knowledge bases in intrusion detection systems come in a collection of different flavors. They provide a means for profiling of users and systems, for capturing attack signatures to be used in detection, and for keeping any information that may be considered useful in the processing, correlation, and analysis of potential intrusion activity. An important research issue in knowledge bases involves the development of common specification means for encoding profile and attack information. The CIDF refers to the implementation of knowledge base storage (as well as that of audit and archive—see below) as a Data-Box or D-Box.

*Audit/archive.* Proper storage of target system activity in audit logs and archives requires considerable thought about the length of time to keep information, the manner in which the information should be protected, and the formats in which the information should be encoded or encrypted for storage and retrieval. Existing tools that generate audit trails are not presently well suited for integration with intrusion detection tools. This is an area in which vendors must do a better job in the future.

---

*Intrusion Detection and Data Warehousing*

Intrusion detection experts agree that long-term storage data will continue to be critical in successful intrusion detection. As a result, the intersection of intrusion detection with data warehousing and mining techniques is inevitable. For information on data warehousing books and resources, visit the Web page of John Wiley and Sons at http://www.wiley.com/ and click on the 'data warehouse' icon. Inside you will find books by Bill Imon, whose brochures proclaim him as the 'Father of the Data Warehouse'.

---

*Alarms.* In current state-of-the-practice intrusion detection systems, alarms are somewhat monolithic in the sense that they typically just alert a human being via a message, email, or page. As intrusion detection system technology matures, alarms must evolve into more dynamic directives from sensor components and processors to other components in the system. For example, alarms should have the capability to automatically initiate intruder traps, to initiate some sort of trace back capability, or to selectively disable access to key assets. In the CIDF, alarms and other information are encoded in a format referred to as the Generalized Intrusion Detection Object (GIDO).

*Graphical User Interface (GUI)/display.* User display is key to the proper human use and analysis of the output of an intrusion detection system. A key issue here is that most GUIs for existing systems are based on R&D guesses about what types of information should be displayed. That is, no experience base exists for determining the types of information displays that are useful to real operators in real situations, as in network management, for example. Hopefully, as more Intranet managers deploy intrusion detection technology, information displays will become more experience-based.

## ISSUE 3: WHAT IS AN INTRUSION?

Invariably, in the development of any new technology, semantics and terminology are problems that hold back progress and impede integration of results by different researchers and working groups. In intrusion detection, the fundamental concept of *intrusion* is unfortunately debated by nearly everyone involved in the field. As an example, many people consider intrusions and attacks to be synonymous, whereas others will argue that the two terms represent completely different concepts.

For the purpose of this book, we propose in Chapter 4 a basic terminology and associated model-based semantics for many different concepts in intrusion detection. The reader must also be warned that the bibliography in this book provides citations to literature and Internet resources that may use terminology in direct conflict with the terms and meanings we define here. This is an unavoidable consequence of the immaturity of intrusion detection.

The terminology proposed in Chapter 4 presumes that attacks and intrusions are synonymous and that they represent a sequence of actions that may be interleaved with other, unrelated actions. Furthermore, the duration between the actions that comprise an attack may be arbitrary. In fact, a longer duration between actions will make it more difficult for intrusion detection systems to detect the attack.

Figure 1-8 depicts this underlying assumption about attacks and their component actions.

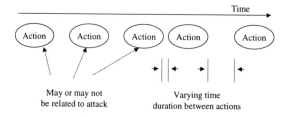

**Figure 1-8**. Attacks and Component Actions

In Chapter 4, this model is expanded and used as the basis for defining what is meant by an attack. We also provide many examples of common Internet attacks with explanations of how and why each step is important.

## ISSUE 4: HOW DO INTRUDERS HIDE ON THE INTERNET (AND HOW CAN THEIR ORIGIN BE TRACED)?

One of the great challenges in intrusion detection involves obtaining accurate information about the identity of a malicious intruder. It is key to determining intrusion technique, intruder intent, and effective security countermeasure procedures. Unfortunately, as we will show, intruders have a variety of methods at their disposal for hiding their identity on the Internet.

In many aspects of life and technology, we have come to rely on certain familiar techniques for determining identity. Consider the following examples:

- In business settings, we rely on visual recognition during human interaction and contact. In fact, many business people will not perform any serious transaction without the physical presence of those involved to reinforce this visual recognition element. I doubt that this will ever change totally, even as electronic commerce becomes more mainstream. Times exist when human interaction cannot be replaced or automated.

- In telephony, we rely on our ability to recognize human voice, with assistance from technology in areas such as caller identification. How many times, for example, are you uncomfortable with the first few moments of a call when you don't recognize the caller's voice? We inevitably are forced to multiplex our attention between the content of the discussion and the quality of the caller's voice to determine identity.

- In travel, we rely on the proper issuance and control of documents such as visas, passports, and work permits to prove our identity. Without such identity-defining tokens, we often cannot get onto airplanes, or into and out of certain countries.

- In electronic commerce, we have come to rely on clients and servers holding cryptographically-signed documents (i.e., ones with digital signatures) that validate reported identity to endpoints. This is a new identity-defining technique, but one that will grow in importance in the coming years.

For general Internet protocol and service interactions between clients and servers, however, accurate identification with strong validation procedures are typically not required to gain access to a large percentage of Internet resources. Simple access to the Internet, for example, requires very little of the user in terms of validation of identity. It is trivial for a user to gain access in some anonymous manner using any number of different techniques. This is in contrast to the somewhat more trusted end-points involved in most telephony settings.

In particular, in Chapter 5, we explore in detail the types of techniques used for hiding one's identity on the Internet, as well as for attempting to trace the real identity of some individual user or set of users. As we will show, these hiding and tracing techniques can be partitioned into two main categories:

- *In-Band Techniques.* The first category includes in-band techniques for hiding and tracing identity that use TCP/IP-based Internet protocols and services. These techniques may use cryptography, certain network weaving approaches, and virtually all Internet hacking/cracking approaches.

- *Out-Of-Band Techniques.* The second category includes out-of-band techniques for hiding and tracing identity that may use methods from the physical and paper worlds, as well as other technologies considered outside the TCP/IP framework such as telephony. Note that physical location is a key issue here; this may explain why Internet cafes, libraries with free access to Internet-connected workstations, and any other kiosk-like access methods are troublesome from an Internet identity definition perspective.

Use of these in-band and out-of-band techniques in combination provides both the intruder and the tracer with a myriad of different approaches to hiding and tracing. This is an important point as it illustrates the usefulness of certain techniques to both the offensive intruder and the defensive protector. The manner in which hiding and tracing are related is depicted in Figure 1-9.

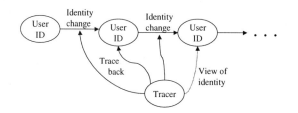

**Figure 1-9**. Interplay Between Identity Hiding and Tracing

---

*Signing Up With An Internet Service Provider (ISP)*

During new account registration, most ISPs are primarily interested in making sure that your credit card validates properly. They rarely bother to make sure that 'Mickey Mantle' living at 'Yankee Stadium, New York' is a valid name and address. This type of provisioning method transfers responsibility for accurate identity to the credit card companies.

---

## ISSUE 5: HOW DO INTRUSION DETECTION SYSTEMS CORRELATE INFORMATION?

Correlation of information is a fifth fundamental issue in intrusion detection; we address this issue in detail in Chapter 6 of this book. As we will demonstrate, the types of correlation that must be performed can be partitioned into a basic taxonomy. This taxonomy is developed around the following three factors:

- Single and multiple session correlation of packets.
- Real time and after-the-fact correlation of information
- In-band and all-band correlation of available information

As a preview of the detailed presentation in Chapter 6, we outline some salient points in these three fundamental correlation factors.

*Single session versus multiple session correlation.* In TCP/IP-based networking, sessions correspond to the TCP or UDP interaction between defined source and destination endpoints. The parameters of the session correspond to the so-called full association in TCP/IP in which the source and destination IP addresses, source and destination ports, and protocol are defined. Clearly, the correlation problem will be different for single sessions in which packets are transferred between the defined session endpoints, and multiple sessions that will involve different endpoint pairs. In the single session case, the correlation is between packets of the same session, separated by an arbitrary time duration. The multiple case, on the other hand, could involve correlation between completely different sessions. The single session correlation approach is represented in the picture in Figure 1-10.

Correlation between packets in single session

**Figure 1-10**. Single Session Correlation

The multiple session correlation approach generalizes the single session problem. This more complex challenge for intrusion detection systems is depicted with three sample sessions in Figure 1-11.

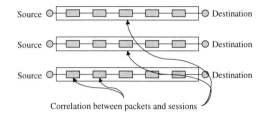

**Figure 1-11**. Multiple Session Correlation

*Real time versus after-the-fact correlation.* The issue of whether the correlation of information is being done in real time versus after-the-fact is key to proper correlation algorithmic design. The basic difference is that in real time correlation, the processing algorithms cannot "look forward" whereas after-the-fact correlation approaches can involve all of the information about an incident. This allows after-the-fact algorithms, common in audit trail analysis tools, to consider time as an index into a complete historical record of all activities. In Chapter 6, we examine the processing and algorithmic implications of this limitation on real time correlation.

*In-band versus all-band correlation.* We define the notion of *in-band* to consist of the computing and networking activity that is inherent to the target system. Since our primary concern in this book is on TCP/IP-based processing, then clearly in-band activity involves packet networking transmission over public and private TCP/IP networks. We must not forget, however, that server-based activity such as file transfers, login information, and process data is considered in-band information for any server-based intrusion detection.

We define *all-band* to constitute all types of information and activity, regardless of whether or not it is in-band. This implies that in-band correlation is just a special case of all-band correlation. Thus, if a user initiates a telnet or ftp command, then this would be considered both in-band and all-band activity in the context of Internet-based intrusion detection. If that same user is stealing cable television, has a police record for physical crimes, and was seen going into a foreign embassy, then this information would be considered all-band.

As we will show, the challenge of all-band correlation is to ensure proper levels of trust, accuracy, and priority, as information becomes available from multiple sources. This should not come as a surprise, however, as these have traditionally been issues in the network management of a non-trivial environment.

---

*Live Television in Network Operations Centers*

Most major communications companies, big government organizations, and large service providers today have high-tech network operations centers that monitor traffic and correlate data for incident response and disaster recovery. In many these centers, live television feeds from news channels are used to increase the all-band information available for correlation.

## ISSUE 6: HOW CAN INTRUDERS BE TRAPPED?

Trapping the bad guys using deception is a topic that has been poorly represented in the secure computing literature. In Chapter 7, we try to rectify this situation somewhat by presenting trap material that should be of use to the intrusion detection system designer and operator.

A simple model for Internet traps involves a user under suspicion, a real system, an intrusion detection system, and a trap system. Presumably, the intrusion detection system would control the interaction between the user and the trap by monitoring the user's actions. A framework in which an intrusion detection system is not diverting traffic from a user to an available dormant trap is depicted in Figure 1-12.

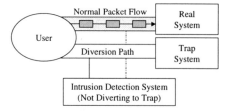

**Figure 1-12**. Dormant Intrusion Detection Trap

In Figure 1-13, we show the diversion of packets from the user to an alternate trap path by the intrusion detection system. Note that the picture shows the diversion directly from the user. This is only a pictorial convenience, as the diversion could be done as part of the transmission, or even as part of the terminating system. In fact, diversion of packets in a protocol sense can be implemented in many different ways.

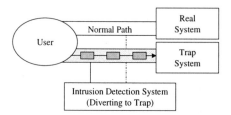

**Figure 1-13**. Intrusion Detection Trap in Use

In Chapter 7, we expand on these basic models and introduce some baseline heuristics for the design, development, test, and integration of effective Internet traps for malicious intruders that can be used to gather evidence and maintain a level of security control over critical network resources. We note here that throughout our presentation on traps, great emphasis is placed on the R&D focus of traps as well as those scenarios for which traps provide a unique detection method. Actual use of trap technology requires careful attention to legal and policy issues in the deployed environment.

## ISSUE 7: WHAT METHODS ARE AVAILABLE FOR INCIDENT RESPONSE?

We can roughly characterize the intrusion detection problem into two phases. In the first phase, activity is scanned and processed to detect whether something is suspicious; in the second phase, appropriate *incident response* methods are followed. This issue of incident response has been sadly neglected in the literature.

The current state-of-the-practice in incident response for most organizations is that when something occurs, management either ignores it and hopes the situation will disappear, or administrators are dispatched to create custom tools for trying to deal with the situation. The phenomenon of ignoring the problem and hoping it will go away should become less prevalent as managers in the ensuing years become more comfortable with Internet environments and how they are secured. Nevertheless, in the current state-of-the-practice for incident response, few aspects of any other engineering discipline are as haphazard.

In Chapter 8, we outline a collection of rational factors that influence the incident response challenge for security managers and administrators. These factors are examined in detail and associated with practical examples from Intranet management, Internet service provision, electronic commerce, and other related environments. It is hoped that these factors will help bring some semblance of order to incident response in some settings.

The set of response factors can be categorized into *information-based observational factors* and *action-based decision factors*. Information-based observational factors are the ones that involve a security manager getting information about the incident. Examples include determining whether an incident is still occurring and determining the extent of damage to an asset. Action-based decision factors involve security managers making determinations as to the appropriate response activity. Examples include deciding whether to bring in law enforcement and whether to sever access to some resource. Obviously, these response methods carry with them a set of associated implications for the organization.

The diagram in Figure 1-14 provides a graphical depiction of these two types of incident response factors.

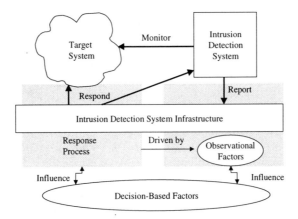

**Figure 1-14**. Observational and Decision-Based Incident Response Factors

As a preview here, we list some of the observational and decision-based factors that determine the response actions for a given incident:

- Does the incident involve critical assets?
- Has this incident occurred before?
- Is it still on-going?
- Has damage, compromise, or blocking occurred?
- Have any community, state, or Federal laws been broken?
- Have any organizational policies been violated?
- Should the connection be broken?
- Are traps available for use?
- Should law enforcement be involved?

Each of the above factors, and many more, are examined in Chapter 8 in the context of the diagram in Figure 1-14. These factors are associated with common examples to demonstrate the challenges inherent in incident response. In addition, we try to identify some basic research and development areas in incident response that hopefully will receive some attention in the near future.

## WHAT INTRUSION DETECTION PRODUCTS AND SYSTEMS EXIST?

Listing and discussing intrusion detection products and systems in this book raises a number of concerns. As we write these words in 1998, the leading intrusion detection product vendors have been kind enough to share with us their product designs and features, as well as their predictions on where the technology is likely to evolve.

We felt this book would be incomplete and too abstract if it didn't include at least some case studies on some real products and systems. We caveat their use to ensure that readers do not base architecture decisions on the information provided here, which can easily be dated and inaccurate as vendors proceed in their normal product life-cycles. Nevertheless, throughout the text, some of the products and systems listed below are used to illustrate the concepts.

---

*Intrusion Detection Systems on the Web*
Michael Sobirey makes available on the Web an excellent list of available intrusion detection systems at http://www-rnks.informatik.tu-cottbus.de/~sobirey/ids.html. At the time of this writing, there were 58 entries in the list, which includes some defunct intrusion detection products, so you have to sift through the list carefully.

---

- *Automated Security Incident Measurement (ASIM).* This often-mentioned system from the Air Force Information Warfare Center (AFWIC) is considered one the earliest systems to be deployed on a major scale. The system is only for use in U.S. Government applications and is not described in any generally-available publication that I am aware of.
- *Bro.* This system was reported recently at the 1998 Usenix Security Conference. It was developed at Lawrence Berkeley Labs; information on the tool is available at http://www.nrg.ee.lbl.gov/nrg/papers.html.
- *Computer Misuse Detection System (CMDS).* This system from the Science Applications International Corporation (SAIC) has the unique feature that it allows multiple audit

trails to be processing in a common environment. Information on CMDS is available at http://www.saic.com/it/cmds/index.html.

- *CyberCop.* Network Associates Corporation makes this tool available. Information can be found at http://www.ngc.com/product_info/cybercop/ccdata/ccdata1.html.
- *Event Monitoring Enabling Response to Anomalous Live Disturbances (EMERALD).* SRI International has long been one of the great research centers for intrusion detection. EMERALD is the descendant of many famous systems including the influential IDES/NIDES systems of the 1980's and 1990's. Information on EMERALD is available at http://www.csl.sri.com/emerald/index.html.
- *Graph-based Intrusion Detection System (GrIDS):* Researchers at the University of California at Davis, including Karl Levitt, Matt Bishop, and Stuart Staniford-Chen, are making huge contributions to intrusion detection technology. GrIDS is their current research platform and detailed information on their product and their excellent research is available at http://olympus.cs.ucdavis.edu/arpa/grids/welcome.html.
- *NetRanger.* The WheelGroup was founded in 1995 by a group of former AFIWC engineers who had worked on ASIM. Their product NetRanger quickly developed into one of the market leaders and has helped result in the company being acquired by Cisco Systems in 1998. This acquisition made each of the founders of the WheelGroup into instant millionaires—so you should study the information in this book carefully and send me a cut of your first million. Information on the NetRanger product can be found at http://www.wheelgroup.com/netrangr/1netrang.html.
- *RealSecure.* The RealSecure product from Internet Security Systems (ISS) is rapidly gaining popularity in the intrusion detection community. Several strategic alliances between ISS and companies like Checkpoint Systems and Optical Data Systems (ODS) have increase the reach of the product. Information on the product is available at http://www.iss.net/prod/rs.html.
- *SecureSwitch.* The SecureSwitch from ODS is a layer 2 LAN switch that provides a range of intrusion detection and network management capabilities including SNMP-based system monitoring. The SecureSwitch can be installed in a non-intrusive mode or as an active switch in the enterprise network. Information on this product is available at http://www.ods.com/.

In addition to these systems, more references to various logging and processing tools are also included throughout the various chapters to illustrate certain key points. My inclusion or exclusion of a product in the book is neither a promotion nor an endorsement of any product. If the description of a given product seemed to help illustrate a point, then it was included.

As the reader will no doubt expect, for more accurate product and system information, contacting the vendor directly would be the best approach. During the writing of this book, it was common to find major redirections for popular products, and even the discontinuance of some interesting tools. So read the following line carefully: *Please do not commit to any system or infrastructure design based on any product feature described here.* The technology is changing rapidly and today's supported architecture may be tomorrow's old hat. Consult your intrusion detection system vendor for product information and get everything in writing—the information still may be neither correct nor accurate, but at least you'll have someone to blame if something goes wrong in your system architecture.

## BIBLIOGRAPHIC NOTES

The quote by Denning is from her landmark 1986 IDES paper at the IEEE Symposium on Security and Privacy [DE86]. The quote from Teresa Lunt is from remarks made at a DARPA research panel report given at the 20[Th] National Information Systems Security Conference. Not many general overviews of intrusion detection exist that we feel compelled to recommend. Teresa Lunt is a name you will get to know if you continue with intrusion detection; she wrote a summary of real-time intrusion detection in [LU89] that is very good. The Lawrence Livermore Labs Web page has a general discussion in [LL96] (see the document at http://doeis.llnl.gov/nitb/docs/nitb.html) that has some useful discussion with outdated references. I can remember reading it some years ago and finding the discussion useful albeit somewhat dated, even then. The following Web sites: http://www.metroactive.com/ and http://www.starlink-dss.com/ were fun to browse and helpful in the discussion on surveillance cameras. Michael Sobirey's intrusion detection page at http://www-rnks.informatik.tucottbus.de/~sobirey.ids.html was a wonderful source of information. You can find information on the Common Intrusion Detection Platform (CIDF) [CI98] at the University of California at Davis computer science Web site at http://seclab.cs.ucdavis.edu/cidf/. Other than this, very little of the intrusion detection information in this chapter was derived from other technical sources. This is good and bad news in that while the material presented in this book may forge some new ground, it is also the case that a consensus on techniques and issues has not formed in the tiny intrusion detection community that exists around the world. Let's hope this changes in the next couple of years.

# CHAPTER 2:
## INTRUSION DETECTION METHODS

*A successful intrusion detection system should incorporate several different approaches.*

Teresa Lunt

*Mechanisms are needed to provide real time detection of patterns in network operations that may indicate anomalous or malicious activity, and to respond to this activity through automated countermeasures.*

Philip Porras and Peter Neumann

### WHAT METHODS ARE USED FOR INTRUSION DETECTION?

Here's an interesting paradox: We know from the previous chapter that commercial and research intrusion detection systems are available for use by security administrators. In spite of this, nearly all *reported* incidents in which an intruder has been caught in real time have involved manual intrusion detection methods used by attentive security experts. Furthermore, these incidents have involved locally developed intrusion detection tools and traps rather than commercial systems. Some examples are listed below.

- In their classic book *Firewalls and Internet Security*, Bill Cheswick and Steve Bellovin describe how manual techniques and locally developed tools were used to catch an intruder dubbed 'Berford' who was wandering around the AT&T Internet gateway. Reading this sort of thing makes many people think that without bona fide Internet geniuses like Cheswick and Bellovin on staff, they really have no chance of ever detecting an incoming intruder.

- The infamous Cliff Stoll reports in various papers and in a popular book called *The Cuckoo's Egg* how the West German intruder he was chasing was ultimately caught via a myriad of custom developed intrusion detection tools and traps. Stoll is another bona fide Internet genius and if you've ever met or seen him, you will agree that there is only one Cliff Stoll. So unless you've already hired him, you won't be able to add him to your staff.

- Tsutomo Shimomura and John Markoff mention in their interesting book *Takedown* that the *tcpdump* utility was hacked during the alleged incident with Kevin Mitnick to allow better monitoring of the intruder's packets. Shimomura may be one of the smartest and most unique people you will ever read about. This certainly does little to ease a network manager's feeling about catching crackers with existing staff.

- As described in the wonderful book *@Large* by David Freedman and Charles Mann, a variety of sites intruded upon by the notorious *phantomd* cracker required highly competent system administrators to hack up some local sniffing tools (often using *tcpdump*) that would be used to deal with future occurrences of the intrusion. This required much time and effort—more than I'll bet most of you will ever have at your disposal at work.

> *Myriad of Books on Internet Cracking*
> Your local bookstore manager can point you to books on Internet cracking by authors like John Markoff, Jonathan Littman, Katie Hafner, and Joshua Quittner (by no means, a complete list). In their books, look for this trend of crackers being caught with hacked software tools created by very special programmers and administrators.

These published accounts raise some fundamental questions for intrusion detection including the following:

- Are intrusion detection methods only inherently suited for manual use by experts?
- Are intrusion detection methods well-defined enough so that automation can be used?
- What are these manual intrusion detection methods that are used to catch intruders by security experts?
- What types of intrusion detection methods are embedded into currently existing tools?

In this chapter, we examine these various questions about intrusion detection in detail.

Recall from our discussion in Chapter 1 that five specific methods were identified for use in practical intrusion detection:

- *Audit trail processing* ("What information can be obtained from an audit trail to detect intruders?")
- *On-the-fly processing* ("What information is available on the system or across the network that provide clues to intrusive behavior?")
- *Profiles of normal behavior* ("What predictive descriptions of users and systems can help highlight intrusions?")
- *Signatures of abnormal behavior* ("What patterns of attack can be described so that they can be recognized when happening?")
- *Parameter pattern matching* ("Do regular behavior patterns exist to help identify when anomalies occur?")

Recall further that these methods are neither mutually exclusive nor mutually dependent. In fact, an effective intrusion detection approach is likely to combine elements of each of these methods. Furthermore, some of the methods interplay quite effectively; signatures of abnormal behavior are useful, for example, in on-the-fly processing. So the reader is advised to interpret each method as contributing to more complete and accurate processing of the target computing and networking activity.

In the sections that follow, we outline the salient aspects of these five methods with liberal use of examples that have been reported in the literature or in available products. In certain cases, we do introduce some new concepts (our vision of parameter pattern matching as an intrusion detection method, for example). However, for the most part, this chapter outlines intrusion detection methods that have had at least a degree of attention in the R&D community.

## HOW DOES THE AUDIT TRAIL PROCESSING METHOD WORK?

As was suggested in Chapter 1, the method of processing an audit trail is fairly common in intrusion detection systems. We enhance here an earlier diagram from Chapter 1 here to present the important features in audit trail processing (see Figure 2-1).

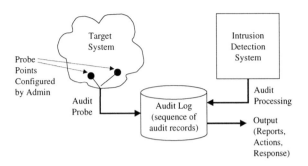

**Figure 2-1.** High-Level Depiction of Audit Trail Processing Method

Apparently, Jim Anderson was the first to recognize in the late 1970's the usefulness of this technique in the detection of external perpetrators, internal masqueraders, clandestine users, and authorized users who abuse their privilege. Anderson suggested that certain patterns might be recognizable in the logs such as multiple failed login attempts and failed access attempts for certain files.

The basic idea in audit trail analysis is that activity is first logged and stored in an audit trail via the selection of *audit probes*. Audit probes are selected by system designers or system administrators based on their view of what constitutes security critical event activity. Presumably, activity is security-critical if it has a potentially significant effect on the security of some valued assets. For example, audit probes in UNIX systems exist in kernel and application level locations that are designed to capture security relevant data (e.g., file opens, login activity). These probes are intended to protect UNIX system files and important applications.

---

*A Brief Note on Auditing and Orange Book Certification*

In the Orange Book B1 security certification of the AT&T UNIX System V/MLS operating system during the late 1980's, the AT&T development team and the National Computer Security Center (NCSC) certification team were constantly debating proper audit probe points and what constituted security-critical events on a UNIX system. The resultant system included 23 selectable channels for UNIX auditing in the kernel (e.g., open for read/write, process fork, creation of interprocess communication (IPC) objects, creation or removal of a file, successful or failed execs) and 14 more user level channels (e.g., unsuccessful login attempts, change of user's password, adding or removing a user, group or label).

---

Security and system administrators have the task of enabling or disabling the use of these audit probes for generation of trails. As a general rule, if the threat environment is severe, then the administrators should enable more auditing than if the threat environment is more benign. Obviously, this will have an impact on the use of the resultant audit trails for intrusion detection. The effect is that if more auditing is enabled, then the intrusion detection processing will have more data to work with. A key trade-off to consider is that systems typically exhibit greatly decreased performance when auditing is enabled. In some cases, this performance decrease is so significant that administrators are loath to enable any audit channels.

The resultant audit trail, often referred to as an *audit log*, provides a basis for the use of automated tools that must understand the semantics of the records in the audit trail. These tools must be accompanied by algorithmic approaches that detect certain attributes of records in the audit trail via an *audit processing* scheme. These attributes correspond to patterns of activity that are considered suspicious.

Our surveillance camera analogy might be helpful here. Imagine, for example, that a camera has taken shots of a target area for some period of time. The film with the captured images can be viewed as comparable to a computer-based audit trail. The period of time the surveillance camera captures images is comparable to the audit trail storage duration. And the types of incidents that can detected on a captured surveillance tape give some indication of the types of intrusions that can be detected on an audit trail. For example, incidents that are captured in audit trails have usually (but not always) long since completed.

## HOW DO GOVERNMENT STANDARDS ADDRESS AUDIT?

The U.S. Government Trusted Computer System Evaluation Criteria (TCSEC), also known as the Orange Book, includes security guidelines for understanding audit in trusted systems in a companion document (this is available as NCSC-TG-001). In this document, recommendations are made on interpretations of audit requirements in the Orange Book, along with practical suggestions for implementation. Although the document was produced in 1987—before most people were talking about Internets—there are enough useful concepts in the work that we include a brief summary here.

The document suggests that audit mechanisms have five primary technical and administrative goals for an operating system:

- *To allow review of patterns of access and usage.* Opening, closing, reading, writing, and executing of files are the most common access and usage activities of interest. One is hard pressed to imagine any non-trivial cracking scenario that does not involve these types of file operations.
- *To allow discovery of repeated attempts to bypass protections.* Failed attempts to open a file often provide good evidence in an audit trail that someone is trying to bypass protections. In some research environments, this type of repeated failure is used to trigger the use of an intruder trap.
- *To allow discovery of any use of unusual privileges.* This may be tough to discern from an audit trail. Some hints that this might be happening include multiple, simultaneous users with system privileges in an environment where this might not be expected or use of a privilege at an unexpected time of day.
- *To serve as a deterrent by its existence as a surveillance tool.* This works best when everyone knows that the audit trail is actually perused by administrators. The existence of tools to provide assistance makes this much more feasible and daunting to a potential intruder.
- *To supply an additional form of user assurance.* Users will be more apt to feel safe in their computing environment if they know that tools for audit analysis are being used.

So you can see that these goals are certainly consistent with the use of audit trails for intrusion detection processing.

In the government document mentioned above, audit requirements are partitioned into three primary groupings:

*Auditable events.* These are the events and actions on a computer system that are deemed security critical and worthy of logging. Typical information included here is:

- Use of identification and authentication mechanisms such as password programs and files.
- Creation or deletion of objects, where objects usually consist of files and directories in an operating system.
- System administrative activity such as file system or process related operations.
- Network activity into or out of the system being audited.

*Auditable information.* This corresponds to the information that must be recorded in the audit trail for auditable events. This includes the following:

- Date, time, type, origin, and result of an auditable event.
- Identification of the subject initiating an auditable event.
- Identification of the object targeted by an auditable event.

*Audit basis.* This addresses the use of the audit information by system and security administrators. A point made strongly in the document is that events should allow definition of accountability to the granularity of an individual.

To date, very few intrusion detection system vendors have paid strict attention to these Orange Book requirements. Some of the firewall vendors, on the other hand, have ported their systems to hardened operating systems that meet stringent B-level Orange Book requirements; but intrusion detection system vendors have not bothered with this approach to date. This may not be a serious problem from an audit perspective, however, since operating systems such as Windows NT, which many intrusion detection systems currently run on, meet the Orange Book C2 requirements for auditing.

If one had to speculate, the tendency would be to presume that the Orange Book will become even *less* important as a measure of audit security in the future. This is not to imply that auditing will become less important as a protection method, but rather that government standards for auditing will have less influence. Instead, commercial approaches embedded in vendor solutions will continue to dominate auditing methods.

## CASE STUDY: FINDING INTRUSIONS IN A HYPOTHETICAL TRAIL

To illustrate the use of audit trails in the intrusion detection process, let's examine the types of intrusions that might be present in a hypothetical audit trail. To keep things simple, let's assume that audit records in our hypothetical audit trail log the initiation of all TCP sessions. This ignores UDP sessions and return packet information, but it provides a framework for demonstrating the basic concept in audit trail processing.

As a further bit of information, let's assume that audit records are coming from a gateway component sitting on the perimeter network of Intranet A which is connected to the Internet. This is a reasonable sample system to examine because most Internet-connected organizations achieve their audit in this manner.

We'll assume that IP addresses from A are *in* addresses and that IP addresses from the Internet are *out* addresses. We'll assume further that *inbound* directed packets come into A, whereas *outbound* packets leave A for the Internet. We'll also presume that the gateway IP address is *gw*. This sample arrangement is depicted in the diagram in Figure 2-2.

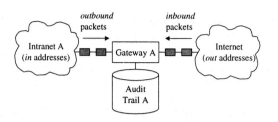

**Figure 2-2**. Hypothetical Illustration Network for Audit Trail Analysis

From this hypothetical network configuration, let's assume that the audit trail builds up over some period of time and that we are now having a look to see if anything looks suspicious. Suppose that the audit records look as follows:

<source IP address, destination IP address, source port, destination port,<br>
protocol, time session initiated,<br>
session initiation direction, success/failure of session>

Thus, if some user in Intranet A successfully initiates an *outbound telnet* session (telnet servers listen on port 23) from some arbitrary user port 3000 at 13:04, then the associated audit record might look as follows:

<*in*, *out*, 3000, 23, TCP, 13:04, *outbound*, success>

With this hypothetical scheme in mind, let's now examine a collection of sample audit records and see if we can derive any intrusion-related information from the trail. As we continue through this small example, you should keep in mind the tediousness of this manual approach—especially in the context of a much larger and more complex audit trail. Keeping this in mind will help you to understand why so many vendors are trying to create automated tools that perform such parsing of audit trails for patterns.

· · ·

<*in*,  *in*, 4050, 80, TCP, 07:36:04,  *inbound*, success><br>
<*out (X)*, *gw*, 6025, 23, TCP, 07:51:12,  *inbound*, failure><br>
<*out (X)*, *gw*, 6025, 23, TCP, 07:51:55,  *inbound*, failure><br>
<*out (X)*, *gw*, 6025, 23, TCP, 07:52:17,  *inbound*, failure><br>
<*out (X)*, *gw*, 6025, 23, TCP, 07:52:58, *inbound*, failure><br>
<*out (X)*, *in*, 3000, 23, TCP, 13:04:22, *inbound*, success><br>
<*out (Y)*, *gw*, 5000, 23, TCP, 23:54:22, *inbound*, success>

· · ·

From the above audit records, we can presume that something suspicious might be occurring. The first record shows an *in* source and an *in* destination IP address for an *inbound* session. This can't be right because *inbound* sessions should have *out* source IP addresses. When this is not the case, we presume that some intruder is changing source IP addresses. This intrusion is sometimes referred to as an IP gateway spoof.

It's worth noting that cases exist where internal users with internal IP addresses connect to the Internet via dial access modems and that return packets sometimes present themselves to a gateway with internal source IP addresses. Intranet managers fear this situation as it tends to place an entire enterprise at risk of unauthorized access around a perimeter firewall. This type of return path for packets isn't an IP spoof, but it's probably not a good idea and should be flagged anyway.

The second, third, fourth, and fifth records in the example show repeated attempts by someone at *out* address X to telnet to A's Intranet gateway. While this may be an innocent sequence, it certainly warrants some attention—especially if the gateway administrators generally do not see this type of activity. In reality, this repetition usually signals some unauthorized activity.

The sixth record shows that the user at address X managed to telnet to an address inside A's Intranet. This also might raise some suspicion, particularly because the source IP address correlates to the previous unsuccessful activity that was considered suspicious. In a true audit trail, this record probably wouldn't show up so close to the previous records because the time is about six hours later than the activity recorded in the earlier records. Audit trail analysis tools must sift through large audit trails to uncover such relationships.

The last record in the example probably would not seem odd in most scenarios. Notice, however, that the time the user at address Y tried to telnet inbound was almost midnight. It might be the case that this is not a normal type of event for this time of night at this gateway. If this is true, then the audit trail provides evidence of an anomaly. Finding this anomaly requires knowledge of this profile information.

---

*UNIX and Internet Advice from Two Noted Experts*

Our example introduces some basic patterns to look for in an audit trail. Simpson Garfinkel and Gene Spafford recommend in their book *Practical UNIX and Internet Security* (Second Edition, O'Reilly, 1996) that the following patterns be considered as potentially suspicious activity in UNIX log files:

- Users logging in at strange hours (this requires some understanding of what constitutes normal activity)
- Unexplained reboots or changes to system clocks
- Unusual error messages from mailers, daemons, or other servers (these can be very valuable)
- Failed login attempts with bad passwords (especially if multiple failures occur)
- Unauthorized use of the *su* command (to gain UNIX root access)
- Users logging in from unfamiliar sites on the network

---

The example above involves a few simple intrusion schemes that were detected. Keep in mind that network security administrators must utilize all sorts of knowledge and tricks to identify attacks in an audit trail. For instance, the IP addresses of certain critical internal resources might be hidden and should never be accessible from the outside. If such an access is attempted from the outside, an intrusion detection scheme could be used to raise an alarm. This sort of clever reasoning must be done by administrators to improve the success rate for detecting intrusions in a trail. It also suggests that automation of the entire intrusion detection process is unlikely in the near future.

## WHAT PROBLEMS MUST BE CONSIDERED IN USING AUDIT TRAILS?

Audit trail processing is not particularly popular with system and network administrators. Most administrators do not collect audit trail information, and if they do, they rarely process it thoroughly. While we certainly cannot give perfect explanations for this common behavior, we suggest here that the reason has to do with the following four practical problems that emerge in the use of an audit trail scheme:

- Potentially large size of the audit trail
- Degraded target system performance due to auditing
- Difficulty protecting the audit trail
- Unknown storage duration for the audit trail

*Potentially large size of the audit trail.* The first problem with the selection of audit probes in a live setting is that the size of the resultant audit trail can become enormous. This is particularly troublesome in environments where audit data is generated in one location and carried to another for processing. Actual estimates of audit trail size are difficult because so many different factors influence size. Some of these factors include the number of audit probes that are active, the number of users on a system, and the amount and types of activity on a system. As a single data point, in one workgroup environment of about a dozen engineers at AT&T, an NCR 3431 computer running a secure version of the UNIX operating system served for a time as a departmental server for email and other services; it generated about five megabytes of audit trail per week, which seems like a pretty typical number, based on purely subjective observations by the author.

*Degraded target system performance due to auditing.* An additional problem is that the performance impact of auditing on the application, operating system, network, or gateway component can be severe as well. The weakest impact the author is familiar with is the UNIX System V/MLS operating system trail, also known as Nighthawk from Concurrent Computer Corporation (previously Harris). This auditing system with all audit probes enabled only impacts performance by 4-6%. It does this by creating a static map of the entire file system so that audit data can be saved with respect to the map. The main penalty is that file system map generation requires some time.

A more typical performance impact was measured by the author and a graduate student a couple of years ago when we ran a collection of off-the-shelf benchmarks on several then current versions of HP/UX and Microsoft Windows NT. With all audit probes enabled, we measured performance impacts of greater than 85% in some of the system call overhead test cases. You can find the paper describing this work at Sam Nitzberg's home page at http://www.iamsam.com/papers/thesis/thesis.htm. For more accurate measurements on current versions of these systems, readers are urged to run their own experiments or to contact their vendors.

*Difficulty protecting the audit trail.* Attackers who don't want to get caught will be motivated to make changes to the audit trail on a target system. One of the most useful heuristics in any audit-monitoring scheme is that the size of an audit trail should never get smaller. If this happens, then one must suspect that someone may be snipping out select audit records. To deal with this problem, some organizations use the low-tech method of spooling audit trails to a printer so that hardcopy output is created (sometimes in a locked closet). Others try to use operating system or network access controls to ensure integrity protection.

*Unknown storage duration for the audit trail.* The fourth problem that we will mention is the duration of storage required for an audit trail. It is intractable to predict how long an audit record must be kept. If it is kept for some arbitrary time duration, then it will always be possible that just beyond the duration, that record is needed for some reason. This problem is somewhat similar to Web administrators and users having to decide how long to cache certain files or links that may be useful in the future.

## CASE STUDY: UNIX SYSLOG AUDIT PROCESSING

A standard UNIX resource is the *syslog* program written by Eric Allman of Berkeley. The program was designed to make auditing of information about running programs easy in a UNIX environment. While the concept associated with *syslog* and its configuration file *syslog.conf* is straightforward, the details of set-up and operation are quite complex. Readers interested in setting up a *syslog* environment for their system are advised to consult the UNIX manual page from their vendor, as well as any of the references cited at the end of this chapter. Our intent here is to report the important aspects of *syslog* processing to illustrate the audit trail processing concepts introduced in our discussion. Note also that we will revisit *syslog* in various other parts of the book to illustrate concepts germane to the discussion at hand.

The way *syslog* works is that a UNIX daemon (i.e., background running process not associated with any terminal or shell) called *syslogd* is executed at startup and essentially sits waiting for log messages. These messages, also referred to in *syslog* parlance as events, can come from three different sources:

- Processes running on the local machine; the source is a UNIX domain socket, named pipe, or streams module called */dev/log*.
- Kernel routines on the local machine; the source is a special device called */dev/klog*.
- Processes on another machine; the source is a domain socket at UDP port 514.

Log messages contain information about the source of the message, the authorizations (called facilities) associated with the message, the priority assigned to the message, and the content of the message. Programmers send data to *syslogd* via a collection of library routines including *openlog*, *syslog*, and *closelog*.

When *syslogd* receives a log message, it consults a file called *syslog.conf* that is usually resident in the */etc* directory of UNIX. The *syslog.conf* file is a relatively simple configuration file that is organized as a sequence of paired entries consisting of the following:

- Selector fields that tell *syslogd* what messages to actually log
- Action fields that tell *syslogd* what to do with the message

The primary resultant actions that are possible using *syslog* are the following:

- Sending the log message to a file or UNIX device
- Sending some message to a user or to all users
- Passing the message to a program using the UNIX pipe interprocess communication mechanism
- Sending the log message to another machine

The overall functionality of *syslogd* and its use of the associated *syslog.conf* configuration file are represented at the conceptual level in the diagram in Figure 2-3.

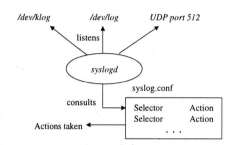

**Figure 2-3**. Depiction of UNIX syslog Operation

Some security considerations that emerge in the context of *syslog* auditing include the following:

- Auditing to a single file may be a central point of vulnerability. For instance, crackers who locate the audit log will have an easier time covering their tracks if all of the auditing is done in one place. To rectify this, many UNIX system and security administrators like to direct their audit log messages to multiple log hosts. The potential also exists theoretically that fake log hosts could be set up as honey pots for potential intruders, but I've never actually seen this done.

- Using the wildcard default * in the *syslog.conf* file to direct all messages to some log host can eat up quite a bit of transmission capacity; UNIX administrators must therefore selectively prune out messages via *syslog.conf* entries that do not cause critical security information to be lost. Compressing of log files using the UNIX *compress* program or something better is a must.

- Security administrators trying to process *syslog* files can make use of simple UNIX tools to detect potential anomalies. In particular, a program called *tail* can be used to deliver the last part of a file to some designated place (e.g., standard output). The program is useful for audit processing because it can be used with the − f ("follow") option to enter an endless loop to monitor the growth of a file that is being written by some other process. As you might imagine, this provides a cheap monitoring tool for *syslog* audit trail files.

From an intrusion detection perspective, the UNIX *syslog* utility is important for several reasons. First, it provides information about UNIX servers that will complement any network or enterprise intrusion detection, processing, and correlation environment. Second, since the utility is probably already present on your UNIX servers, very little time and resource investment is typically required to obtain this functionality. And finally, although *syslog* is by no means a standard, especially if incompatible Windows NT-based auditing is being done in the local environment, it *does* serve as a common means for auditing on a UNIX system. As a result, common expertise, tools, and knowledge are beginning to emerge with respect to *syslog* among UNIX system administrators.

## CASE STUDY: SWATCH AUDIT PROCESSING

One of the more useful programs that helps UNIX system and security administrators deal with *syslog* audit trails is the *swatch* program (the tool is available at ftp://coast.cs.purdue.edu/tools/unix/chrootuid). The *swatch* program goes through *syslog* audit logs, or other files, as they are created. The program initiates action when certain patterns are detected. This can be done in batch mode after log files have been created and stored, or in real-time as a more dynamic scanning function. Most security administrators we are familiar with use the *swatch* program in a network environment that passes multiple log files to a central log processing system.

The program is controlled via a configuration file that consists of three fields: 1) audit trail patterns to look for, 2) response actions to take as a result of audit trail pattern matches, and 3) optional time and duration settings that allows repeat log entries to be ignored for a specified period of time. The specific format for *swatch* audit configuration file entries is as follows:

/pattern/[,/pattern/,…] action[,action,…][[[HH:]MM:]SS[start:length]]

In this format, patterns are regular expressions that are examined in turn until a match if found; the action corresponding to the matched expression is then taken. Actions recognized by *swatch* include an *echo* action that causes a line to be echoed to *swatch*'s controlling terminal, a *bell* action that sends a bell signal to the controlling terminal, an *ignore* action that causes *swatch* to ignore the current line and move on to the next one, *write* and *mail* actions that send the current line to a user list via the write or mail commends, and *pipe* and *exec* actions that allow sending a line to a particular command or to execute a command with selected fields from the matched line as command arguments.

An example pattern from a *swatch* configuration file (derived from the *swatch* manual description located at http://starwww.rl.ac.uk/~cac/security/ssn67.htx/node21.html) is shown below:

/permission denied/ echo,bell 00:30 0:16

In this example, if the pattern 'permission denied' is matched, then a bell will sound to the controlling swatch terminal. Multiple instances of this pattern will be ignored if they appear within thirty seconds of the first one, which, incidentally, would not be a good idea for 'permission denied' matches.

The program also includes modifications to some network service daemons to enhance their ability to work in concert with the *sysylog* auditing function. These daemons include *ftpd* and *telnetd*. It is also worth noting that *swatch* is written in the popular Perl programming language which raises questions about whether this environment on an intrusion detection system might provide too much power to a potential cracker gaining access to the system.

The reason we mention *swatch* in the context of our audit trail processing discussion is to highlight the fact that some simple, effective tools are being created and used. The familiar complaint that audit trails are too complex, too large, and too unwieldy to handle is becoming less and less true. What is missing, however, is a more coherent paradigm for audit processing than just some simple tools used in an ad hoc manner by system administrators. The new paradigm that emerges may be related to the use of data mining tools in a data-warehousing environment as a powerful concept. We believe this will become a more accepted notion and more tools will be created to extract information from program output like that of *syslog*. In spite of this, we believe that simple tools like *swatch* will continue to play a role in such security mining applications because they are gaining acceptance and will probably continue to improve with use.

## CASE STUDY: SECUREVIEW FIREWALL-1 AUDIT PROCESSING

For those of you who are more comfortable paying for software, rather than just finding it on the Web, many vendors have created audit-processing tools that they are willing to support commercially. The SecureIT Corporation, for example, (you can visit their Web site at http://www.secure-it.net/) provides an audit trail processing tool called SecureView for Checkpoint Firewall-1 audit trails.

The SecureView tool focuses on Firewall-1 trails and offers some representative features worth examining briefly here. The baseline presumption is that an administrator would have a Firewall-1 component at their gateway, or somewhere in the network. This is not a bad assumption since at the time of this writing Checkpoint is considered by many to be the market leader in the Intranet gateway market.

Firewalls such as Firewall-1 provide security gateway functionality via traffic filtering based on TCP/IP header information as well as content and other factors such as time of day. In addition, firewalls such as Firewall-1 generate their own audit trails of events that occur at the gateway. These trails would be generated in addition to the trails for the underlying operating system. This is an important point because the underlying operating system trails and application firewall trails are generally incompatible—a point that drives network security administrators absolutely nuts.

The on-line auditing and audit processing arrangement for SecureView is sketched in Figure 2-4.

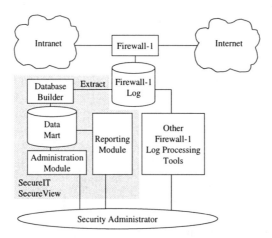

**Figure 2-4**. SecureView Audit Processing at a Firewall-1 Gateway

Since the Firewall-1 component is already in place generating audit trails, the SecureView tool would be used to augment existing Firewall-1 real time alerting and Checkpoint log viewer functionality to extract and process gateway audit trails. It would also obviously be used to augment any tools such as *swatch* being used for underlying operating system audit processing.

The SecureView audit processor provides a means for analyzing and reporting information derived directly from the Firewall-1 audit trail. The design notion is that a so-called *data mart* is created from the raw audit trail. This is done by a *database builder* component that performs some clean-up activities such as resolving IP addresses and adding URL categories and cost information. An *administration module* is available for managing, administering, and archiving the database. As you can see from these components, SecureIT has already recognized that data warehousing and mining techniques are directly applicable to security audit trail analysis.

A *reporter module* is used for the generation of reports. These reports allow queries into the audit trail including identifying the following:

- Most used Internet services
- Top users (by workgroup, location, etc.)
- Certain known attack strategies
- Network traffic patterns
- Capacity utilization
- Accounting and costing reports

The product comes with a standard GUI display that has attractive graphics for reporting. Downloading a sample from the SecureIT web site is recommended as it will give you an idea of what the tool can provide. There's a nice little demo that you can download with the sample.

As audit trail analysis technology becomes more important in practical intrusion detection, we expect to see more tools like SecureView become available for more audit trail formats. In particular, the functional capability to process multiple audit trail formats will be an important product discriminator. In particular, product vendors are strongly encouraged to consider the potential for dealing with audit records from all the various places in a typical enterprise environment where data is being generated. These enterprise locations include the following:

- Routers on local area networks
- Data and network servers
- Workstations and PCs
- Private Branch Exchanges (PBXs)

Security managers have to deal with the audit trails from each of these components separately. This represents a huge market opportunity for vendors.

---

*A Note on Lossy and Lossless Audit Data Reduction Methods*

If you have too much audit data to store, then you would like to reduce its volume for storage. The problem is that you don't want to lose critical information. Here is where some subtleties emerge: If the data includes only certain nuggets of information that are required, then by storing only the nuggets, you have certainly *lost* information (i.e., it is lossy with respect to the total volume). However, if you decide that the lost information was not required, then you have done lossless data reduction with respect to your requirements.

---

## CASE STUDY: COMPUTER MISUSE DETECTION SYSTEM (CMDS)

As was suggested in the previous section, the ability to process multiple audit trails represents an important market opportunity for vendors. The SAIC Corporation provides a product that does perhaps the best job to date in this area with their Computer Misuse

Detection System (CMDS). CMDS is a host-based system that deals with multiple audit trails by creating an intermediate representation of audit that is dealt with by the CMDS processing tools in a uniform manner. The basic architecture of CMDS is sketched in the diagram in Figure 2.5.

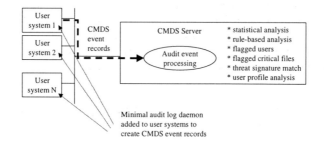

**Figure 2.5**. CMDS Architecture

Audit formats that are included in CMDS as of this writing include the following:
- ANS+CORE InterLock Firewall
- Data General/UX B2 4.11 trails
- HP/UX 10.X
- IBM LAN Server
- Lotus Notes
- Raptor Eagle Firewall
- SunOS 4.1.2/3 C2, Basic Security Module
- Sun Solaris 2.4/5
- Sun Trusted Solaris 1.1
- Windows NT 3.5.1

This is an impressive list, but it illustrates the difficulty network managers will have dealing with multiple audit formats. For example, if you have any other firewalls generating audit trails, then you will have to deal with these separately, perhaps by writing scripts yourself.

The types of statistics that CMDS provides can be described in terms of the UNIX-specific implementation. The categories of statistics include, but are certainly not limited to, the following:

- *Executions*: A measure of programs run with some indication as to whether the computer system was used in interactive mode or in an automated session. This may provide valuable hints during the analysis of incidents that are related to a break-in.
- *Networking*: Any remote system networking will be recorded and analyzed. The importance of this category should be evident.
- *Browsing*: Reading and changing of files or directories is examined in the common trails on CMDS. This also provides important evidence, particularly for certain files such as /etc/shadow.
- *Superuser attempts*: You would expect this to be included as most UNIX cracking activity includes attempts to gain root privilege.
- *Device allocations*: This examines and measures devices allocated to a system.

- *Failed logins and reads*: The value of this should be evident in any audit processing.
- *Warnings and alerts*: This is also an invaluable measure on a UNIX system.
- *Firewall-specific sources*: Measures of connections to various servers for HTTP, NNTP, SMTP, FTP, and Telnet are included as well.

We believe that CMDS is the first of a new breed of audit trail analysis engines that will be invaluable in an intrusion detection environment. The ability to deal with this myriad of audit data in such incompatible formats begs the use of automation to ease the analysis burden and to make certain correlations possible. As we've alluded earlier, the real benefit will come with the ability to include multimedia trails from components such as PBXs.

## HOW DOES ON-THE-FLY PROCESSING WORK?

This second intrusion detection method we will examine in this chapter involves on-the-fly processing from a direct traffic feed of information. On-the-fly intrusion detection roughly corresponds to real time processing of information to initiate response activities in a more timely fashion than in audit trail processing. One must be careful, however, with this distinction because audit trail processing can also be performed in pseudo real time. The limiting factor is processor and memory capacity and size, rather than some algorithmic limitation.

We enhance an earlier diagram from Chapter 1 in Figure 2-6 below to outline the high-level aspects of the on-the-fly processing method.

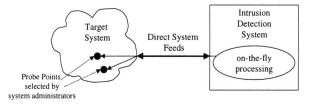

**Figure 2-6**. High-Level Depiction of On-the-Fly Processing Method

---

*A Brief Note on Real Time Processing*

Most people find the notions of real time processing, pseudo real time processing, and non-real time processing very confusing. Keep in mind that real time processing must be considered in the context of an environment. Real time response for humans is counted in seconds (or minutes) whereas real time for electronic components may be measured in milliseconds (or smaller increments). Pseudo real time is used to refer to methods that are on the boundary of what is required in a given environment.

---

We can summarize the key differences between off-line audit trail processing and on-the-fly processing in the context of the following attributes:

*Timeliness.* On-the-fly techniques are designed to provide indications and warning before real damage can occur in an infrastructure or protected domain. This is in direct contrast to off-line audit trail processing that parses through logs after activity has probably completed.

*Processing methods.* Since on-the-fly techniques must produce results quickly, the types of algorithms that can be used are limited to fast and efficient procedures. Obviously, as processing hardware is increased in power, perhaps even to huge signal processing engines, the capacity to perform more involved algorithmic analysis increases.

*Storage requirements.* Off-line audit techniques typically allow greater storage of information. Buffers for on-the-fly method can only be as large as the processing complex can handle. In many cases, software solutions in on-the-fly methods are notorious for dropping packets.

*Information capacity.* The capacity of information in the target system to be monitored increases dramatically for off-line audit analysis. When fat, broadband pipes are the target of intrusion detection processing in an on-the-fly manner, the best that can be done in most cases is to sift through the reams of data, looking for specific patterns or sentinels that can be used to create warnings.

## CASE STUDY: SNMP REMOTE MONITORING (RMON)

One area of intrusion detection R&D that has received much too little attention has been the similarity between on-the-fly network management functions and on-the-fly network intrusion detection. In particular, the emerging Remote Monitoring (RMON) Management Information base (MIB) defined in RFC 1271 provides an excellent basis for performing some intrusion detection collection and processing. This is especially important because such an embedded base of network management applications already exists for RMON.

RMON defines a standard for the Simple Network Management Protocol (SNMP)-based information passed between sensors known as segment monitors that are placed around a network and the centralized management station. By utilizing standards such as SNMP and RMON, network system designers can use multiple vendors for their data collection and processing functions, without having to worry about incompatibilities.

As an example, HP OpenView provides three useful SNMP and RMON tools for supporting data collection and processing:

- NetMetrix distributed monitor and analysis system
- LanProbe noninvasive data collectors for Ethernet and Token Ring
- Power Agent data collectors that provide enhanced collection capabilities

These HP OpenView components provide a powerful means for implementing many useful intrusion detection functions in a network managed environment. The key issue is that by detecting changes in the normal network management environment, anomalies may be uncovered. This is a somewhat controversial notion in intrusion detection because it has not been validated widely in many large networking environments. Nevertheless, if this concept of deviation from normalcy warrants any attention, the use of network management tools is likely to play an important role.

Figure 2-7 shows a typical environment architecture using these HP OpenView tools for RMON-compliant remote network management functionality with attention to intrusion detection.

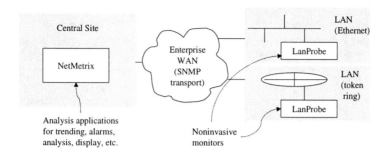

**Figure 2-7.** Sample RMON Environment with HP OpenView Tools

These three tools are fully RMON-compliant and as such, they provide network managers with the capability to perform the following management tasks:

- Analyze historical statistics on the network
- Examine and report on network trends
- Initiate alarms for certain network conditions
- Provide view of traffic loads by time, nodes, and services
- Perform end-to-end traffic analysis
- Packet filtering and saving of trace files
- Network File System (NFS) monitoring and control
- Traffic generation for testing

As should be obvious, each of the above network management functions is directly analogous to on-the-fly intrusion detection functionality. They also provide exactly the type of monitoring that is likely to be the most useful in measuring changes from normal environment activity. That more researchers and developers have not begun to explore this interplay between intrusion detection and network management is curious. Hopefully, in the ensuring years, more work will be focused in this area.

We should point out that some intrusion detection system vendors have, in fact, noticed the relationship between intrusion detection and network management. Most vendors have even based their product offering on some underlying network management system. HP OpenView, for instance, provides an underlying transport and control framework for the NetRanger system. Similarly, the RealSecure intrusion detection system is compliant with several network management platforms including CA-Unicenter from Computer Associates.


## CASE STUDY: NETWORK FLIGHT RECORDER PROCESSING

Network Flight Recorder (NFR) (visit their Web site at http://www.nfr.net/) is a generalized network-monitoring tool designed by one of the great pioneers in Internet firewall technology, Marcus Ranum. If you ever get the chance to meet Marcus or see him talk, I strongly recommend it. And you should listen to what he says—his style of pulling no punches and offering complete technical details on NFR is refreshing, particularly in contrast to the way most companies market their products.

His tool, NFR, is essentially a toolkit for building network traffic analysis and statistical event records. It works by sniffing Internet packets from a target network medium and processing them via a decision engine. The decision engine processes traffic feeds based on user-programmed scripts that direct results to back-end loggers and statistical analyzers. To date, NFR is more a user-programmed engine than a traditional intrusion detection system with canned attack signatures, but plans may be in the works to incorporate some of this functionality into future generations of NFR. Contact the company for details.

The general set-up of the NFR system at a high-level is sketched in Figure 2-8.

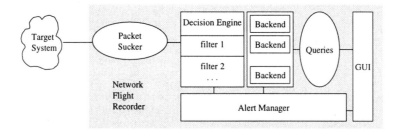

**Figure 2-8**. High-Level NFR Architecture Set-Up

Some unique security and architectural aspects of the NFR system include the following:

- So-called packet suckers operate to capture network traffic and forward copies of packets to the decision engine. According to on-line discussions among NFR users on the Internet, the designers of the packet sucking mechanism are currently addressing practical issues of how best to buffer high volumes of data using device drivers. This author believes that NFR and other systems will benefit greatly from plug-ins for more robust packet capture facilities based on hardware devices. The marriage of the flexible NFR software with fast, hardware-based packet capture is something the intrusion detection community will benefit from.

- The decision engine is based on a collection of filters written in a special programming language called N that Marcus Ranum claims to have evolved from a dungeon game language called UberMUD. Filters are bound in N to target packets. Once all filters have been applied to the packet, the binding is dropped and the packet discarded. The ability to customize filters in N is one of the great advantages of NFR. More intrusion detection systems are likely to come out with their own programming languages for filter configuration.

- Extraction of data from N filters is via an *alert* primitive that passes alarms to a designated alarm management system and a *record* primitive that passes a data structure to a backend to perform intrusion processing. This modularity is useful as it allows potentially the use of third party routines to perform alarm management or recording.

- Backend processing is done via a small collection of general-purpose programs that provide histograms of data as well as lists of chronological records of information. These backends also promote modularity in NFR that is very attractive.

- A set of query backends is used to analyze data. Some of the initially designed queries for NFR are reported to have produced too much data, which prompted the design of a so-called threshold cutoff for queries. Query capability is provided via external database access with structured query language (SQL).

- A graphical user interface (GUI) is provided with a collection of packages that are groupings of backends that operate independently or may include some communication or sharing. This allows for flexible analysis of different types of information on different backends.

- An alert queue manager subsystem is used to provide alerts. A custom daemon called *alertd* is used to prioritize and route alerts. As one might expect, the types of alerts that NFR uses include delivery mechanisms such as alarm printing, email, and fax.

One of the more attractive features of NFR is that it can be downloaded for free from the NFR site for non-commercial use. As a result, a growing number of security and gateway administrators are beginning to use the tool and to discuss their experiences on the Internet. This is a great service for the intrusion detection community as it promotes the use of the technology in environments where financial investment may be impossible.

As more users are introduced to intrusion detection through the popular NFR product, hopefully we in the intrusion detection community can begin to educate them in the various methods that are available. In fact, the on-the-fly nature of NFR for detecting anomalies is actually complemented by its back-ends that may be somewhat more like the off-line audit trail processing methods described in the previous sections.

## HOW IS TRAFFIC EXTRACTED FROM THE NETWORK FOR PROCESSING?

In order for on-the-fly intrusion detection to be performed, information must be extracted from the target system in a timely manner. In a TCP/IP-based networking environment, this implies that packets must be extracted from target network media in one of the following ways discussed below.

*In-line diversion of packets by network components.* In-line network components that can be used for diversion of packets include the following:

- Firewalls that can direct packets to intrusion detection systems based on header information such as source and destination IP address, source and destination port, protocol, and other available information processed by either packet filtering or proxy software.

- Routers that can direct packets to intrusion detection systems based on routing table information, access lists, or some other internal mechanism native to the router.

- Server components that can direct packets to intrusion detection systems based on network service routines (e.g., device drivers), application routines, or operating system services. These applications often require that the hardware interface be configured in a so-called promiscuous mode, an approach common in Ethernet environments. Servers operating off-line and passively in this mode are often referred to as sniffers (see discussion below).

- Other network components such as hubs and bridges that could potentially be used to divert traffic to intrusion detection system segments.

In considering the deployment of the above cases, several engineering trade-offs must be considered. First, the issue of legacy or existing components should be examined. Organizations with existing components that could be used to divert traffic might consider this approach. Second, the issue of stealth or undetectable intrusion detection should be considered. Within an Intranet, this may not be an issue, but in more hostile settings, the need for techniques that are more stealth (see below) should be examined. Third, if an organization has multiple security needs such as the need for a firewall, then traffic diversion via a firewall that can also serve as a network filter makes sense.

*Off-line extraction of packets by network taps.* This approach is well known to the cracking community as passive network sniffing. In a passive sniffing scenario for a simple cable-based Ethernet configuration in which multiple stations are connected into a single segment, a sniffer can be installed that accepts *all* traffic that passes along the cable. This is done by configuring the sniffer to listen in so-called promiscuous mode to passing traffic.

We call this technique off-line because it is evocative of traditional wire tapping techniques in telephony. That is, the sniffing device can be installed into an existing network without effecting applications and user activity. Readers will note, however, that the difference between in-line and off-line techniques is subtle. Readers should also note the potential misuses of off-line extraction because it merely requires access to network media. Malicious administrators of Internet backbone nodes, for example, could utilize their unique access to cause this type of packet capture. Obviously, laws exist that restrict this type of activity in certain environments.

Figure 2-9 depicts a typical sniffer configuration in a cable-based Ethernet.

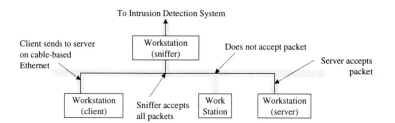

**Figure 2-9.** Off-line Extraction Using Promiscuous Sniffing

Engineering trade-off issues also emerge in the use of off-line techniques for diverting traffic to intrusion detection systems. First, the use of sniffers only works in network environments for which target traffic is readily available. In a typical LAN-based environment, for example, traffic can usually be sniffed without much difficulty. In smart hub-based LANs, however, segment traffic may be controlled and users might have more trouble listening in promiscuous mode. Second, off-line components tend to be less intrusive and hence less detectable than in-line components. This stealth attribute makes this technique attractive in law enforcement settings. Third, an off-line technique is more mobile and more easily integrated into an existing network. This also explains the attractiveness of this technique in law enforcement settings.

## CASE STUDY: BORDERGUARD FIREWALL EXTRACTION FOR NETRANGER PROCESSING

The earliest generation of the WheelGroup's NetRanger intrusion detection system made use of a BorderGuard firewall as a means for diverting packets from a target network to their NSX intrusion detection component. As the WheelGroup product integrates into the Cisco product line in 1998 and beyond, the use of the BorderGuard in their architecture remains uncertain. Nevertheless, an installed base of BorderGuard/NetRanger users exists and will likely continue to use their installed systems for some time. We therefore caution the reader to contact the Cisco Systems before making any system integration decisions based on information described here.

In particular, the BorderGuard diverts traffic to an NSX device that performs a good portion of the local intrusion monitoring function. Figure 2-10 depicts this approach.

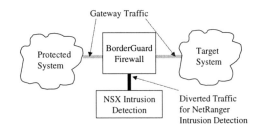

**Figure 2-10**. NetRanger Traffic Diversion Using BorderGuard Firewall

The use of a firewall in the NetRanger configuration is particularly interesting because WheelGroup customers have had the option of using the BorderGuard as both a firewall and as part of the intrusion detection system, or simply as a non-intrusive, in-line traffic diverter to the intrusion detection system. Cost issues, application-processing environments, legacy interoperability, and system engineering estimates of environmental risk should govern this decision. Obviously, as the WheelGroup integrates with the Cisco product line, the use of the Cisco PIX firewall or some other device could be considered a potential architectural direction—but this remains to be seen. This is another example of the exciting changes that are occurring in the intrusion detection community.

To illustrate this use of the BorderGuard as a firewall, consider that if the environment is some intra-organizational choke point through which a variety of applications must pass, then firewalls may not be appropriate or needed. In this case, the BorderGuard might be used to divert packets to the NSX without filtering. However, if a firewall is desired, perhaps in response to an identified security risk, then the use of the WheelGroup product is particularly attractive because it offers the option of inserting both a firewall and an intrusion detection system into the selected choke point. More and more Intranet managers are beginning to view border defenses as consisting of both firewall and intrusion detection functionality.

By the way, a unique feature in this arrangement is that the system can also provide real time policy monitoring for violations of the gateway security policy. Many intrusion detection environments spend a great deal of time and energy developing a security policy for their firewall. When an intrusion detection system is then introduced to their processing environment, it should be obvious that any policy violation constitutes a security-critical event. Without a degree of integration between the firewall and intrusion detection system, however, this may not be the case. This dynamic, on-the-fly policy monitoring component is a powerful concept that will hopefully remain in the evolving Cisco implementations of NetRanger.

## HOW DOES THE NORMAL BEHAVIOR PROFILE METHOD WORK?

Profiles of normal behavior are used in intrusion detection to capture expectations about user and system computing activity. This may be the most well known paradigm for intrusion detection in the computing and networking community. A baseline strategy for user profiling is depicted in Figure 2-11.

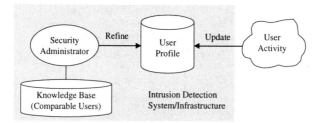

**Figure 2-11.** User Profiling Method

Note that this user profiling technique easily extends to groups of users and complete systems. For instance, to profile a system, the knowledge base would have to focus on characteristics of the system such as peak processing time, number of users, service mix, and so on.

Regardless of the target, the creation of profiles involves three basic concerns:

- Initial profiling for new users and systems should require some estimation of expected behavior.
- Observed user and system behavior should be used to fine-tune existing profiles.
- Information should be used from any relevant source to more accurately predict expected behavior.

Each of these tasks represents a nontrivial challenge. Initial profiling, for example, requires prediction that may not be feasible.

Once profiles are created, the intrusion detection processing compares these profiles to observations of real behavior. This fundamental approach to intrusion detection is depicted in Figure 2-12.

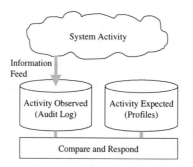

**Figure 2-12.** Concept of Profile-Based Processing

Note that this concept of comparing expectations (i.e., profiles) with observations (i.e., audit trail information or on-the-fly derived information) is central to every intrusion detection method. As we will discuss in Chapter 6, profiles must be interpreted in the context of available correlated information. For example, in long distance telephony, profiles of typical network usage are readily available and are used to monitor health and status of networks. Mother's Day is an example of a day in which the profile suggests a particularly heavy traffic pattern. Thus, if network managers detect something strange, such as heavy traffic, then their interpretation must include correlated information, such as whether today is Mother's Day or a similar heavy traffic day. Major events such as the Super Bowl, verdict announcements of major trials (e.g., the OJ Simpson trial verdict announcement), or major televised speeches or funerals (e.g., that of Princess Diana) may tend to affect observed service behavior as well.

## CASE STUDY: IDES MODEL

One of the more influential researchers in computer and network security during the past fifteen years has been Dorothy Denning—now with the Department of Computer Science, Georgetown University. In the mid 1980's she published an abstract model for profile-based intrusion detection at the IEEE Symposium on Security and Privacy, which at the time, was the only legitimate conference for computer security researchers to publish major results in a timely fashion (see references at the end of this chapter). Now, of course, there are many security conferences, but at the time, this was the premier.

Her published model called IDES had quite an effect on the community. In fact, in the decade that followed, Denning's IDES model was the basis for the vast majority of products, systems, and research tools in intrusion detection including the important IDES systems developed at SRI International. In fact, my own group at AT&T Laboratories got caught up in this approach in the late 1980's and created an IDES-motivated audit trail analysis tool for our secure UNIX system. Thus, Denning's work stands as perhaps the most influential work to date in the field of intrusion detection.

The basic philosophy espoused in the IDES model is that as audit trail information is collected into a protected log, profile-based statistical and other types of analysis are possible using off-line tools and techniques. In Denning's paper, an intrusion detection system is modeled as the following six-tuple mathematical object:

$$<\text{subjects, objects, profiles, audit records,}$$
$$\text{anomaly records, alarms}>$$

*Subjects* and *objects* denote the traditional INFOSEC view of the initiators and targets of system activity. In operating system parlance, subjects would correspond to the basic processes that initiate activity and objects would correspond to the files and directories used to store information.

*Profiles* in the model denote characterizations of behavior. These characterizations are most accurate if they are based on a large sample of suitable behavior. This may not be possible, however, and profiles are often based on statistical relationships. This is really the first explicit inclusion of normal behavior-based profiles in a computing intrusion detection model.

*Audit records* are included to model those data structures used to capture observed behavior on a system. Operating system security involves the use of audit trails that are composed of sequences of audit records. Each record is intended to contribute to a temporal view of system or user activity in the target environment.

*Anomaly records* are included to model data structures used to capture program decisions based on intrusion analysis. In the context of a system development environment, activity records are reminiscent of trouble tickets or configuration change requests that are based on analysis.

*Alarms* denote in the model the manner in which potential problems are actually reported. Alarms usually correspond to response actions taken after an anomaly has been detected.

The schematic in Figure 2-13 below sketches the major components of and interconnections of such a model.

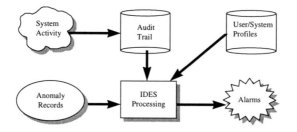

**Figure 2-13**. IDES Design

It is worth noting that even after Denning left SRI, work continued on this model and resulted in a long series of intrusion detection models, prototypes, platforms, and systems—the most recent being the Emerald system, discussed in various places throughout this text.

## CAN TOLL FRAUD INTRUSIONS BE DETECTED?

Toll fraud is a particularly troublesome network security problem for telephony providers, data network service providers, and local service managers—not to mention the *users* of all these services as well. Toll fraud involves a myriad of different motivations, strategies, and gains to the intruder. One popular approach involves crackers trying to gain access to voice messaging systems. Voice mailboxes are particularly troublesome targets for system managers when toll free 800 or 888 inbound access is required. This is very attractive to crackers.

The attack technique typically involves first gaining information about voice mail system manufacturers, defaults, menu structures, and other useful information. Social engineering to the organization may be useful in gaining some information. The idea then is to gain access to a mailbox, which is often simple, especially if some unused mailboxes have no passwords. Where there are passwords, common defaults are often used, such as the digits of someone's home phone or a social security number.

Once an intruder compromises a mailbox, the mailbox can then be used for outbound calls if the feature is implemented at the PBX or Centrex server, personal messaging, and other unauthorized services. The problem is really bad when an administrator's mailbox is compromised. This puts the entire voice messaging system at risk. So administrators have an added responsibility to be more careful.

Approaches to dealing with such problems include proper system administration of passwords, careful configuration of potentially dangerous services, and certain types of intrusion detection. In fact, the use of intrusion detection for toll fraud security is a growing application with lots of promise. In particular, the intrusion detection features in some of the systems designed to detect toll fraud include the following:

- Capture of call record information into a historical file for analysis and perusal; this is where the real profiling is done. That is, profiles of normal usage would be used as the basis for algorithms that parse through call record files. A industry could easily emerge in which tools for processing telephony records are sold to users of this technology.

- Construction of calling patterns of authorized users for comparison with historical files; profiles are important here as well. Historical files would also serve to help establish accurate profiles. Certain calling patterns might be suspicious in any environment (e.g., late night calls to known improper numbers). Other patterns might require comparison with the local environment.

- Automated response capability including reconfiguration of certain services such as outbound access. Response will almost always involve some degree of human intervention; a research goal is to produce better response tools that minimize the need for manual processing.

Such intrusion detection services in emerging products and services provide a powerful means for dealing with the ever-increasing toll fraud problem.

## CASE STUDY: XIOX HACKER PREVENTION TOOLS

The XIOX Corporation (their Web site is http://www.xiox.com/) provides a collection of tools that is useful in the monitoring and detection of toll fraud. They refer to these tools as their Fort Knox Series. In particular, the XIOX Hacker Preventer, Hacker Deadbolt, and Hacker Tracker offer some attractive intrusion detection features including the following:

- Tracking of call activity including all unauthorized calls and call attempts; this can be done with hardware-based solutions such as Hacker Preventer or software solutions such as Hacker Tracker. Keep in mind that caller activity involves end points that are somewhat more stable and known than IP addresses in Internet environments.

- Real time monitoring and automated restriction of suspected fraudulent calls; such monitoring is done in conjunction with the PBX or Centrex system. PBX systems are important components in an enterprise network because they are such valuable sources of connection information. For organizations with dial access problems around their firewall, the PBX or Centrex service may provide the best available means for increasing security.

- Historical profiling of authorized users based on calling patterns; these patterns correspond to profiling of normal behavior for the enterprise. A common type of pattern that suggests toll fraud involves repeat calls from the enterprise to a country that is not normally called. Many small countries find it attractive to try to encourage incoming calls (e.g., via sex phone operators) in order to collect their portion of the customer toll revenue from the long distance company. The image of a small country realizing that they can make money in this manner is somewhat ironic.

- Phone call-based response capability for shutting down suspicious user IDs. This type of simple response is not very involved, but it works well.
- Comprehensive report generation for perusal of potentially fraudulent activity; XIOX makes a library of useful reports available as part of the Hacker Tracker product.
- Archival subsystems for storage of call records and similar information. Archives of this information will provide useful data for correlation with other intrusion detection activities.

These features work together with simple authorizations (call-back features are implemented and all users are assigned user IDs and passwords) to provide an effective intrusion detection system for enterprise telephony.

### HOW DOES THE ABNORMAL BEHAVIOR SIGNATURE METHOD WORK?

As was suggested in Chapter 1, the use of abnormal behavioral signatures, sometimes also called attack signatures, is particularly common in on-the-fly intrusion detection systems. These signatures come in two different types:

- *Attack Signatures.* These are dynamic attack profile signatures of related activity patterns that might constitute a security problem. These attack signatures usually involve some temporal relation on a sequence of actions that might or might not be interleaved with unrelated actions. (Ironically, the best source of attack signatures is the plethora of hacking and cracking sites on the Internet.)
- *Select Character Strings.* These are the character string signatures that might be considered suspicious in any service query across a network (such as the strings '/etc/passwd', 'Financial Proposal', or 'Competitive Analysis'). The proper identification of strings to include requires an analysis of attack critical paths. Thus, if a security analyst comes to the conclusion that some attack cannot proceed without the attacker invoking command 'ABC' with arguments '–XYZ', then the pattern 'ABC –XYZ' would be a good candidate for inclusion in the intrusion detection string database.

The use of signatures is depicted in Figure 2-14 (note that this is an enhancement to an earlier depiction from Chapter 1).

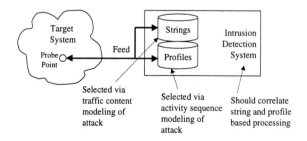

**Figure 2-14.** Abnormal Behavior Signature Method

Each of these types of abnormal behavioral signatures will play a role in most practical intrusion detection systems. In the section below, we demonstrate the use of a generic firewall as the basis for attack profile specification to detect attack. Then we demonstrate how the NetRanger NSX sensor component is used to detect select character strings in target system traffic.

## CASE STUDY: FIREWALL INTRUSION DETECTION RULES

Perhaps the most common use of a known abnormal behavior involves the use of firewall rules for detection of known attacks. Unfortunately, the richness of firewall rule languages remains immature, which severely limits the degree to which intrusion detection can be performed with an off-the-shelf firewall. Nevertheless, some known intrusions can be detected with a firewall.

The most common such intrusion involves an IP spoof attempt by an intruder. Suppose, for example, that an intruder exists somewhere on the public Internet outside a protected organizational gateway with registered IP addresses that we will refer to as *in* addresses. If a firewall exists at the organizational gateway, then the rule shown in Figure 2-15 can be included in the rule base (often the first rule) to try to detect known abnormal IP spoof attempts to gain access via a reported in source IP address for inbound packets.

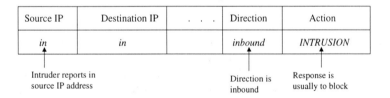

**Figure 2-15**. Firewall Rule to Detect IP Spoof

We know the above to be an attack because many external intruders know that some gateways allow packets to be passed to internal addresses if they emanate from an internal source address. This is particularly true in older routers that do not recognize the direction of their interfaces. It is also true in environments in which the perimeter devices are not properly configured. Thus, we can presume that packet direction as in the example shown above probably is associated with some improper activity (although, in reality, this is becoming less and less common as more administrators have learned to include this rule in their base).

While this example certainly introduces nothing new to any gateway, system, or security administrator, it does provide an existence proof that intrusion detection via firewall rule bases can be done. As we suggested earlier, the great barrier to the expansion of this functionality in firewalls is the primitive rule specification type of language used in firewalls today. Even with point and click GUI interfaces, the behavior that can be specified is minimal. One would expect that very soon, the research and product community will begin to focus on more general and effective ways to specify and implement the behavior of gateway devices such as routers and firewalls.

## CASE STUDY: STRING MATCHING IN NETRANGER NSX SENSOR

A powerful technique that is employed in several intrusion detection systems today involves on-the-fly matching of a collection of character strings with target traffic. The idea is reminiscent of the so-called "dirty word checkers" that sometimes emerge in security filters. Traffic passes the intrusion detection system, it is compared on-the-fly to each of the strings, and if a match occurs, then the specified response is initiated.

The WheelGroup implements this on-the-fly heuristic in their NetRanger product. The way it works is that a database of WheelGroup-provided strings comes embedded in the product internals. Security administrators have the option of adding to this list via a configuration file called *sensord.conf*. A sample *sensord.conf* entry is shown in Figure 2-16.

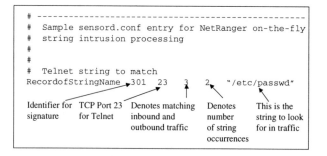

**Figure 2-16**. Sample NetRanger *sensord.conf* File

Note from Figure 2-16 that the *sensord.conf* configuration entries include the following:

- The specific string to be looked for in target traffic; in the example, the entry specifies that the string '/etc/passwd' would be considered suspicious.
- The port number for the service being examined; TCP port 23 in the example is Telnet.
- Specification of the direction in which to look for a given string; the directions include inbound, outbound, and bi-directional.
- The number of times a string must be seen before a given response action is taken.

NetRanger provides the capability for security administrators to define their own strings. This is powerful as it allows customization to environment-specific traffic. Not all intrusion detection systems include this functionality, but more and more are embedding this into their base system.

Some research needs to be done in the intrusion detection community to provide a set of common string patterns that we can all include as a baseline in our intrusion detection systems. It can be argued that this would simply alert the cracking community to those strings to avoid, and this is certainly true. However, in reality, this sort of activity makes cracking more difficult by raising the low-water mark for most systems. Local administrators can really raise their own security by including locally defined strings that they do not share outside their community. One might imagine clearinghouses of string patterns emerging and network administrators using this information with local knowledge to identify an effective set of string sentinels to key on.

## HOW DOES THE PARAMETER PATTERN MATCHING METHOD WORK?

Of all the methods used for intrusion detection, this one is the most subtle. The basis for this method is that in an operational setting, system operators and administrators will monitor a variety of different system and network attributes. This monitoring is usually not focused on security and may be explicit as part of a network or system management discipline (e.g., using an SNMP-based tool). As a result, predictable, periodic reporting of information from this disciplined monitoring will often be available.

To complement this disciplined monitoring, system operators and administrators usually also perform arbitrary monitoring of various attributes that may not provide information relevant to anything important. Sometimes, however, it is this type of monitoring that directs an administrator to malicious activity. Recall Cliff Stoll's account in his book, *The Cuckoo's Egg* (Doubleday, 1992) in which an small, seemingly unimportant accounting error led to a multi-year chase of a West German cracker.

As a result, this method involves the use of day-to-day operational experience as the basis for detecting anomalies. From a logical perspective, it can be viewed as a special case of the normal profiling method. It is separated out here because the explicit development of profiles may not be included in the approach. Instead, operators doing normal system and network management activity might or might not detect some sort of change in the parameters they typically monitor. This explains our use of the pattern matching term for this method.

Such pattern matching constitutes an especially powerful approach because it provides an intrusion detection capability for attacks that might not be predictable. In fact, human operators might detect subtle changes that they can neither explain nor understand. It is these types of changes, however, that could lead to detection of a problem. In network operations centers where not everyone is a network security expert, this arrangement can be very helpful. It is also helpful in environments where intensive network management information is readily available on a regular basis.

A high-level view of this subtle parameter matching intrusion detection method is depicted in Figure 2-17.

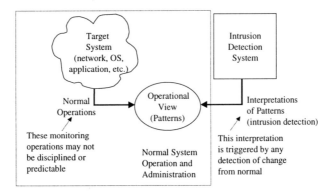

**Figure 2-17.** Pattern Matching Method of Intrusion Detection

### CASE STUDY: HP OPENVIEW NETWORK MANGEMENT

We've mentioned earlier the important relationship between intrusion detection and network management tools, particularly for detecting anomalous behavior in monitored environments. HP OpenView network management environments provides many opportunities for monitoring in an operational environment that may be useful in intrusion detection. Some of the functions available in a typical OpenView environment include the following:

- *Performance monitoring.* This can identify unusual performance attributes in traffic; in fact, performance problems are often the only available signal that some attack is taking place. The crypto community has known for many years that intensive processing on many servers over weekends and holidays sometimes means that cracking is going on. (Or that RSA is running yet another cryptanalysis contest.)

- *Capacity planning via analysis of historical data.* This may uncover certain anomalies not noticed elsewhere; throughout our discussions on intrusion detection, we will repeatedly point to the importance of examining historical data to detect pattern changes. If your network management tools are already doing this, then you should take advantage of the results.

- *Traffic monitoring for Ethernet, NetWare, and Token Ring.* This can be in probes, Hubs, routers, bridges, or other devices; this is important in modern Intranets that include multiple protocols and LAN network components. Too much intrusion detection R&D is focused entirely on TCP/IP, without attention to the link transport protocols or to protocols such as IPX.

- *Network tuning and capacity planning.* This may uncover anomalies not noticed elsewhere. If the network tuning methods are not performing as usual, this may signal an anomaly.

- *Network management functions.* This includes ping, Telnet, protocol analysis, packet capture and decode, network node discovery, and network mapping.

In addition, one of the features of OpenView is that network managers have the option of adding their own tools to their OpenView environment. A development environment is provided a means via the HP OpenView SNMP Developer's Kit for creating applications to manage SNMP-TCP/IP devices. This allows for the introduction of customized tools that may have useful intrusion detection implications. This is especially important because in most of the security environments that we are familiar with, good network security administrators almost always employ locally developed monitoring tools that are viewed as invaluable to their environment.

### A RECENT CRITICISM OF INTRUSION DETECTION METHODS

The intrusion detection community was buzzing with discussion and debate in early 1998 with the Internet publication of a technical article by Thomas Ptacek and Timothy Newsham from Secure Networks Inc. of Canada. It's rare that a published criticism hits on something significant, but I think this paper establishes some valid and interesting points. Their article summarizes a series of specific criticisms of network-based intrusion detection methods such as the ones described in this chapter. In this section, we extrapolate and generalize their remarks somewhat. The essence of their intrusion detection method criticism can be summarized as follows:

*On-the-fly traffic interpretation problem.* The first point is that transit bits captured by network intrusion detection methods don't provide enough information about target server activity to determine if an attack is really occurring. This really strikes at the correlation issue because they are saying that without context information, network intrusion detection systems cannot reliably determine the intent of something potentially suspicious.

Consider, for example, the case in which an intrusion detection system is watching traffic into a LAN environment with two servers, A and B. If server A is in an attack state such that some transit message which flies past the intrusion detection system is enough to complete the attack, then the intrusion detection system should note this fact. It is possible, however, that this same message could be perfectly reasonable for server B which is not in any attack state.

Our response here is that by correlating information between the server-based auditing subsystem and the network-based intrusion detection system, this problem largely goes away. The authors' contention that current intrusion detection systems do not do this is well taken. Only in customized, carefully integrated environments can this sort of thing be done properly.

*Server audit interpretation problem.* Their next point is that a server analyzing data relevant to its local processing will have difficulty correlating such activity with real-time network activity. This is essentially the same problem as the previous one, but with the roles of server and network intrusion detection system reversed.

This problem stems from the fact that security-relevant network events may be invisible to the server. It must be noted again that in environments where servers and network intrusion detection systems share information across an infrastructure, this may not be a problem.

*Fail-open nature of intrusion detection.* This criticism focuses primarily on on-the-fly network capture methods of intrusion detection. The idea is that if an enterprise uses a passive, off-line intrusion detection for protection, then if the intrusion detection system fails, the system becomes open to attack without any protection.

The presumption here is that intrusion detection systems are being used as the sole security mechanism. This is rarely the case. In fact, if a firewall exists and is being complemented with an intrusion detection system, then this fail-safe argument weakens to the case in which intrusion monitoring is not available if the intrusion detection system fails.

*Intrusion detection methods may be vulnerable to insertion attacks.* Another criticism is that if an intrusion detection system is configured to detect strings in on-the-fly traffic, then an attacker may be able to insert data into traffic to camouflage the target string. This technique plays on the fact that a target server and an intrusion detection system may treat incoming packets differently. This implies that under the appropriate set of circumstances, an attacker can insert noise that the intrusion detection system will see, but that the target server will not.

One of the examples provided in the paper is that if an intrusion detection system is keying on some string such as '/etc/shadow', then the attacker in this context can insert noise destined for the intrusion detection system to camouflage the real string. The real string sent would be something like '/eXtXc/XsXhXaXdXoXw', and the destination server could be set-up to ignore the X's in a tunneling arrangement, or the invader would utilize knowledge of the destination servers network drivers to find noise that would likely be ignored by the server, but picked up by the intrusion detection system.

A comment here is that such odd transmission strings might be detected by a clever intrusion detection system databases. For example, command-line traffic that looks so odd with so much noise in an environment where this is not normally seen might actually be picked up. In reality, I've never seen this or experimented with it. Perhaps this might be a good project for a graduate student.

*Intrusion detection methods may be vulnerable to evasion attacks.* Using the argument just made (i.e., that an attacker can take advantage of the fact that an intrusion detection system and target server may be interested in different things), an attacker might embed an attack in traffic ignored by the intrusion detection system. This is the same issue as discussed previously but with the insertion destined for the server, rather than the intrusion detection system.

*Intrusion detection methods may be vulnerable to denial of service attacks.* Finally, the case can be made that if an intrusion detection system is expecting some series of actions, then an attacker can wreak havoc by simply arranging for lots of the expected actions to occur. If the response portion of the intrusion detection system involves considerable activity, then the overhead of dealing with all this planted activity may make the system incapable of dealing with a real attack. The result is a denial of service attack to the intrusion detection system as a protective method.

We've experimented with detecting flood-like attack behavior and one technique for dealing with this is to respond to initial flood behavior with your baroque response processes. Perhaps a threshold can be set for initial activity. Subsequent activity of the same type is then ignored for a specified period of time until your internal processes can catch up. This is a patch solution, but it seems to work in some cases. Never forget that denial of service and flood-type attacks are often the toughest to deal with.

## BIBLIOGRAPHIC NOTES

The quote by Teresa Lunt is from her 1988 survey of audit trail and intrusion detection tools [LU88]. The quote from Porras and Neumann is from their EMERALD paper [PN97]. The *HP OpenView* text by Huntington-Lee, Terplan, and Gibson [HU97] was useful in the development of the RMON example. The WheelGroup's 1997 NetRanger Training Manual was used in the development of the NetRanger examples. Information from the XIOX and SecureIt Web sites was useful in preparation of the materials on the SecureView tool, the XIOX tool, and the toll fraud discussion. The paper by Ranum et al. [RA97] was found on the Internet and used for the NFR material. The security text by Simpson Garfinkel and Gene Spafford [GS96] had nice Swatch and Syslog explanations that were helpful in the preparation of the associated sections. Their audit processing information was also helpful. The National Computer Security Center "Guide to Understanding Audit in Trusted Systems" (NCSC-TG-001, July 28, 1987) [NC87] was used in the preparation of this chapter. The Secure Networks article by Ptacek and Newsham entitled "Insertion, Evasion, and Denial of Service: Eluding Network Intrusion Detection," [PN98] is available on the Web at http://www.securenetworks.com/papers/ids.html. This is highly recommended reading for students of intrusion detection. During the writing of the sections on audit trail processing, I found myself referring to the Final Evaluation Report for AT&T System V/MLS Release 1.2, issued 29 September, 1990 from the National Computer Security Center (NCSC) and available as CSC-EPL-90/003 (C-Evaluation Report No. 17-91).

# CHAPTER 3:
## INTRUSION DETECTION ARCHITECTURE

*Intrusion and anomaly detection tools are more effective if they can provide the system administrator information on the status of the network in real time.*

J. Alves-Foss

*The various intrusion detection efforts (funded by ARPA) should be usable and reusable together and have lasting value to customers of intrusion detection systems.*

From the CIDF specification

### AN INTRUSION DETECTION SYSTEM ARCHITECTURAL SCHEMA

Recall that back in Chapter 1, we introduced a simple architectural model for intrusion detection with some high-level descriptions of basic functionality. The use of a highly simplified architectural model is common in computer science as a means for describing complex systems, as long as students and readers are cognizant of the details that are being abstracted. Our goal in this chapter is to extend the simple notion to a more in-depth analysis of intrusion detection architectures. We do this by first introducing a architectural schema for a practical intrusion detection system. Later in the chapter, we will examine the Common Intrusion Detection Framework (CIDF) architecture and relate it to our discussion.

Note that architectures for intrusion detection will differ based on the products used, the types of attacks being countered, the legacy network environment, the preferences of the network security administrators involved, the budget of the target environment, the assets to be protected, and many more relevant factors. One should recognize, however, that these differences will be found in virtually any computing or network system. Also note that we focus here primarily on the functional aspects of intrusion detection as they are realized in computing and networking components. In real intrusion detection for a nontrivial enterprise, much of the intrusion detection that takes place involves people, processes, and procedures that may not involve any functionality. So this further complicates the presentation of a generic intrusion detection architecture in this chapter.

Nevertheless, some pedagogical value is provided in a baseline schema for an intrusion detection functional architecture, one that captures the salient aspects of practical intrusion detection that are likely to be present in any realistic case. In this section, we introduce such a schema and we focus on those functional elements of intrusion detection that we believe will continue in prominence as intrusion detection techniques mature. The fact that intrusion detection technology and products are changing so rapidly certainly reduces the likelihood that we will be correct in our estimation; but we proceed in any event. The basic intrusion detection architectural schema we propose is shown in the diagram in Figure 3-1 below.

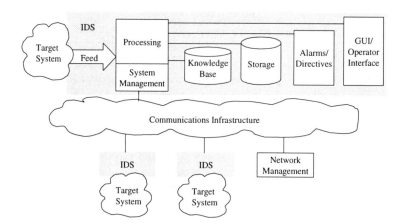

**Figure 3-1**. Intrusion Detection Architectural Schema

Some issues that are important to highlight with respect to the schema in Figure 3-1 include the following:

- The details of each component in the diagram will be addressed in this chapter. This schema is introduced here to give you a first look at how a typical intrusion detection environment might look.

- The shaded portion of the figure represents a single intrusion detection system (denoted IDS in the diagram). We purposely blurred the shading into the target system to denote the fuzzy demarcation points that typically exist between intrusion detection monitoring and target environments. Sometimes, for example, the intrusion monitoring requires that code be inserted directly into the target operating system. Other times, passive monitoring on the network is possible without changes to the target system.

- The schema suggests that multiple intrusion detection systems can be integrated into an infrastructure. This will require the usual network management functions, some providing enhanced security protection (e.g., event correlation support), others providing generic management functions (e.g., configuration control, status monitoring).

- For most Intranet environments, access points from separate networks like the Internet to the organizational Intranet serve as attractive locations for intrusion detection systems. Nevertheless, nothing prevents the schema from having a single or many intrusion detection systems. In fact, as most security engineers come to recognize that the internal threat to their resources is often much greater than the external threat, the use of intrusion detection on internal choke points should increase dramatically.

## WHAT ARE THE FUNCTIONAL COMPONENTS OF INTRUSION DETECTION SYSTEMS?

The major functional components included in an intrusion detection system architecture can be derived directly from the diagram in Figure 3-1. These components are as follows:

*Target system.* The system on which activity and behavior is being examined from an intrusion detection perspective is considered the target system. Clearly, the target system must have assets worth protecting before any intrusion detection system can even be considered. Corporate Intranets are good examples of typical target systems for intrusion detection. As the United States National Information Infrastructure (NII) becomes more dependent on computing and networking, it too becomes a good candidate for intrusion detection.

*Feed.* The abstract notion of "feed" is meant to represent some means for deriving information from a target system for intrusion detection system processing and analysis. Obviously, in a network setting, this feed might constitute a live, dedicated network connection in the traditional sense; but it could also mean a flow of information through any number of interim storage points and processing components. A key issue with respect to feeds is whether to carry monitored traffic from a sensor to a central correlation site for processing or to perform processing locally and carry alarms back to the central correlation site for processing. Intrusion detection experts should be able to rattle off the pros and cons of distributed versus centralized feed processing (see below).

*Processing.* We refer to processing as the execution of algorithms designed to detect malicious activity to some target system. These algorithms will typically make use of basic principles and heuristics to direct the types of processing performed. Furthermore, the underlying physical architecture associated with processing must have sufficient power and storage to implement the selected algorithms. Later in this chapter, we will present a collection of high-level pseudo coded routines to demonstrate the types of algorithms embedded into modern intrusion detection systems. The algorithms are simpler than the reader might expect; this stems from our belief that complicated algorithmic analysis looking for deep statistical relationships is not as effective as routine processing of information from probes in properly selected locations.

*Knowledge base.* In an intrusion detection system, knowledge bases are used to store information about attacks as signatures and strings, user and system behavior as profiles, and other related information. These knowledge bases must be designed with appropriate protection, capacity, and processing queries to support the desired intrusion detection functions. They also must be associated with an update function so that information about new attacks can be installed into existing knowledge bases. A new industry is likely to emerge for knowledge base modules from third parties for insertion into your intrusion detection system (not unlike the way updates to virus detection packages can be downloaded and used).

*Storage.* The types of information that must be stored in an intrusion detection system will vary from short term cached information about an on-going session to longer term event-related session information that must be sent to an audit trail or archive. Storage capacity requirements will obviously be environment specific. A key issue here is that as network capacities grow from slow Ethernet to much greater rates, short term cached information will require more memory. Hardware packet capture routines will also greatly increase the need for interim storage as target system capacities increase.

*Alarms/directives.* The most familiar response in an intrusion detection system is to send an alarm to an interested party, processing component, or other intrusion detection system. This may or may not be enough in a given target environment. For example, the inclusion of alarms that automatically reconfigure parts of the intrusion detection based on detected activity are becoming more feasible. As this trend continues, we believe that intrusion detection systems will require messaging architectures for transmitting information between components. Such messaging is a major element of the Common Intrusion Detection Framework.

*GUI/operator interface.* Display (graphical or otherwise) by an intrusion detection system for an operator or administrator requires attention to proper presentation, combination, and representation of information. Most commercial intrusion detection systems are migrating to a point-and-click interface for administration and interpretation, which may be viewed as bad news by hard core UNIX administrators. In reality, operational environments only achieve a proper user interface after considerable live experience and feedback to and from interface developers and the operational users. Few intrusion detection researchers and system vendors understand this subtle point. Instead, they continue to point to a glitzy user interface as a salient feature of their system.

*Communications infrastructure.* Different components of an intrusion detection system and different intrusion detection systems require a means for communication. This may involve infrastructure protections such as encryption and access control to protect information such as alarms in transit between intrusion detection system components. It also requires standard messaging between components to ensure that information or requests from one part of the intrusion detection infrastructure get delivered reliably to the appropriate destination. For the average Intranet with multiple intrusion detection probe points, the communication infrastructure is the actual Intranet, perhaps with virtual private network (VPN) transport. Alternatives include dial access transport for low volumes or frame relay private virtual circuits (PVCs) for greater volumes.

*Multiple intrusion detection systems.* As was just suggested, some environments may involve the use of more than one intrusion detection system. When this is true, the overall infrastructure must support the types of care and maintenance required to deal with multiple systems. Efforts such as the Common Intrusion Detection Framework (CIDF) are being organized to ease the use of multiple systems from different vendors. The US National Information Infrastructure (NII) is a classic example of a collection of resources requiring multiple intrusion detection systems.

*Network management.* Network management systems are commonly found in any nontrivial environment performing intrusion detection. The network management system may be embedded into the intrusion processing or it could be used to complement intrusion detection via remote monitoring and administration activity. Most intrusion detection system researchers forget this interaction between intrusion detection and network management.

## TARGET SYSTEMS FOR INTRUSION DETECTION

Determining the types of systems that are good targets for intrusion detection is a part of the more general system security engineering challenge. Specifically, security engineers have the task of trying to reduce security risk in a cost-effective and practical manner. If intrusion detection system technology is now considered practical, then such technology must be assumed to be present in the security engineer's risk management toolkit.

Once a system has been deemed fit for intrusion detection, the feed components and back-end processing, storage, and other components can be integrated into the environment. Figure 3-2 depicts how target systems fit into this overall intrusion detection system architectural schema. Note that the input feed of information and the output response activities represent the primary interfaces between a target system and the intrusion detection system.

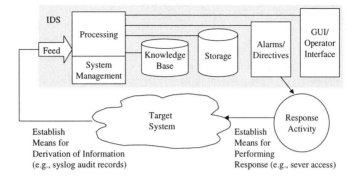

**Figure 3-2.** Target Systems in Intrusion Detection Architectural Schema

We can provide a criteria for determining when intrusion detection is appropriate. Specifically, the types of systems that tend to be good targets for intrusion detection include those computing applications, operating systems, and network systems that exhibit at least the following features:

- *Critical assets.* The presence of critical assets of interest to malicious intruders or compromised insiders signals that intrusion detection may be appropriate. If no such assets are present, then the likelihood of intrusions would not be great. But in reality, do any environments exist without *some* assets of interest?

- *Management perception.* The perception by management and staff that security protections need to be augmented with monitoring, intrusive or non-intrusive is an important criterion. Intrusion detection requires time, resource, and effort investments. The perception by management that monitoring is needed will be required to overcome this practical hurdle.

- *Existing feeds.* The ability to utilize existing information feeds or insert new ones for intrusion processing will determine the success of an intrusion detection project. Without the ability to extract information, intrusion detection cannot be performed effectively. If existing information feeds are present this is great. If not, then support is required to create new ones.

- *Personnel.* Appropriate personnel must be available that can interpret information about target system activity. The notion that intrusion detection can become fully automated is controversial. Certainly, present systems require extensive human support, particularly in terms of correlation and interpretation of information. We believe this will continue, even as systems gain functionality.

- *Response.* An environment must exist where some form of response can be initiated based on detected intrusion information. Since the overall goal is risk reduction, response procedures represent the means by which this goal can be achieved.

The presence or absence of these features will help security managers decide if an intrusion detection system is required.

In practice, however, virtually all intrusion detection is performed either in an Internet-based network such as an organizational Intranet or as part of an operating system security scheme, usually on a UNIX or Windows NT-based system. Hopefully, as intrusion detection technology evolves, additional target systems such as database systems, real time controls systems, and office automation systems will be integrated with practical intrusion detection.

It is also worth noting again that as national information infrastructures become more dependent on public Internet and TCP/IP-based technology, they also become more attractive frameworks for intrusion detection systems. Considerable attention has been placed in the research literature on techniques for performing this integration.

## CAN INTRUSION DETECTION BE PERFORMED IN NON-TCP/IP SETTINGS?

The vast majority of intrusion detection systems to date are built directly for TCP/IP-based environments where Intranet managers want to monitor their Internet gateway traffic. Engineering issues must be dealt with in intrusion detection environments for which this Intranet gateway model does not apply (e.g., IPX LAN environments, telephony signaling systems, IBM SNA protocol environments).

Two approaches exist for intrusion detection systems in non-TCP/IP target system environments:

- Front-end processing can be used to create interfaces between the TCP/IP and non-TCP/IP processing environments. This allows use of existing off-the-shelf intrusion detection systems in these target systems. The use of virtual private networking is a special case in that the "outer wrapper" could be TCP/IP, but the "inner wrapper" could be the target TCP/IP traffic for intrusion detection processing. Front end virtual private networking servers would be required to gain access to this tunneled traffic for intrusion processing.
- Custom intrusion detection systems for non-TCP/IP target systems can be constructed based on the unique attributes of the target protocols and processing approaches. Simple war dial intrusion detection systems for organizations based on their PBX or Centrex call detail records is an example.

The diagram in Figure 3-3 shows the use of intrusion detection system approaches for TCP/IP and non-TCP/IP environments.

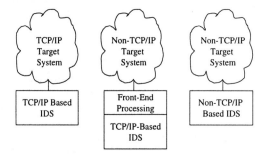

**Figure 3-3.** TCP/IP and non-TCP/IP Target Environments

---

*Intrusion Detection and Signaling System 7 (SS7)*
Most people equate packet networking with TCP/IP. Anyone familiar with telephony, however, knows that a major, non-TCP/IP packet network exists to provide signaling for public switched telephony. This global network uses the Signaling System 7 (SS7) packet protocol. Intrusion detection methods that are protocol independent such as flood pattern detection and end point analyses easily apply to packet protocols such as SS7. No vendors to our knowledge have implemented this scheme, however.

## INFORMATION FEEDS FOR INTRUSION DETECTION SYSTEMS

We have said several times throughout this text that without a means for extracting information from a target system, intrusion detection cannot be performed. Recall also that we described some methods in Chapter 2 by which traffic can be diverted for on-the-fly and off-line audit trail processing. Figure 3-4 depicts these two approaches—audit trail and packet feed—for producing information feeds for target systems.

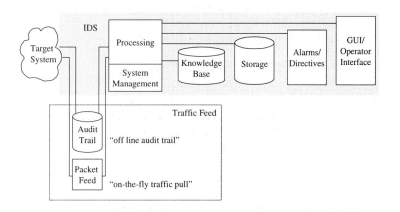

**Figure 3-4.** Information Feeds for Intrusion Detection Systems

In this section, we continue our discussion on information feeds by examining some different architectural means by which such information can be obtained for intrusion processing. Architectures for intrusion detection systems will typically include information feeds that are directly based on the following factors:

- The type of target system will obviously affect the manner in which information feeds are designed. The two major types for consideration include dynamic feeds from network media and transfers of records from audit logs.
- Any real time requirements that are present based on the application environment will have an effect on the type of information feed used. If, for example, no requirement exists for timely processing of information, then off-line batch transfers of information can be used as the feed approach. If more timely processing is required, then in-line traffic feeds may be required.

- Network capacity will influence the manner in which dynamic traffic feeds are pulled for intrusion detection. If the target system network environment is based on the Asynchronous Transfer Mode (ATM) protocol over fiber, then the traffic feed components must be capable of handling the potentially large capacity. (Intrusion detection system vendors can provide information on the types of server capacities that are required for different types of media.)
- Target system activity will also have information feed capacity implications. An operating system, for example, that includes lots of network activity will require probes in network internals (e.g., device drivers) whereas stand-alone servers may get by with a set of probes that are more focused on local system resource activities (e.g., basic file operations).
- Information feed implementations can consist of a variety of different approaches including physical choke point taps, distributed information collection through operating system, network system, or application probe points, and explicitly derived information from audit trail processing systems.
- In UNIX-based TCP/IP environments, the *tcpdump* utility is frequently used for monitoring traffic via a workstation in promiscuous mode. A general language for specifying which packets are to be recorded is included; presumably Tsutomu Shimomura was running a modified version of *tcpdump* when he helped catch Kevin Mitnick (according to certain published reports). The tool is available via ftp at *ftp.ee.lbl.gov*. A common practical question that emerges is whether the program is keeping up or dropping packets on the target media. The intrusion detection community remains relatively immature in answering these types of performance related questions.

## CASE STUDY: NETWORK FLIGHT RECORDER PACKET SUCKERS

Network Flight Recorder (NFR) is a network monitoring and processing tool designed by Marcus Ranum that is becoming widely used and that exhibits some unique intrusion detection features. In this section, we focus on the promiscuous packet transfer component called, interestingly enough, the NFR packet sucker.

The development of the NFR packet sucker is based on the *libpcap* packet capture interface, which offers a degree of operating system independence, hence improving NFR portability. An issue that arose is that the packet capture facilities in *libpcap* could not keep up with high capacity bursts of network traffic. This issue of maintaining monitoring buffers in the presence of the typically bursty nature of data network traffic is an important design challenge for intrusion detection system designers.

When NFR packet suckers grab packets from the network, they send the packets to the decision engine. NFR is designed in a modular manner with application programmer interfaces (APIs) that allow packet suckers to operate autonomously from other components. This loose decoupling of monitoring and processing is not always found in available intrusion detection systems. Such decoupling also improves concurrent buffering in different packet suckers.

At the time of this writing, NFR code is being made available on the Web. This will no doubt result in considerable experimentation on various networks and operating systems with this *libpcap*-based method of packet sniffing (also known as sucking). As was suggested in the previous section, an obvious intrusion detection research area in which more experimental results are needed is system performance for different network capacities.

We are of the belief that serious packet capture in modern internetworks is almost always done with dedicated hardware. As intrusion detection systems mature, it seems inevitable that novel applications like NFR will be married with fast packet capture routines implemented in hardware. Appropriate filtering and buffering in a proper hardware/software combination would bridge the gap between the huge capacity for network feeds and the more modest ability of computer-based applications to process this traffic. This is not a new concept, however, as certain digital signal processing applications have worked this way for many years.

## PROCESSING IN INTRUSION DETECTION

Once information feeds are provided to the intrusion detection system, the next functional component in our architectural schema is the processing element. Figure 3-5 depicts processing in the context of our intrusion detection architectural schema.

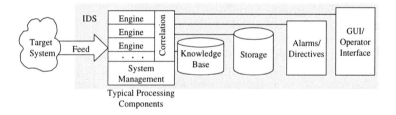

**Figure 3-5**. Processing in Intrusion Detection System Architecture

The processing component is certainly the most complex and difficult to understand aspect of any intrusion detection system. The diagram in Figure 3-5 suggests that the processing component include three primary components. These are discussed below.

*Engines.* The processing component of the architecture is represented as a collection of engines, also referred to as filters in some systems. This approach is becoming a de facto approach to the challenges inherent in intrusion processing. That is, intrusion detection system designers have begun to arrange their processing elements into a series of autonomous engines that each perform a specific task. This architectural approach is reminiscent of object oriented design, and thus carries all the associated benefits of modularity, complexity avoidance, and so on.

*System Management.* A system management element is included to coordinate processing. Nothing in this system management arrangement is unique to intrusion detection technology, but proper security protection of this management function is obviously required.

*Correlation.* The processing complex also includes a correlation component to combine results from the individual processing engines. The correlation component needs an interface to other elements in the intrusion detection system so that information from other systems can be included in the correlation.

## WHAT ALGORITHMS DO INTRUSION PROCESSING ELEMENTS IMPLEMENT?

No single approach exists for intrusion detection system processing. Vendors continue to search for better, faster, and more effective processing approaches to detecting intrusions in target system activity. Nevertheless, a collection of processing algorithms can be identified from recent research, development, and product experiences. These algorithms collectively comprise the present state-of-the-practice and state-of-the-art in intrusion detection system processing internals.

In this section, we describe several algorithmic approaches to intrusion processing. It is possible in a given intrusion detection system that some or all of these would be actually implemented. Our intention is not to provide a complete record of all possible algorithms but rather to offer some insight into the types of concerns that the intrusion detection algorithm designer must consider.

The notation we use is standard pseudo-code; we ignore low level details in favor of illustrating high level ideas. As a result, it is doubtful that anyone reading these algorithmic descriptions could go off and implement them without considerable additional work. Nevertheless, we remind the reader that these algorithms are based on reported R&D and from product literature. Thus, they should not be viewed as what *could* be implemented, but rather as what is currently being done.

*Algorithm 1: Baseline Processing.* We can describe one approach to intrusion detection processing at the highest level by the following baseline processing algorithm in Figure 3-6 (where we select function and parameter names suggestive of their intended meaning):

```
1    repeat                    /* iterative loop forever */
2          target_system_feed (info)
3          intrusion_processing (info, result)
4          if (result = intrusion) then
5          initiate_response (result) fi
6    forever
```

**Figure 3-6**. Baseline Processing Algorithm Sketch

Annotation of the Algorithm in Figure 3-6:

- Line 1: Throughout our algorithmic presentations in this chapter, we will repeatedly use repeat/forever loops to demonstrate the continuous, embedded systems-nature of intrusion detection. Note that we also underline words that are viewed as reserved words in our pseudo-code language.

- Line 2: The function target_system_feed (info) is intended to represent a means by which information is obtained from some target system feed in a suitable format for processing. This abstracts *quite a bit* of detail.

- Line 3: The function intrusion_processing (info, result) is intended to represent the manner in which processing accepts an information stream, processes it, and returns a result.

- Line 4: The comparison of the result to some representation of intrusion is a key component in intrusion detection. This might be incorporated into the function intrusion_processing (info, result) which might encode some representation of an intrusion into the result.

- Line 5: The function initiate_response (result) represents whatever response activity is required for the result.
- Line 6: This ends the loop.

This small code sketch provides a useful means for identifying some of the processing challenges in intrusion detection. For example, consider that the sample algorithm is encapsulated by a single process that repeats itself and includes information feeds, processing, and response. An issue highlighted by this repetitive loop is how the intrusion detection system maintains a continual and vigilant processing presence in the target system. Some approaches to this required vigilance are described below.

*Tight coupling of monitoring, processing, and response.* In this approach, the intrusion detection system combines the monitoring, processing, and response activities into a cohesive cycle. Processing of extracted information is performed by components that carry through the monitoring, analysis, and response initiation activities. The image of a single process comes to mind in this tight coupling scenario.

*Loose coupling of monitoring, processing, and response.* In this approach, the intrusion detection system separates monitoring, processing, and response functionality into different architectural components. This separation could be logical, physical, or both. The image of multiple processes perhaps in different locations for this scenario comes to mind. Figure 3-7 shows the basic notions of tight and loose coupling in intrusion detection processing.

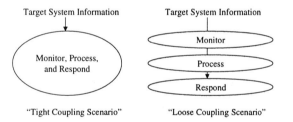

**Figure 3-7**. Couplings of Monitoring, Processing, and Response

It should be noted that the reason tight and loose coupling is useful in the consideration and design of intrusion detection systems is that it provides insight into architectural designs. For instance, we can see that in computing environments where existing platforms extract information via existing monitoring functions (e.g., HP OpenView) and off-line tools are used to process these trails, this corresponds to a loose coupling of the monitoring and processing functions. From this, we can see the obvious benefits of loose coupling such as easier integration with existing components and perhaps better use of available resources.

On the other hand, in off-the-shelf intrusion detection systems such as RealSecure or Emerald, the various components fit together into a cohesive system. Furthermore, these components are interdependent; that is, the system will not work with replacement parts. The obvious benefits of this include a more optimized set of components for the intrusion detection job as well as a more uniform monitoring, processing, and response initiation environment.

*Algorithm 2: Dynamic Association.* An additional algorithmic approach that is worth mentioning here involves the dynamic creation of so-called associations. The idea in the association algorithm is that as traffic is monitored, it is compared with previous monitored activity to determine if correlation is possible. This algorithm is sketched in Figure 3-8.

```
1        repeat
2            target_system_feed (info)
3            if suspicious (info)and new (info) then
4                create new association fi
5            if suspicious (info) and not new (info) then
6                add info to relevant associations fi
7        forever
```

**Figure 3-8.** Dynamic Association Algorithm Sketch

Annotation of the Algorithm in Figure 3-8:

- Line 1: Begins the iterative loop.
- Line 2: This is the same function used to obtain information from the target system in the previous algorithm. As we'll see in the Common Intrusion Detection Framework (CIDF) later in the chapter, there are many opportunities for reuse of components in different intrusion detection settings.
- Line 3: We're checking to see if the observed information is suspicious and new. This implies that perhaps we have not seen this sort of thing before.
- Line 4: If the conditions in the previous line are met, we're going to create a so-called new association.
- Line 5: If the information is suspicious, but not new, then we must have seen it before. The key here is that the definition of information being not new is that at least one active association is being kept for something similar.
- Line 6: In this section of the code, we include the new information in the relevant active associations.
- Line 7: This ends the loop.

The idea here is simple: if information becomes available that is considered suspicious (for whatever reason), then it must be examined in the context of previous information. As suggested in the annotation, we call the data structures used to record previous suspicious activity an *association*. The algorithm in Figure 3-5 shows how associations can be built on the fly.

Note that when suspicious information is considered suspicious and new (i.e., not related to any previous activity), it is used to create a new association. Likewise, when suspicious information is considered not new (i.e., somehow related to previous activity), then it is appended to an existing association. This is a powerful concept that has its roots in basic network management and fraud detection.

As an example, imagine that an intrusion detection system implementing the association concept notices that user EVE has attempted to guess a root password. Suppose that this is the first time it has occurred for this user and for this type of activity, but that it is considered suspicious. The processing engine would thus create an association with one entry: <EVE guess root password> (this presumes that the implementation of an association is a sequence).

If soon after, EVE tries to guess the root password again, then this suspicious activity might be appended to the association to produce the resulting: <EVE guess root

password, EVE guess root password>. Processing would be required to determine when this association has captured sufficient information to trip a response action.

Note also that if user EVE attempts some other suspicious action such as performing a port scan or a ping sweep, this might be appended to the existing association. It may also, however, be considered a new association at the same time. We recognize that our algorithmic presentation is informal, but it is our intention that the semantics not preclude some information from being both appended to multiple associations and also used to create a new association at the same time.

From this example, it should be evident that all sorts of processing issues emerge such as how to determine if information is new, how to determine if information is suspicious, and how to determine if information is relevant to a given association. These issues do not include the myriad of possibilities that exist for the processing that is required to determine if active associations correspond to known intrusions or if an association has become sufficiently stale that it is best discarded.

These processing decisions comprise a field within intrusion detection that is known as *correlation*. The technology of correlation is sufficiently rich that we devote an entire later chapter to this important topic. Amazingly, this topic has been severely ignored in computing and networking security literature.

*Algorithm 3: Statistical Profile Processing.* In the statistical processing of profiles, the general goal is to monitor behavior of some target system and to learn in an adaptive manner what constitutes normal behavior (and correspondingly what constitutes abnormal). A simple, high-level algorithm for statistical profile processing is sketched in Figure 3-9.

```
1      initial
2          expected = pattern_X  /* guess for new target */
3      repeat
4          target_system_feed (info)
5          if not consistent (info, pattern_X) then
6                  initiate_response (info) and "update pattern_X with respect to info" fi
7      forever
```

**Figure 3-9.** Statistical Profile Processing Algorithm Sketch

Annotation for Algorithm in Figure 3-9:
- Line 1: In our pseudo-code, we presume that initial values can be set for certain variables of use in the algorithm.
- Line 2: We set the initial value for some variable expected to be a guessed pattern. This pattern should incorporate everything known about the target system and what should be expected. This is the familiar profiling approach.
- Line 3: This begins the loop.
- Line 4: Recall our function for obtaining information from the target system.
- Line 5: Here's where we check to see if the observed information feed is consistent with the expected pattern. This typically involves pattern matching with respect to defined thresholds.
- Line 6: Here we initiate response using a function used in previous algorithms; we also update the profile based on what we are seeing. This is a design decision intended to reduce repetitive response alarms in an adaptive manner.

- Line 7: Ends the loop.

In the sketched algorithm, note that for some target system an expectation is created initially for what would be considered normal behavior. This may or may not be correct, and in fact, the purpose of the statistical processing is to make this determination and adaptively update the estimate based on observed behavior.

Note that a function called consistent is included in the algorithm sketch. The idea is that some functional means would be considered for determining if the observed behavior is consistent with the expected behavior. As suggested in the annotation, the most common such means for implementing this notion involves the use of *profiles*. Profiles are normally specified for either specific users or entire systems. The update action specified in the algorithm would typically involve changing these user or system profiles to match the observed behavior.

*Algorithm 4: Audit Trail Data Reduction.* In audit trail data reduction processing, the basic concept is to reduce the volume of data in the log files without losing any security relevant information. The motivation for this data reduction is to make the typically large volume of data more manageable for a security administrator as well as to highlight important trends or attack-related activities that may be obscured by less relevant information.

Obviously, the amount of information in the audit trail can be throttled by the auditing subsystem. For instance, in UNIX *syslog* auditing, the *syslog.conf* configuration file can be set to reduce the volume of audit records based on specific insights or knowledge. This helps to make audit trails more manageable.

When an incident occurs, security administrators want to focus on the relevant audit log information. Intrusion detection systems often provide this functionality via an audit trail data reduction processing scheme as depicted roughly in Figure 3-10.

```
1      initial
2          audit_log = <record1, record2, . . . , recordN>
3          report = <>
4          incident_info = "relevant info to incident"
5      for each combination of records (C) do
6          if relevant (C, incident_info) then
7            append (C) to report fi
8      od  /* report is now the new, reduced audit trail */
```

**Figure 3-10.** Audit Trail Data Reduction Algorithm Sketch

Annotation for the Algorithm in Figure 3-10:
- Line 1: Some initial values for variables are needed in this algorithm
- Line 2: The audit log is initially set with an arbitrary list of N records.
- Line 3: The report is initially an empty sequence (denoted <>).
- Line 4: The relevant information used in this line is that data supplied in a user query or directive that focuses in on the information in the log that must be examined. This is an important point because the reduction of volume in an audit log will only be as good as the parameters used to save, combine, or remove data.
- Line 5: Note that the loop examines combinations of records. This implies that audit records in isolation might have a different meaning than audit records in combination.

- Line 6: Here we compare the audit record combination to the relevant information.
- Line 7: If the record combination is relevant, then a new, smaller record log is used to house that information. In this sense, audit trail reduction can be viewed as a function on sequences that takes large sequences to (hopefully) smaller sequences.
- Line 8: Ends the loop; note that this is not a continuous loop.

In the algorithm, audit_log is initially a sequence of N audit records. We presume that a specific incident has occurred that has some associated incident_info that is relevant to the incident. The algorithm parses and processes combinations of audit records with respect to the incident-specific information. A report is constructed from this processing and this becomes the new, reduced volume audit trail.

Obviously, this algorithm sketch abstracts considerable detail. For example, the representation of incident_info is generally based on some security administrator provided query. In addition, audit trails are often so large that processing all combinations of audit records is generally impossible in any reasonable processing environment.

---

*Audit Trail Reduction Tools*

In the late 1980's several developers in my group at AT&T Labs constructed a tool called the Audit Trail Analysis Tool (ATAT) for UNIX System V/MLS trails. The technology, algorithms, and reports associated with that tool were not dramatically different than the tools being purported as breakthroughs today. Both ATAT and current tools suffer from weak methods for massive reduction without losing key information. They also suffer from incompatible audit trail formats for routers, firewalls, and servers. Considerable research is needed to make these data reduction tools truly represent advances in intrusion detection.

---

*Algorithm 5: Out-of-Band Correlation Processing.* The concept of correlation is examined in detail in Chapter 7. In this section, we provide a basic high-level algorithm that would be used to determine if pulled traffic from a target network or audit trail is somehow related to information made available out of band from the intrusion processing. Out of band information is any type of data derived from a source other than the target traffic feed. Figure 3-11 sketches a simple view of this processing.

```
1    repeat
2      target_system_feed (info)
3      if "operator has some out of band info" then
4        get_out_of_band (operator_input)
5        if relevant (info, operator_input) then
6          "combine out of band with target feed"  fi
7      fi
8    forever
```

**Figure 3-11.** Out of Band Correlation Processing Algorithm Sketch

Annotation of the Algorithm in Figure 3-11:
- Line 1: We put this in a repetitive loop to show that this type of correlation should be done continuously.
- Line 2: In-band information is pulled from the target system.
- Line 3: Here it is denoted that an operator has out of band information.

- Line 4: A function is presented here that accepts data from the operator. This abstracts many different issues related to the insertion of out of band information into an in-band data stream.
- Line 5: This function compares the out of band data with the stream to determine relevance.
- Line 6: Combining the information is done here. This could be as simple as insertion of the information into a database or it could be much more complex.

The concept of our out of band algorithm is simple: if an operator (or security administrator) has some information that may be considered critical, then it should be examined in the context of pulled traffic. For example, if the United States has just gotten itself into a war on the morning that a barrage of suspicious traffic is detected at some military base, then these two pieces of information require the obvious correlation in order that a proper interpretation be obtained.

*Algorithm 6: Attack Filter Pattern Matching.* This algorithm follows a typical pass-through semantics for a collection of ordered attack filters in an intrusion detection system engine. The approach is reminiscent of typical firewall rule processing semantics in which the processing engine examines successive rules until a logical match is made, after which the processing passes through the remainder of the attack filters (as in a case or switch statement in a programming language like C). The obvious challenge in such an algorithm is to maintain a collection of accurate, up-to-date attack filters. Figure 3-12 depicts the high-level algorithm sketch.

```
1       initial
2          filters = <filter(1), . . . filter(N)>
3          found_attacks = Ø
4       for i in 1 . . N do
5          if match (filter(i), target_system_feed (info)) then
6          "add i to found_attacks" fi
7       od
```

**Figure 3-12.** Multiple Filter Pattern Matching Algorithm Sketch

Annotation of the Algorithm in Figure 3-12:
- Line 2: These filters are the known attacks arranged in a sequence.
- Line 3: This set variable will be empty initially and will contain the indices of the filters matched to the input stream.
- Line 4: The loop parses through each of the attacks in the filter sequence.
- Line 5: Here, the input feed from the target system is compared with an attack in the filter sequence. Implementing this is non-trivial.
- Line 6: The index of any matched attack will be added to the set.

Obviously, the true complexity and richness of an attack filter processing match algorithm lies in the representation of the filters and how they are compared in real time to derived traffic. This is an area of active research in the intrusion detection community, especially since the primary complaint of many commercial intrusion detection users is that the ability to extend attack filters is typically not well-developed.

## INTRUSION DETECTION SYSTEM KNOWLEDGE BASES

The intrusion detection system components that maintain the knowledge used in processing and correlation of information are presumed to be resident in a collection of knowledge bases. We view these knowledge bases as being more than transient storage; instead, they would house data with a more lengthy usefulness. The information one expects to find in intrusion detection system knowledge bases includes the following:

- *Profiles of normal and abnormal user and system behavior.* This information includes descriptions of users and target systems to support the processing paradigm of detecting abnormal behavior as an attack indicator. Profiling user behavior often involves identifying activity patterns such as types of services and commands used, typical periods of activity, and amount of CPU usage. Profiling system behavior often involves identifying peak load periods, minimum processing periods, and amounts of CPU and memory usage.

- *Signatures of known attacks and intrusions.* This information represents attack signatures for known sequences of malicious action. The sources of these signatures includes security clearinghouses and cracking community dissemination in conferences, bulletin boards, available tools, and publications. A key research issue is how to represent these attacks.

---

*Intrusion Detection Information and CERT*

The Computer Emergency Response Team (CERT) offers valuable information to security administrators about known vulnerabilities and attacks (see http://www.cert.org/). A natural extension of their current activities would involve CERT offering attack information for direct insertion into an intrusion detection system knowledge base. This may be a lofty goal as the specification of attacks is in its infancy, and standards for knowledge base representation in intrusion detection systems may be a long way off. Nevertheless, this is a service that some suitable clearinghouse-type organization should consider providing.

---

- *Strings that denote suspicious traffic patterns.* This involves so-called "dirty word checking" in which sequences of characters are specified that correspond to suspicious actions. Very little research has been done in the area of methodologies for identifying string patterns. Some guidelines that may be useful include inclusion of any local security information markings, inclusion of file names of critical resources, and inclusion of any services that are specifically precluded in the security policy. In some company FOO, for example, the string 'FOO Proprietary' would be a good candidate for inclusion in the string-matching scheme.

- *Information used to initiate response actions.* This information typically directs the desired processing and response actions that correspond to the various anomalies and attacks that the intrusion detection system has been set up to accept. For intrusion processing centers that may deal with multiple sources of data, different response processes might be maintained for each source.

In Figure 3-13, we depict the role that the various knowledge bases of the type described above play in our intrusion detection system architectural schema. Note that this information is considered static, in the sense that it is set by the intrusion detection system administrator based on available knowledge.

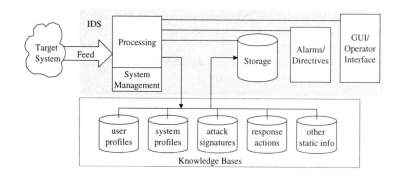

**Figure 3-13**. Knowledge Bases in Intrusion Detection Architecture

A challenge in intrusion detection research involves procedures for general reuse of attack, profile, string, and action knowledge bases. For example, if one organization develops and uses a profile for their environment using one tool, the challenge is for this to be potentially provided to another organization in another environment using a different tool. One can envision an entire industry in which attack profiles are sold for insertion into an off-the-shelf intrusion detection system.

## STORAGE TECHNIQUES FOR INTRUSION DETECTION

As in virtually every computing and networking application, the storage of information plays a critical role in intrusion detection processing. Information is stored to maintain system state values, attack progress, data for historical recording, evidence for cracker conviction, and many more possibilities.

A key attribute in the storage of information for intrusion detection is the length of time the information is maintained and considered available and relevant. We propose here that three specific types of information storage exist in current state of the art intrusion detection systems:

*Archives.* This type of storage is considered long-term and generally corresponds to the types of information that would be required for intrusion correlation long after an event has occurred (e.g., months or years). Archived information must therefore be subject to careful selection since such consideration will ease the archive storage requirements and will help to ensure that the archives only contain critically relevant information.

*Audit logs.* Intrusion detection systems often provide an audit log of their own, particularly in on-the-fly systems. This audit log is not considered as having long-term value as is the case with archive data; however, most archived information originates as audit log information. Audited information is, however, generally considered security critical and deemed suitable for storage in a protected log. The relevant duration will depend on the environment, but typical audit log storage is measured on the order of days, weeks, and perhaps months. Storage beyond months is considered archived.

*Dynamic buffers.* As intrusion detection systems process information, many of the processing schemes employed require some sort of short term storage. This is considered buffering (or cache storage) and requires that fast hardware and software be available to keep up with target system capacities and performance. An obvious example of this is in the on-the-fly traffic feeding of packets into an intrusion detection system. Buffers are typically required to maintain processing synchrony with the typically bursty nature of data network traffic. In fact, in many cases, buffer size will determine if an intrusion detection system can even be employed in the target environment.

The role that each of these three storage cases plays in the context of our architectural schema is depicted in Figure 3-14.

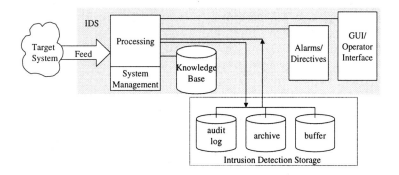

**Figure 3-14.** Storage Techniques in Intrusion Detection Architecture

Two engineering issues that arise with respect to these intrusion detection storage approaches include the following:

- The degree of functional and procedural security and integrity protection required for stored information must be considered. Access controls are the obvious means by which this protection would likely be implemented. Whether these controls are weak discretionary techniques such as the UNIX *chroot* facility, or stronger methods such as a properly administered firewall should be determined by a security risk analysis.
- Proper disaster recovery and business continuity functions associated with storage approaches (especially archives) must be considered. Obviously, back-up strategies for critical storage must be included, as well as the mundane (but critical) issues of physical disaster recovery where data is housed.

## CASE STUDY: OKLAHOMA CITY BANK CAMERA ARCHIVE

In the trial of Timothy McVeigh for the terrible Oklahoma City bombing incident, the prosecution offered as evidence a surveillance tape from an Automated Teller Machine (ATM) near the Federal building. In the tape archival, an image of a Ryder rental truck was captured passing by the street behind the ATM machine. This truck was captured as part of the normal surveillance by the ATM camera, even though the camera was not focused on the street.

Several philosophical and technical issues arise with respect to this incident that are applicable to the storage challenge in an intrusion detection system:

- As we've suggested, the ATM camera was not focused on the street, but rather on the customers using the system. The camera picked up the key evidence by accident. In computing and networking surveillance systems, this is bad news because it suggests that *every* possible audit record could eventually be significant and should be saved. This is clearly an intractable goal and represents a fundamental limitation in any surveillance application.

- The tape archive would likely have raised no eyebrows if prosecutors had not made information about the truck available. Thus, correlation of the tape with other incidents surrounding the truck rental was needed. This is an example of correlation of out-of-band information. It is also an example of how fragile important information about an incident can be.

- No alarm mechanism could ever have been conceived to trigger a response after a truck passed by on the street behind the ATM. This is a normal action with no unusual attributes. But when combined with knowledge about the bombing, this normal action was anything but normal. In the computing scenario, it is conceivable that correlation processing could produce knowledge that would result in a directive to intrusion detection sensors to look for an otherwise normal activity.

- No significant rationale would have existed (independent of the bombing) for saving the video based on the Ryder truck. This follows our earlier comment that storage of everything is not tractable, even if we concede that no audit record can ever be identified as useless without some degree of uncertainty.

We introduce this surveillance camera example because it demonstrates several issues with respect to intrusion detection systems for computer and network systems. It shows, for example, that predefined intrusion processing methods for archived audit information may not be possible. It also shows that an intrusion detection system focused on one type of intrusion pattern, may in fact be useful in the processing and interpretation of another type of intrusion. And finally, it demonstrates that archival time for audit data cannot be easily predicted. For example, if the ATM surveillance video of the Ryder truck had been thrown out, then it would not have been available for the trial.

## INTRUSION DETECTION SYSTEM ALARMS AND DIRECTIVES

Once intrusions or suspicious actions have been detected via the processing capability of the intrusion detection system, the response action most often found in available systems involves alarms. These alarms can range from simple textual messages to more involved procedures such as the sending of email to specified users, the initiation of phone calls or faxes to specified locations, or the execution of arbitrary programs in a local or remote computing environment.

From a more foundational perspective, alarms can be viewed as generalized directives that provide back end processing for intrusion detection. Furthermore, these directives can be organized into a taxonomy of termination objectives. That is, alarm directives can be modeled as one of the following three types:

- *Human terminating alarm directives.* (No, these are not alarms that terminate humans.) These types of alarm directives provide an automated message that results in some direction to a human being. These types of directives often involve email, fax, or phone messages sent to an administrator. The key notion is that the termination of the directive is with a human being who must interpret the alarm and initiate some response. These are the most common types of alarms in current intrusion detection systems.

---

> *Disaster Recovery and Business Continuity Processes*
> Most businesses have well-developed notions of responding to disasters and interruptions to
> normal business. After floods, fires, and other catastrophes, for example, most businesses
> resume their normal operation based on well-defined procedures, processes, and tools. Now
> that security attacks have become a reality in computing environments, alarms must be
> included to initiate security response activities. A key issue is that security attacks do not
> always result in visible damage as in floods and fires.

- *Automated process terminating alarm directives.* These types of alarm directives cause a message to be sent to some automated system for subsequent processing. Thus, instead of a message terminating with a human being (as in the previous case) these types terminate in some automated process that can initiate a programmed response. An example would be an alarm directive that causes the monitoring function to dynamically focus in on a specific target.
- *Hybrid terminating alarm directives.* These types are combinations of human and automated process-terminating alarm directives. This case introduces no new functionality, but must be included since the best available intrusion detection systems provide this hybrid functionality.

In Figure 3-15, we depict the role these alarm directives play in our intrusion detection architectural schema.

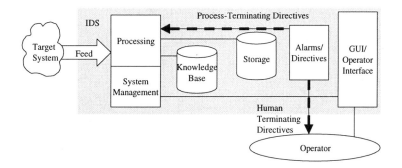

**Figure 3-15**. Alarm Directives in Intrusion Detection Architecture

## CASE STUDY: UNIX SYSLOG ACTIONS

In this section, we outline some of the response actions in UNIX *syslog* to illustrate the general alarm concepts introduced earlier. UNIX *syslog* implements a response action functional mechanism via a collection of related utilities. First, audit probes from UNIX processes, applications, and other systems are obtained by the *syslog* daemon *syslogd*. As was discussed earlier, this daemon monitors /dev/log, /dev/klog, and UDP port 512 for this information. This audit information is associated with a collection of *syslog* priorities as follows (more information on *syslog* priorities can be obtained from your UNIX vendor documentation):

- *emerg* (emergency condition)
- *alert* (correct immediately)
- *crit* (critical condition)
- *err* (ordinary error)
- *warning* (non-critical warning)
- *notice* (special handling)
- *info* (informational)
- *debug* (messages for debugging)
- *none* (message negation)

The UNIX *syslog* actions associated with various process, application, and network alarms at their defined priorities are defined in the *syslog.conf* file. The baseline response alarm directive for *syslog* is to write a record to a specified log file. The *syslog.conf* file specifies several more types of response alarms including the following:

- It directs where to send these log messages. For example, if all notice messages are to be sent to the system console, then the *syslog.conf* file will include a line as follows: '*.notice /dev/console'. The presumption here is that a system administrator would interpret the console message and take some action (i.e., a human terminating directive).
- It sends messages to users. For example, if all emergency messages from the system daemons should result in every user's UNIX terminal getting a message, then the *syslog.conf* file will include a line as follows: 'daemon.emerg  *'. Note that this *syslog* case is also human terminating.
- It can pipe messages to programs. For example, if all alert messages from the authorization system should be sent to some special (hypothetical) program we will call *hypoth*, then this would be specified in the *syslog.conf* file as follows: 'auth.alert   |hypoth'. This case is process terminating and may be used to initiate some automated response activity (e.g., a honey pot).
- It can send messages to *syslog* daemons on other systems (listening to their UDP port 512). For example, if some remote system called logsystem.school.edu is the specified *syslog* collector, then a local system could send all debug messages from the kernel as follows: 'kern.debug  @logsystem.school.edu'. This case is also process terminating.

## INTRUSION DETECTION SYSTEM GUI TECHNOLOGY

The technology associated with graphical user interfaces (GUIs) for intrusion detection systems is more than just the soft issues of screen look and feel for users. Intrusion detection systems are used in operational settings as a means for indications and warning (I&W) in target environments. As a result, the human computer interface (HCI) must be designed to support the basic target system I&W mission.

In particular, a GUI for an intrusion detection system must have the following attributes in live, operational settings:

- *Rapid operator response.* Support for rapid interpretation of data by operators must be included. In the most extreme cases, such as information warfare, rapid response to indications and warning data could have serious implications. Consider, for example, the types of GUIs that have evolved for use in telecommunications operations. These GUIs typically result from the operational experience and feedback of operators who are part of the infrastructure.

- *Clarity and conciseness.* Avoidance of incorrect or misleading representation of information is an important factor. GUIs must be designed to provide information in a clear and concise manner so as to avoid mistakes. In air traffic control settings, for example, GUIs must be present that avoid operator error.

- *Clutter avoidance.* Avoidance of cluttered presentation that may obscure critical patterns is an important consideration. This is often found in many vendor systems that are designed by marketing personnel intent on cramming every possible feature into the GUI.

- *Response initiation.* Simple procedures must be included for initiating critical response functions. A good metric for how well the GUI supports simple response is to examine the documentation and manuals that come with the system. If you cannot easily identify in the documentation the procedure for simple response to a detected intrusion, then something may be wrong.

The problem with current GUIs for intrusion detection systems is that most have not been deployed and used routinely in large-scale operational settings. As a result, features included in available GUIs are based on engineering and developers making estimations as to the types of display information that is useful. Obviously, the only way this can be rectified is through experience with these GUIs in real environments. The next few years should prove useful for intrusion detection GUI technology as such systems are deployed in different environments.

---

*Marketing GUIs*

One area of GUI design that few people like to talk about is the inevitable marketing "dog and pony" GUI. This GUI has a specific purpose: to impress and educate observers, customers, and managers. In intrusion detection, such GUIs should be expected, since security screens used to deal with day-to-day incidents and trouble tickets can be pretty boring.

---

## INTRUSION DETECTION COMMUNICATIONS INFRASTRUCTURE

Intrusion detection systems typically require communications between a collection of distributed components such as monitors, processing engines, knowledge bases, and response functions. As a result, some means for secure communications transport of messages is required as part of the intrusion detection system infrastructure.

Some of the security and functional requirements for this intrusion detection component communications infrastructure include the following:

- Reliable, secure transport of alarms and directives between intrusion detection system components as well as different intrusion detection systems; these intra and inter-system alarms and directives would be used to carry information about detected events as well as directions for processing and response. For this to work, standard means for communication between different intrusion detection systems would be required. As of the time of this writing, the Common Intrusion Detection Framework (CIDF) may be the only real work in this important research area (see below).

- Reliable, secure network management of intrusion detection system information between components and systems; this information would be used to manage the operation and functionality of the components in the system. SNMP-based transport is common in commercial intrusion detection systems.

Note that reliable transport implies that design faults do not introduce system failures to the degree that the intrusion detection components cannot perform their duties. Secure transport implies that malicious intruders cannot subvert the intrusion detection infrastructure via the communications mechanism (e.g., remote dial access).

The most common means by which current intrusion detection systems provide secure, reliable transport over insecure communications media is via a secure, virtual private network (VPN). A secure VPN will encrypt payload and real header information between VPN client and server stations. A VPN header is used to route the secure message packets between the stations and key exchange algorithms are used to negotiate a session key for encryption and decryption.

As suggested above, some standards for this type of communications have begun to emerge. The S/WAN approach to remote station private communication is an example approach that has been largely driven by the firewall vendor community. As commercial intrusion detection systems and efforts such as the CIDF become more successful, they will likely influence future computing and networking standards efforts.


## CASE STUDY: EMERALD ARCHITECTURE

SRI International has been a leading center for intrusion detection research and development for many years. Researchers such as Peter Neumann, Philip Porras, Alphonso Valdes, and Harold Javitz have been lead contributors to intrusion detection advances for years. The EMERALD system (referenced earlier in Chapter 1) is their current research platform that provides many interesting and important features. In this section, we outline the basic EMERALD system architecture as a case study in the concepts introduced earlier in this chapter.

The interested reader is strongly encouraged to closely examine EMERALD, perhaps through the references noted in the Bibliographic Notes at the end of the chapter. This may be the premier research intrusion detection system and quite a bit of thinking has gone into its design and that of its predecessor systems.

To understand EMERALD, one must understand their notion of hierarchically layered network surveillance. In the EMERALD system, monitoring is performed in three separate layers:

- *Service-specific analysis monitoring* is performed via a collection of dynamically deployable, highly distributed, and independently tunable *service monitors*. This is considered the lowest tier in the hierarchy.
- *Domain-wide analysis monitoring* is performed within a domain of services. Service monitors pass information to each other and to *domain monitors* via a subscription-based, duplex communications interface with both a push and pull semantics. These domain monitors are responsible for correlating available service monitor information, as well as for various configuration and reporting actions. This is considered the middle layer in the EMERALD surveillance hierarchy.

- *Enterprise-wide analysis monitoring* is done with a collection of *enterprise monitors* that correlate activity reports across monitored domains. This allows for detection of network-wide threats such as worms and coordinated attacks across multiple domains. Enterprise-wide analysis is the top layer in the hierarchy.

To realize these three layers of monitoring, EMERALD employs a generic monitoring component architecture that is sketched below in Figure 3-15.

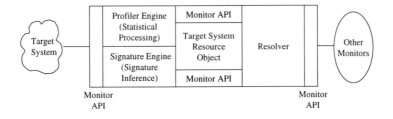

**Figure 3-15.** EMERALD Generic Monitor Architecture

Note in Figure 3-15 that information feeds in EMERALD are pulled directly from a target system. This is done via target specific feeds such as audit trail information, network packets, SNMP traffic, and other means. The EMERALD monitor architecture tries to abstract the means by which information feeds are obtained to produce a more general scheme. This is a novel concept and one that other intrusion detection system vendors would be smart to adopt. Performance remains an issue, however, with this method.

In addition, at the center of the EMERALD architecture is a so-called target specific resource object that is intended to provide an independent processing environment for EMERALD in the target system environment. This is done through a pluggable library of target specific configuration data and methods. Resource objects are important because they represent the only non-generic component of the EMERALD architecture. One might imagine an EMERALD integration involving the specification of a proper resource object, integration with the general EMERALD components, and the insertion into the real target environment. SRI is currently producing a library of available resource objects (e.g., for certain routers) that may be useful for EMERALD users. In particular, the EMERALD resource object includes the following components:

- *Configurable event structures.* This allows the resource object to define the specifics of the event streams for the target system. As a result, EMERALD becomes portable to many different streams via this input specification.

- *Event collection methods.* These are the filtering and low-level processing routines that handle the raw streams obtained from the target system.

- *Engine configurations.* Many analysis engines can be included in a resource object; The operating configurations of the data structures and variables in these engines are defined as needed for the target streams.

- *Analysis unit configurations.* The specific types of intrusion processing methods to be used in the resource object engines are specified as well.

- *Subscription list.* This supports EMERALD's communications infrastructure; information about subscriptions including address and public key information is typical in such a list.

- *Response methods.* Programmed responses for the resource object are included for identified events.

Target system-fed information is then forwarded to the EMERALD analysis engines for processing. The so-called *profiler* engine is tasked with performing statistical profile-based anomaly detection (in accordance with SRI's history of successful research in this area through the NIDES statistical component). A corresponding *signature engine* is tasked with matching and inferring specified signature sequences that correspond to attack streams with target system activity.

A resolver component is used to coordinate analysis reports from the EMERALD profiler and signature engines and to initiate specified response activities. The resolver must also deal with information that may be provided by other engines in other service, domain, or enterprise monitors to which a subscription is available for information. This resolver concept may be the closest any available commercial or research system has come to actually producing globally correlated views from a collection of distributed, local views.

## CASE STUDY: COMMON INTRUSION DETECTION FRAMEWORK

In January of 1997, Teresa Lunt of the Advanced Research Projects Agency (ARPA) organized a group of researchers, vendors, and users that would address the issue of interoperability between different intrusion detection systems. The work that has emerged from this group is called the Common Intrusion Detection Framework (CIDF). This work represents a major advance in the intrusion detection community and will likely become more significant as more vendors recognize its potential.

Furthermore, as the work matures, it provides a common means for developers, researchers, and students to discuss intrusion detection. At the time of this writing, final plans are in the works to develop an Internet Request for Comments (RFC) from the existing draft. In the following section, we provide an overview of the architectural features of the CIDF with an emphasis on how it addresses interoperability.

---

*The CIDF Text on the Internet*

The CIDF document is being managed by Stuart Staniford-Chen from the University of California at Davis and is available at http://seclab.cs.ucdavis.edu/cidf/spec/cidf.txt.

---

The CIDF is described in its specification as consisting of the following components:

- A set of architectural conventions for how different parts of intrusion detection systems can be modeled. This is a useful contribution as it may ease the semantic inconsistencies inevitable in discussions where multiple intrusion detection vendors and researchers interact.
- A messaging specification called generalized intrusion detection objects (GIDO) that allow event description, action direction, event query, and component description. GIDOs appear to be general enough to allow for somewhat flexible implementation, but that remains to be seen.
- A means for transmitting GIDOs between CIDF functional components.
- Protocols for CIDF components to interoperate.

- An application programming interface (API) for CIDF component reuse. This may open new commercial opportunities for vendors.

At the heart of the CIDF is a simple architectural model that includes several primary functional components. The presumption is that an interpretation would be done by the product vendors to associate their system components with CIDF components from the model. These CIDF components include the following:

- *Event generators (E-Boxes)*. These components represent the functionality in an intrusion detection system that obtains information about events streams from the target system. Such events could originate from audit trail files, from raw binary transmission from networks, or from some other intrusion detection system. All of the packet sucking, packet sniffing, and traffic feed generation functionality described thus far would likely be interpreted as E-Box functionality. It's worth noting that the blurred distinction in many systems between feeds and processing, particularly in hardware implementations, may make this interpretation difficult.

- *Analysis engines (A-Boxes)*. These components process information about events provided by E-Boxes. This is where the heart of the intrusion detection algorithmic analysis occurs in an intrusion detection system. A good portion of current research and development in intrusion detection focuses on this component. In an enterprise intrusion detection system, it is likely that A-Box functionality will be distributed across a given system. For example, the EMERALD research system provides distributed processing and functionality across many different components.

- *Storage mechanisms (D-Boxes)*. These components represent the storage functionality in an intrusion detection system. The types of information that must be stored in an intrusion detection system includes data about on-going events, data about previous events that can be correlated with on-going analysis, and archived information about profiles and attacks that is used for detection of intrusions in an event stream. Flavors of storage are somewhat blurred in the CIDF as most practical systems require storage of short term cache information, longer term audit, profile, and attack signature information, and very long term archive data.

- *Response components (R-Boxes)*. Intrusion detection systems respond to detected intrusions in a variety of ways. R-Boxes represent this functionality which in many cases involves cutting off access from suspected source IP addresses, a technique that is highly vulnerable to error. One area in which the CIDF raises some questions is when the R-Box functionality is inherently embedded in some other functionality such as A-Boxes.

Another attribute at the heart of the CIDF model is a messaging protocol that presumes a common so-called *generalized intrusion detection object* or *GIDO* that is passed between the components. The various types of GIDO messages that are required between each types of component are included in the CIDF specification. This collection of inter-component message specifications forms an application programming interface (API) that developers of CIDF-compliant systems can build upon and use. Furthermore, great pains are being made to include specified directory support for CIDF-compliant intrusion detection systems. As one might expect, interoperability would be greatly increased with common directory APIs.

As an illustration, the manner in which E-Box and A-Box CIDF components in an intrusion detection system might interact via GIDO messages is represented in Figure 3-16.

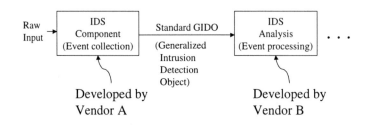

**Figure 3-16**. E-Box and A-Box CIDF Component Interaction

As you can see from the diagram, GIDOs provide a means for intrusion detection systems to interoperate and communicate. It is this notion that the CIDF authors hope will spur the design of modular intrusion detection objects that can eventually plug into and out of other objects, perhaps developed by other teams. The problem with this notion in practice is that the intrusion detection system vendors have not been intimately involved in the CIDF. It has been an academic exercise instead.

Possible speculations as to why the vendor community might not be as interested in the CIDF as researchers are many. For instance, from a business perspective, one might argue that vendor A would want its customers to purchase only vendor A intrusion detection system components, rather than having the flexibility of plugging and playing with many vendors. Another speculation is that the intrusion detection system market is so new and these product houses are so competitive, that none of the vendors have time to worry about speculative efforts like CIDF that may or may not be useful to their business bottom line.

Another concern with respect to the CIDF is the omission of functionality critical to the proper operation of intrusion detection systems in real enterprises. In particular, the use of deceptive honey pots and the use of trace back facilities are not mentioned in the CIDF. Systems that employ such means would have to figure out some reasonable interpretation for their systems to be interoperable with the CIDF.

In any event, readers interested in the CIDF are urged to download the specification and the RFC materials at the URL listed above. Whether the CIDF becomes an important factor in intrusion detection does not change the fact that it is a good piece of computer science. As is the case for any such specification and RFC, technical comments continue to be welcomed as the work becomes more mainstream. All of my intrusion detection graduate students are now required to study the CIDF. (By the way, I should warn you that this is not easy reading, especially the grammars and the API descriptions. So don't fret if you have some trouble.)

## BIBLIOGRAPHIC NOTES

The quote by Alves-Foss is from [AL95]. The second quote is from the Common Intrusion Detection Framework (CIDF) document. The full text is available for download on the Web at http://seclab.cs.ucdavis.edu/cidf/spec/cidf.txt. Don't be upset if you find the specification tough reading. One of its current drawbacks is that very little tutorial material and examples are included. I've been reading the CIDF carefully and slowly; I've come to the conclusion that there is excellent computer science involved in the work, but not enough vendor participation. Hopefully, the major intrusion detection system vendors will become more interested in the CIDF. If they do not, then the future of the CIDF as a useful standard is uncertain. The NFR paper by Ranum et al. [RA97] was useful in the preparation of the material on NFR. The material on Emerald is from the excellent paper by Porras and Neumann [PN97]. I've had my graduate students read this paper now for a couple of semesters and most report the paper useful. The text by Garfinkel and Spafford [GS96] was useful for the UNIX *syslog* material. I saw the Oklahoma City ATM camera information on CNN shortly after the incident.

# CHAPTER 4:
# MODELS OF INTRUSION

*It can be very hard to tell the difference between genuine messages, ordinary failures, and enemy action.*
Bill Cheswick and Steve Bellovin

*Something didn't look right. To get more information, the programmer ran the ps command. That's when things got stranger still—the mysterious program didn't appear when the ps was run.*
Simson Garfinkel and Gene Spafford

## WHAT IS AN INTRUSION?

In order to understand intrusion detection properly, one must first have a reasonable understanding of *intrusions*. If this is not the case for intrusion detection system designers, then the likelihood of so-called *false positives*—detecting and responding to benign events—or *false negatives*—ignoring activities that are significant—in their systems increases greatly. In fact, the most often-cited criticism of intrusion detection is that false positives and false negatives are so prevalent that they invalidate the usefulness of the technology. Great motivation therefore exists to address this question of what constitutes an intrusion.

To demonstrate how tough it is to define intrusions, let's examine the non-computing analogy of potential intrusions into your home. Some candidates for intrusion into your home include the following:

- Someone pries open a window where you live, climbs inside, and rummages through your belongings. This is a clear case of intrusion unless you live in a really weird neighborhood.

- Someone is found pointing a flashlight into your window from the street, presumably checking to see if anyone is inside. This would seem terribly suspicious, but it is unclear whether an intrusion has been committed. Most people would say that an intrusion has not occurred, but that the preliminary information gathering for a subsequent intrusion may have occurred. The result is a warning of an impending intrusion.

- Someone is heard saying that they intend to break into your home when you are not there. This is clearly not an intrusion, but is certainly a threatened one. This is another example of an intrusion warning.

- Someone with a history of breaking and entering convictions goes to the municipal building in your town to look at the property map of your home. This would be suspicious, but perfectly legal. It would also make me nervous as heck if I knew about it. I would consider this an intrusion warning as well. By the way, try telling this to the police—I suspect they'd think you were crazy to be worried.

- Someone slows down as they drive by your house, peering out the window at your property. This is legal as well, but might raise some suspicion. This is a less strong warning, but may be worth noting, especially in the context of other information. Suppose, for example, that a rash of neighborhood break-ins has recently started. Under these circumstances, you'd pay more attention to someone peering at your home from a car than you ally might

- A salesperson comes to your door and peeks inside as you decline to purchase any of their wares. Nothing wrong here on the surface, unless you can correlate it with some other related information.

It's easy to imagine any of the above cases being a component of a real intrusion into your home. You can see, however, that in a subset of the cases, you really don't know for sure if anything has happened or is about to happen. Clearly, you can initiate some response by heightening your property security, but you would hate to have to run and lock all the doors and windows every time someone slows down in a car on your street.

The key issue in all of these scenarios is the notion of an *indication and warning* of some impending intrusion. Indications and warning are so commonly desired, particularly in government applications, that the phrase has even become yet another acronym: I&W. So keep this important concept of I&W in mind. It will be the driving force behind much of the intrusion detection activity in practical settings.

For the purposes of this book, as has been implicitly evident in our discussions to this point, intrusions will correspond to a malicious adversary gaining unauthorized access to a protected resource in a target domain. The notion of an adversary *actively intruding* into a domain is the right thought process to maintain in trying to understand the purpose of intrusion detection. Thus, intrusions will include activities such as outside cracking through a gateway into a protected domain, Internet probes from remote crackers that result in obtaining domain services, scanning of advertised resources and services in a protected domain resulting in unauthorized access, and so on.

Throughout our discussion in this chapter, we will therefore assume the following definition:

---

*Definition of Intrusion*
An *intrusion* is a <u>sequence</u> of <u>related actions</u> by a <u>malicious adversary</u> that results in the <u>occurrence</u> of <u>unauthorized security threats</u> to a <u>target computing or networking domain</u>.

---

Let's go through the underlined portions of the definition to make sure we are clear in our definition.

"*Sequence*". An intrusion is presumed to be a sequence. This implies some sort of time-ordering on the activity comprising the intrusion. The time-ordering of logically or physically concurrent actions is generally not considered a critical concern. What is considered critical is that intrusions are rarely instantaneous or atomic; they may require activity spanning seconds, minutes, hours, days, months, or even years. Sequences are also important because I&W is driven by the early actions in an intrusion sequence. In fact, the earlier one can pick up on the sequential pattern, the more timely the I&W becomes for the intrusion detection infrastructure.

"*Related actions*". What we mean by this is that the actions comprising an intrusion are *by definition* related. That is, unrelated actions are not considered part of the intrusion. By the way, seemingly unrelated activity designed by the intruder to divert attention away from the real intrusion is also by definition related to the intrusion. Furthermore, sometimes the best way to make related activity seem unrelated is to ensure a reasonable time duration between them. The notion of going very slowly through an attack makes intrusion detection considerably more challenging.

"*Malicious adversary*". We presume that intrusions do not occur by accident. Intentional maliciousness is always present on the part of the intruder. In cases where damage, compromise, or blocking occurs by accident, other disciplines such as reliability engineering, safety engineering, and proper system engineering are focused on damage control and prevention. Some people have begun to combine all these terms in the context of computing and networking into a new term called *information assurance*. This broad term encompasses malicious and innocent problems that can occur in an information infrastructure.

"*Occurrence*". An intrusion only occurs if it occurs. (This sounds like something Yogi Berra would have said if he'd studied computer science.) This simple statement implies that suggested intrusions or the preparation work involved in planning and setting up an intrusion is *not* considered an intrusion. This is not to say that such activity does not provide valid I&W information that an intrusion might occur in the future. The difference between unsuccessful (referred to here as *attempted*) and successful intrusions is shown in Figure 4-1.

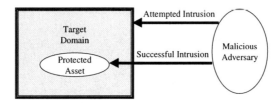

**Figure 4-1**. Intrusions as Unauthorized Domain Accesses

Note from Figure 4-1 that we differentiate *successful* intrusions from *unsuccessful* intrusions, which we also refer to as *attempted* intrusions, by whether or not protected assets are actually accessed by the intruder. Intrusion detection systems will typically want to obtain indications of both successful and attempted intrusions. This allows security managers to better understand the threat environment on their system.

> *Do Intrusion Detection Systems Belong Inside or Outside the Firewall?*
> This is a really common question. If you put them on the untrusted side of the firewall, then you have a better chance of seeing attempted intrusions that may be blocked by the firewall. If you put them on the trusted, inside network, then you will see only those intrusions that are successful. Some vendors like ODS Systems recommend configurations in which both locations are examined.

"*Unauthorized security threats*". We use this term because it implies that a security policy is present to define authorized and unauthorized activity. Without such a security policy, the notion of intrusion is arbitrary. With the existence of a security policy, however, we can specifically denote security policy violations as intrusions. Clearly, this suggests that the term attack can be used synonymously with intrusion, and this is precisely what we will do throughout our discussions. One additional point worth making with respect to unauthorized security threats is that many commercial intrusion detection system products include a series of hard-coded intrusion indicators in their functionality. This is fine, unless the indicators are not consistent with the organizational security policy.

"*Target computing or networking domain*". A domain implies that a well-known set of resources has been identified as the target of the security policy. It should be obvious by now that our focus is on computing and networking resources.

## A TEMPORAL MODEL OF INTRUSIONS AS ACTION SEQUENCES

One useful means for representing intrusions involves modeling them as temporal orderings of actions. The word temporal is intended to denote the passing of time. In fact, time is a critical element in intrusion modeling as we will demonstrate below. In a temporal model of intrusion, an intruder begins with some initial action, the first element of the sequence. This action is followed by supporting actions that occur later in time and which are represented later in the sequence.

Response and other actions may also be involved, and these may be initiated by virtually anyone, including the protected asset manager, other intruders, normal users, and so on. The resultant sequence of actions models the exploitation of vulnerabilities to bring about the unauthorized security threat. This notion is depicted in Figure 4-2; we simplify the drawing somewhat by denoting that all actions are initiated by the intruder.

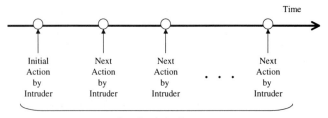

**Figure 4-2**. Temporal Model of Intrusion

As an example of temporal intrusion modeling, consider that if an intrusion involves some unauthorized remote *read* by intruder $x$ of some remote protected resource $y$, then this might consist of a sequence of actions between the endpoints. These actions will correspond to the implementation of the remote *read* operation used in the target environment.

For example, most remote *read* implementations require that a *read* request be followed by an acknowledgement, which is followed by some sort of channel being opened, over which the *read* data is passed. This may be followed by some closing or terminating of the data channel connection. Using this example, we might model the remote *read* intrusion as consisting of the actions shown in Figure 4-3.

&lt; ($x$ requests remote *read* of $y$), /* x unauthorized */
($y$ allows remote *read* by $x$),   /* y *should* disallow */
($x$ and $y$ agree on a data channel),
($y$ transfers the information being read by $x$),
($x$ and $y$ close the data channel) &gt;

**Figure 4-3**. Example Intrusion Action Sequence for Remote *Read*

---

*Behavioral Signatures*

The sequence in Figure 4-3 is an example of a behavioral signature. As you will see, intrusion detection relies to a great extent on the ability of security engineers to model intrusive behavior as signatures. As a simple illustration, suppose that you could write down the series of actions that correspond to some intrusion. You could then parse audit trails looking for that pattern, and in fact, many intrusion detection systems work in precisely this manner.

In the example in Figure 4-3, the security effect of the intrusion is that some unauthorized intruder has managed to penetrate the ineffective security protections to remotely *read* an unauthorized file. Detection of the first or second read actions allows prevention of the more damaging subsequent read actions that produce a *security effect*. It is this notion of having some security effect take place through a vulnerability exploitation that characterizes an intrusion. Thus, we can say that once some security effect has taken place and a policy has been violated, an intrusion has occurred. This is depicted in Figure 4-4.

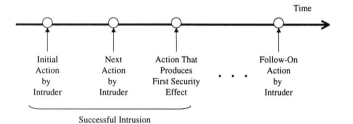

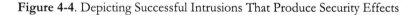

**Figure 4-4.** Depicting Successful Intrusions That Produce Security Effects

Note that the definition of security effect will be environment-specific. For example, in some environments such as government repositories, the disclosure threat to sensitive information is considered the major concern. In fact, for many years, government organizations were obsessed with disclosure. Thus, if someone manages to read sensitive government information, then a security effect will have occurred. In other environments, the disclosure threat might not be considered significant for target content (e.g., in the content pages of a Web server). It is also important to note that after an intrusion has become successful, follow-on activity can certainly occur. This activity could result in addition security effects to a target resource, as shown in Figure 4-4.

Earlier in this discussion, we introduced the notion of an unsuccessful intrusion. This corresponds to a sequence of actions by an intruder that never produces a security effect on some target resource. This may be because the skill of the intruder is low, the security protections in place are significant, or the motivation on the part of the intruder changes during the attack (e.g., the intruder loses interest). Such unsuccessful intrusion attempts are a problem for intrusion detection systems because they produce the same indications as successful intrusions. This notion of unsuccessful intrusion is depicted in Figure 4-5.

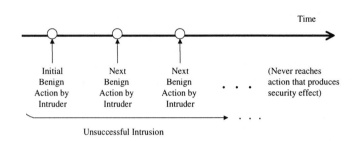

**Figure 4-5**. Depicting Unsuccessful Intrusions

The intrusion modeling examples we've examined thus far have ignored one of the major challenges inherent in intrusion detection. This challenge involves differentiation of what is relevant and part of the intrusion sequence from what is not relevant and not part of the sequence. This may involve, for example, an intruder initiating some malicious action, but then doing something unrelated and benign. The purpose of such unrelated, benign actions would be to obscure the temporal relation on the real malicious actions in the sequence. This is depicted in Figure 4-6.

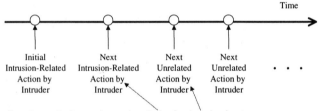

**Figure 4-6**. Differentiating Related and Unrelated Actions in an Intrusion

Similarly, the actions of other malicious intruders and other benign users, must be identified, sorted out, filtered, and correlated by the intrusion detection system to provide an accurate picture of the intrusion environment. The interleaving of different intruder actions is depicted in Figure 4-7.

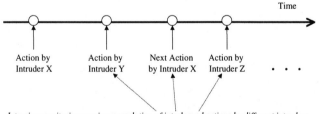

**Figure 4-7**. Interleaved Actions by Different Intruders

As should be evident by now, these simple temporal models are useful in identifying general concepts and issues in the identification and definition of intrusions. We use them here for their pedagogical value and also to highlight some of the challenges inherent in understanding intrusion. As one might expect, the practical design of an intrusion detection system will require considerably more attention to detail in the categorization of system intrusions.

## CASE STUDY: TAXONOMIES OF INTRUSION

Before we talk about intrusion taxonomies in this section, we'd better provide a rigorous definition of the basic concept.

---

*Definition of Intrusion Taxonomy*
An *intrusion taxonomy* is a <u>structured representation</u> of <u>intrusion types</u> that provides <u>insight</u> into their respective <u>relationships and differences</u>.

---

As has been our custom with definitions throughout this text, let's examine the underlined components the definition.

"*Structured representation*". This implies that some order , pattern, or grouping is used to describe intrusions. This is important for intrusion detection systems because any patterns that are meaningful will assist in the automated detection process.

"*Intrusion types*". This is an easy thing to *say*, but a difficult thing to actually *do*. For example, most attacks are combinations of common activities. Thus, if one attack comprises actions A, B, and D, whereas another attack comprises actions B, C, and D, then are these considered the same type of attack? Later in this chapter, we introduce a collection of heuristics on types of intrusion that we believe is a contribution in this area.

"*Insight*". That's why you bother to produce a taxonomy in the first place. The more insight gained, the better the taxonomy.

"*Relationships and differences*". These are the fundamental issues with respect to the various intrusions that must be detected. If we can identify patterns in common or major differences between intrusions, then we will have a better time of automating the detection process.

Over the year, many have attempted to create useful taxonomies of intrusion. In this section, we outline the results of three different efforts:

* SRI intrusion taxonomy research
* Lindqvist and Jonssen's taxonomy research
* John Howard's research investigations

The following sections examine these works in the context of the insights gained for intrusion detection research, development, and operation.

*SRI intrusion taxonomy research.* Several years ago, SRI International researchers Peter Neumann and Donn Parker, both of whom are major contributors to computer and network security, created an intrusion taxonomy that has proven useful to researchers in intrusion detection. Their taxonomy categorizes intrusions into a collection of separate classes (see Figure 4-8).

| Class of Intrusion | Brief Description |
| --- | --- |
| NP 1 External Misuse | Nontechnical, physically separate intrusions |
| NP 2 Hardware Misuse | Passive or active hardware security problems |
| NP3 Masquerading | Spoofs and identity changes |
| NP4 Subsequent Misuse | Setting up intrusions via plants, bugs |
| NP5 Control Bypass | Going around authorized protections/controls |
| NP6 Active resource misuse | Unauthorized changing of resources |
| NP7 Passive resource misuse | Unauthorized reading of resources |
| NP8 Misuse via inaction | Neglect of failure to protect a resource |
| NP9 Indirect aid | Planning tools for misuse |

**Figure 4-8**. Intrusion Taxonomy of Neumann and Parker

In the taxonomy of Figure 4-8, nine classes of intrusion are defined (NP corresponds to the initials of the authors). For intrusion detection system design, the fundamental issue is identifying the key *indicators* associated with each intrusion type. Defining such indicators is considered an active and fruitful area of intrusion detection research. Here are some indicators one might expect for the nine classes in their taxonomy:

- *NP1: External Misuse Indicators.* Indicators for non-technical, out-of-band intrusions will be based on the characteristics of the external misuse being performed, and this can be virtually anything. For example, an indicator that someone might be breaking into a laboratory could be a physical alarm that is set off.
- *NP2: Hardware Misuse Indicators.* Indicators that hardware is being misused or attacked include physical, observable evidence, flaky hardware behavior, or out-of-band information from an informant.
- *NP3: Masquerading Indicators.* Indicators that suggest masquerading could be occurring include multiple, simultaneous instantiations of an identity (e.g., multiple logins), as well as behavior uncharacteristic of a stored profile.
- *NP4: Subsequent Misuse Indicators.* An obvious indicator here is if one finds a plant or bug; more subtle indicators include any type of hacking-style behavior in which a plant or bug could be inserted into a system. Software development environment would be ripe for such misuse.
- *NP5: Control Bypass Indicators.* Indicators for detecting control bypass include detection of multiple paths to the same resource as in network discovery tools that find different paths, as well as any significant improvement in the performance of the control, as one might find in a firewall which users have found a way around.
- *NP6: Active Resource Misuse Indicators.* Any unexplained behavior or odd functionality in a resource is an indicator that some active misuse could be occurring.
- *NP7: Passive Resource Misuse Indicators.* Any unusual or unexplained knowledge on the part of an individual or group could signal that passive reading of unauthorized information is occurring.
- *NP8: Misuse Via Inaction Indicators.* Incidents that should have been prevented but were not are indicators of this type of problem.
- *NP9: Indirect Aid Indicators.* Any odd behavior on a system normally used for mundane purposes could indicate that it is being used for off-line planning or support of an intrusion (e.g., running crack off-line to break password files).

It's worth noting that the SRI taxonomy and its associated indicators are particularly important because they are based on a large collection of reported incidents to the Internet risks forum over a long period of time. Thus, the categories are based more on observed behavior than on the perceptions and engineering judgement of an intrusion detection researcher.

*Lindqvist and Jonssen's taxonomy research.* In a recent paper given at the IEEE Symposium on Security and Privacy, Ulf Lindqvist and Erland Jonsson suggest a taxonomy refinement based on the SRI work of Neumann and Parker. In the creation of their taxonomy, Lindqvist and Jonsson differentiate between intrusions, attacks, and breaches. The claim is made that an intrusion consists of an attack where a security flaw is exploited and a breach is where a defined security policy tenet is violated. They further define attacks that do not lead to breaches as unsuccessful intrusions. The reader will note that these definitions are consistent with our general presentation to this point.

To produce the proposed new taxonomy, Lindqvist and Jonsson conducted a series of intrusion experiments with students in which security intrusions were attempted on a test bed. In classifying the results of the student activity, the following refinements were made to the taxonomy of Neumann and Parker:

- The bypass of intended controls class (NP 5) was divided into subclasses corresponding to password attacks, spoofing privileged programs, and utilizing weak authentication.
- The active resource misuse class (NP 6) was divided into subclasses corresponding to exploitation of write permissions and resource exhaustion.
- The passive resource misuse class (NP 7) was divided into manual browsing and automated browsing using either personal or publicly available tools.

The reason that intrusion taxonomies and refinements such as this are so valuable to intrusion detection system designers and users is that they provide insight into the target objects being detected by these systems, particularly in the area of indicators of intrusion. In fact, one might imagine intrusion detection systems being organized based on some taxonomy of expected intrusions. The two research efforts cited above in particular are useful because they involve empirical results based on real and experimental data.

*John Howard's research investigations.* John Howard's Ph.D. thesis from Carnegie Mellon entitled "An Analysis of Security Incidents on the Internet 1989-1995" has been widely circulated across the Internet. (You can get a copy at http://www.infowar.com/.) In his work, Howard performs numerous statistical analyses of intrusions and in some cases, patterns emerge.

Unfortunately, it may be that the most startling result of Howard's work is the sheer increase in intrusions, thus making the intrusion detection problem more difficult. Howard points to clear trends in the growing nature of the security problem for all of us. In any event, this thesis is worth reading, if only to marvel at the sheer volume of charts and graphs in the work.

## HOW ARE INTRUSIONS INDICATED?

You might expect that the key requirement for an intrusion detection system would be to characterize *every step* in an intrusion. Interestingly, this is not really the case. Instead, intrusion detection systems are obliged to provide indication and warning (I&W) information that an intrusion is taking place so that response can be initiated properly. This

I&W information is obtained and gathered via evidence that is visible to the intrusion detection system infrastructure. Such evidence can come from a variety of indicators. This notion of indicators providing evidence of intrusion to an intrusion detection system is depicted in Figure 4-9.

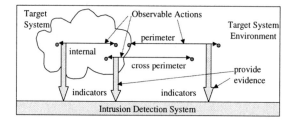

**Figure 4-9**. Detection of Evidence from Intrusion Indicators

In the previous section on intrusion taxonomies, you will recall that we went through some sample indicators for the SRI intrusion taxonomy. We did so as a prelude to the more rigorous attention we will pay to indicators in the next sections. In particular, some key evidence-based indicators that an intrusion detection system might use to determine that an intrusion might be taking place are listed below.

- Repetition of a suspicious action
- Mistyped commands or responses during an automated sequence
- Exploitation of known vulnerabilities
- Directional inconsistencies in inbound or outbound packets
- Unexpected attributes of some service request or packet
- Unexplained problems in some service request, system, or environment
- Out of band knowledge about an intrusion
- Suspicious character traffic on a network

In the ensuing sections, we will provide detailed discussion and illustrations on these intrusion indicators in practical Internet intrusion detection environments. We will also emphasize the protocol independence of these indicators. As more emphasis is inevitably placed on additional protocols such as SS7, these indicators will guide intrusion detection system developers to the proper types of information to be keying on.

## REPETITION AS AN INTRUSION INDICATOR

One of the best ways to detect intrusions involves recognition of unexpected repetitive behavior of some sort. The motivation for using repetition as an indicator is that unless an intruder knows exactly how to gain unauthorized access to a target resource on the first try, some degree of trial and error will be needed. Intrusion detection algorithms need to recognize this repetition and decide how many instances of the repeat behavior would constitute a potential intrusion (see Figure 4-10).

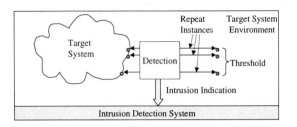

**Figure 4-10**. Depiction of Repetition Detection

Repetition detection is a powerful concept because it comes close to being able to detect intrusions without knowing their details. For example, if some intruder dreams up an intrusion that involves trying something over and over until it succeeds (e.g., guessing Simple Network Management Protocol (SNMP) community names), then this may be detected as an intrusion indicator without even knowing the rationale for the repeat behavior. Some of the technical issues related to the detection of intrusions by repetitive behavior include the following:

- *Repetition thresholds.* In the detection of repetitive behavior as indicators of intrusion, some numeric threshold must be identified to differentiate normal repetition from suspicious repetition. For example, if some user is trying to gain access to a system via an authentication response to a challenge, then a couple of unsuccessful tries might be considered normal. On the other hand, twenty or thirty unsuccessful attempts to supply a response to a challenge may be an indicator of an intrusion. Operational experience would provide the best means for fine-tuning initial thresholds for target user or system services.

- *Time between repeat instances.* In the detection of repetitive behavior, the more time between repeat instances, the more difficult it becomes to recognize the pattern. From an intrusion detection system design perspective, if the first instance of some potentially suspicious behavior occurs, then this would be stored somehow (e.g., in a buffer). The lifetime of this buffer would correspond to the expected time between potential instances of the behavior. For example, suppose that repeat attempts to guess passwords at a server are identified as a suspicious pattern, and that knowledge of one guessing instance is detected and stored in a buffer. If, after every few seconds, additional guesses are detected, then it is likely that the intrusion detection system will recognize the pattern. If, on the other hand, several days pass between successive instances of password guessing, then this might be more difficult to detect as the buffers would likely be cleared.

- *Repetitive patterns.* If the behavior being repeated by an intruder is more complex than a simple service request (i.e., a password guess), then detection may be more difficult. For example, if an intruder is trying to gain access to some target asset by connecting through a series of intermediate systems, and performing a series of set-up operations that may or may not be suspicious, then the detection of the repetition cycle may not be easy. Similarly, if some attribute of the intruder changes (e.g., different Internet Service Providers (ISPs) are used for subsequent steps of an intrusion), then detection becomes more difficult.

---

*Intrusion Indicators and Protocol Independence*

It should be clear from our example that this indicator is independent of the actual protocol. TCP/IP is certainly vulnerable to this sort of problem, but other packet (and even non-packet) protocols should be expected to be vulnerable to the same patterns. The specifics of the repetition might be different, but the concept should remain the same. This is an important point for security engineers attempting to derive vulnerabilities in new protocols.

## CASE STUDY: SYN FLOOD ATTACK

The well-known SYN flood attack is a good example of a repetition-oriented attack. Recall that the TCP/IP protocol involves a TCP handshake in which a three-step exchange of packets between end points is used to establish a session connection over IP. The protocol involves the initiator (which we will call a client) creating a so-called SYN packet with an associated initial sequence number and then sending this packet and sequence number to a receiver (which we will call a server). The server then creates a second sequence number and sends a so-called SYN-ACK sequence back to the client. The SYN includes the second sequence number and the ACK includes an acknowledgement of the first sequence number sent from the client. The third step in the handshake involves the client then acknowledging the second sequence number with an ACK packet sent back to the server.

The whole three-step TCP/IP sequence is illustrated in the diagram in Figure 4-11.

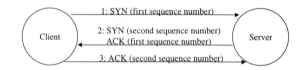

**Figure 4-11**. TCP Three-Step Session Handshake

In the SYN flood attack, an intruder needs some program that will generate TCP packets at will. Several security sites, hacking sites, and vendors on the Internet advertise these sorts of tools. (One vendor site that offers a tool that is valid as of the time of this writing for generating these sorts of packets is http://www.ballista.com.) It shouldn't take more than a couple of minutes to find more sources of this kind of program; you can also write one yourself.

The repetitive SYN flood attack involves the client using such a program to generate a large number of TCP initial connection requests (i.e., the initial SYN packet with sequence number). This repetition of requests is intended to fill up the connection queue at the server with so-called half-open connections. Note that many SYN flood attacks target TCP privileged port 513 which allows remote login. Firewalls should either block this type of incoming service request or use it as the basis for a honey pot or trap.

The flood attack requires that the client ensure that responses to the SYN-ACK sequence sent from the server are not acknowledged. An easy way for the attacking client to do this is to simply advertise a nonexistent source IP address. Note that this is really the essence of the attack: Starting the connection handshake repeatedly and then not completing the sequence for any of the requested sessions.

When the server is in this flooded state, two important conditions become true. First, the server will no longer respond to any new connection requests. In this sense, a SYN flood attack is an example of a denial of service attack. Second, since the server is now unable to respond to new requests, it cannot generate TCP resets to unexpected packets and it is now vulnerable to related attacks such as TCP sequence number guessing attacks.

An excerpt is shown below (with a minor modification) from a log of the SYN flood attack that was alleged to have been initiated by Kevin Mitnick against Tsutomu Shimomura in a well-publicized recent incident.

> 14:18:22.516699 10.92.6.97.600 > server.login: S
>     1382726960:1382726960(0) win 4096
> 14:18:22.566069 10.92.6.97.601 > server.login: S
>     1382726961:1382726961(0) win 4096
> 14:18:22.744477 10.92.6.97.602 > server.login: S
>     1382726962:1382726962(0) win 4096
> 14:18:22.830111 10.92.6.97.603 > server.login: S
>     1382726963:1382726963(0) win 4096

Note that the IP address 10.92.6.97 in the four repeat instances of the flood shown above is always a non-existent address (10.anything is the indicator). In the actual log from the alleged Mitnick incident, a slightly different, but still non-existent address was used. Such non-existence of source IP address ensures that the server will not have the capability to issue a reset command to the source. If enough of these happen in repetition, then the resultant flood can take a target server out of server. Internet and Intranet managers are rightly concerned with this activity.

## MISTYPED COMMANDS OR RESPONSES AS AN INTRUSION INDICATOR

Another indicator of potential intrusion involves the detection of mistyped commands or responses that are expected from an automated process (see Figure 4-12).

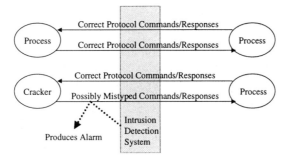

**Figure 4-12.** Normal Process Protocol Versus One Spoofed Endpoint

This indicator is particularly interesting because it is not easy to characterize exactly the kind of mistyped information that one would expect to find. Nevertheless, since computer and network processes don't mistype commands or responses, an intrusion detection system can conclude from these cases that a human being may be trying to spoof a process at one end of a protocol. Suppose, for example, that an audit log stores the results of a *sendmail* handshake between mail processes. The sequence of *sendmail* protocol commands involved is regular and predictable for the different handshakes and mail operations. If the audit log shows that one of the processes is not offering proper commands or responses, then it may be that this process has been corrupted for non-malicious reasons (e.g., software faults, system failure). On the other hand, it may also be that a human being is trying to spoof one end of the mail protocol.

Some practical hints that a human being may be trying to spoof one end of a protocol include the following observations:

- Detected attempts to delete and then retype misspelled commands or responses; as was suggested above, this would be difficult to characterize in advance of the actual mistyping incident; as a result, using the string matching feature in many intrusion detection systems would not be easy for this type of detection.

- Detection of several protocol attempts with mistypings followed by a correct protocol handshake; this is also tough to characterize ahead of time.

- Detection of *learning* by one end of the protocol as mistakes are made and then as they are corrected, these mistakes are no longer made in subsequent attempts.

---

*Mistyping of URLs*

Many marketing organizations have long since learned the value of owning a URL that differs by one character from a popular sites; furthermore, the difference should be set with a character that is next to the one being replaced on the keyboard. For example, suppose 'top_site' is the most popular site on the Internet; an organization would therefore be smart to reserve 'yop_site' because 'y' is next to 't' on the keyboard and might be mistakenly entered by unknowing potential customers.

---

## CASE STUDY: BERFORD ATTACK AT AT&T

Bill Cheswick and Steve Bellovin recently reported an intrusion at the AT&T Internet gateway in their now-classic firewall book. The incident began when a cracker that they named Berford tried to obtain a copy of the AT&T gateway machine password file. This is perhaps the most common indicator in log files that some intrusion attempt has occurred. It is also an indicator that the intruder probably does not possess great skill (since this is such an obvious action). In the Berford case, the cracker tried to obtain the file using a well-known debug mode security vulnerability in the UNIX *sendmail* program. Here is a snippet of the actual Berford *sendmail* attack log (widely disseminated on the Internet):

```
19:43:10 smtpd: <--- 220 inet.att.com SMTP
19:43:14 smtpd: ---> debug
19:43:14 smtpd: DEBUG attempt
19:43:14 smtpd: <--- 200 OK
19:43:25 smtpd: ------> mail from:</dev/null>
19:43:25 smtpd: <--- 503 expecting HELO
19:43:34 smtpd: ---> HELO
```

```
19:43:34 smtpd: HELO from
19:43:34 smtpd: <--- 250 inet.att.com
19:43:42 smtpd: ------> mail from:</dev/null>
19:43:42 smtpd: <--- 250 OK
19:43:34 smtpd: ---> rcpt to:</dev/^H^H^H^H^H^H^H
19:43:34 smtpd: <--- 501 syntax error in recipient name
```

Note in the above log that the Berford hacker tries to enter the address of the mail recipient, but mistypes the response. You can see this from all the ^H characters in the log. Cheswick detected this mistyping via a series of traps in the AT&T research gateway (including the code that provided the 250 OK response in the log). This detection prompted a long and interesting sequence of interactive cat and mouse actions between Cheswick and his cracker. (The story in their book provides the details and is highly recommended). The point of this story for the purposes of intrusion detection is that mistypings and misspellings provide a useful protocol-independent means for detecting potential intrusions.

## EXPLOITATION OF KNOWN VULNERABILITIES AS AN INTRUSION INDICATOR

Several years ago, Fred Grampp from AT&T created a clever tool called Quest for scanning UNIX systems for vulnerabilities. It was based on known vulnerabilities such as accounts with no passwords, unused accounts, and the existence of setuid-to-root programs in a file system. Fred's tool was soon popularized around AT&T and several development efforts ensued in this area. My department at AT&T even provided a now-defunct service in the late 1980's called ComputerWatch that centered on this notion of scanning a system for vulnerabilities.

Recently, many popular integrity-scanning tools have appeared and are used all around the world and Grampp rarely gets credit for having originated such a widespread notion. Some of the more popular scanners include the following:

- SATAN (freeware)
- Tripwire (freeware)
- SAFEsuite (commercial tool from Internet Security Systems (ISS))
- NetSonar (commercial tool from Cisco Systems)

Scanning tools can be partitioned into those that run on servers, looking for application or even kernel-visible information, and those that run on networks, looking for network-level events. Security administrators find these tools invaluable in evaluating the security of their systems.

Unfortunately, malicious crackers also have access to these scanning tools. Virtually every hacking and cracking site on the Internet advertises a plethora of scanning tools for UNIX, Windows NT, and many other systems. As a result, crackers may use these and other tools as a means for obtaining information about target system vulnerabilities. Furthermore, once these vulnerabilities are detected, crackers may try to exploit them to gain unauthorized access.

As a result, a powerful intrusion detection approach involves monitored searches for any unexpected use of scanners or any exploitations of known, popular security vulnerabilities to gain access to a target system. These intrusion detection approaches raise the following technical issues:

- *Detection of scanning tool usage.* Known scanning tools exhibit a regular pattern that can be modeled; tools can be implemented to identify incoming scanning based on these modeled patterns. For example, SATAN scans can be detected via a freeware tool known as Courtney developed at the Department of Energy (DOE) Computer Incident Advisory Council (CIAC) (Courtney can be downloaded at http://www.ciac.org). The tool tries to identify the incoming regular vulnerability search pattern embedded in a SATAN scan in order to alter administrators of a possible malicious scan.

- *Detection of vulnerability exploitation.* The hundreds of known vulnerabilities embedded in tools such as SATAN or ISS SAFEsuite offer a useful guide to the types of cracker activity one might expect for a target computer system. The problem with this approach is that new vulnerabilities and attacks are discovered, tested, exploited, and disseminated across the Internet with great frequency. Intrusion detection systems that try to keep up with these new malicious attack methods require diligent monitoring of best practice cracking techniques to know what to monitor (CERT advisories on the Internet at http://www.cert.org are a useful resource in this regard). Such intrusion detection systems also require flexible means for implementation of new vulnerability exploitation detectors.

- *Correlation between scanning and exploitation.* If scanning is detected for a target system, then follow-on exploitation of an existing vulnerability may be a strong indication that a cracker is present. Suppose, for example, that some system requires Trivial File Transfer Protocol (*tftp*) access for whatever reason. Perhaps the site is using *tftp* for their routers, as is so often found. If a scan is detected, followed by an incoming *tftp* request for service, then the intrusion detection system might correlate these events to produce a suitable alarm directive.

## DIRECTIONAL INCONSISTENCIES AS AN INTRUSION INDICATOR

One indication of a potential intrusion is a directional inconsistency in network protocol traffic. By 'directional', we refer to either packet direction or session direction.

*Packet Direction.* IP packets coming into an Intranet from the public Internet would be considered incoming (or inbound) with respect to that Intranet. Similarly, packets leaving an Intranet for the public Internet would be considered outgoing (or outbound) with respect to that Intranet.

*Session Direction.* A process initiating a service from the public Internet into an Intranet would be initiating an incoming (or inbound) service with respect to that Intranet. Similarly, a process initiating a service from an Intranet out to the Internet would be initiated an outgoing (or outbound) service. Note that session direction can be confusing because inbound sessions will usually involve both inbound and outbound packets (same for outbound sessions).

Some types of protocol inconsistencies that might be considered intrusion indicators include the following:

- *Inbound initial packets with internal source IP addresses.* In this case, the inconsistency is that an inbound service request from an inbound source does not make sense. If packet direction can't be determined as in routers that don't look at their physical interfaces, then this IP spoofing intrusion indicator cannot be used. Most modern routers, nearly all firewalls, and most intrusion detection systems, however, provide the ability to detect packet direction. This common IP spoof intrusion is depicted in Figure 4-13.

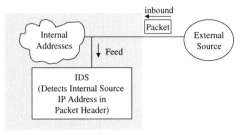

**Figure 4-13**. IP Spoof (Inbound Packet Directional Inconsistency)

- *Outbound initial packets with external source IP addresses.* This indicator is the same as above with inbound and outbound sources reversed. The issue here is that insider intrusions may be detected as opposed to external intrusions (as in the previous case).
- *Packets with unexpected source or destination ports.* If the source port for some incoming or outgoing service request is not consistent with what is being requested, then this may flag a potential problem. Examples include Telnet requests from well-known server port numbers in an environment where this is not expected. In addition, packets presumably from servers with non well-known port numbers may flag a potential intrusion attempt.
- *Packets with unexpected acknowledgement settings.* If a packet is detected that has its ACK bit set, but for which no associated service request can be easily identified, then this may be an example of an attempted intrusion.

It's important to note in the above cases, that these packets may be faulty, spurious packets from malfunctioning network components or software. Firewalls and routers routinely drop these packets and generate audit records that may or may not be detected via the log files. Nevertheless, since these inconsistencies represent unexpected conditions, one might become suspicious of a potential intrusion attempt.

## UNEXPECTED ATTRIBUTES AS AN INTRUSION INDICATOR

When a network, system, or service request exhibits a collection of expected attributes, we often combine these into what is generally referred to as a profile (recall the discussion in Chapter 2). Such profiles provide a basis for comparison with observed behavior. Some commonly used profile-based attributes that help intrusion detection systems detect potential intrusions through unexpected attributes are discussed below.

*Calendar and time attributes.* It may be the case that in a particular environment, certain types of events should occur regularly at specified times or dates. Similarly, in a particular environment, certain types of events might be expected to *not* occur regularly at specified times or dates. Some financial institutions, for instance, make regular, predictable payments to other organizations on Friday afternoons to avoid late payments for waiting until after the weekend. Thus, large financial electronic data interchange (EDI) transfers would be considered a normal type of traffic at this time in this environment. If Friday were a holiday, however, then one could imagine that this type of detected transfer would be exactly the type of subtle, unexpected traffic that one might see in a clever intrusion.

*System resource attributes.* Some intrusions require a unique mix of computing system resources to operate properly. Brute force cryptanalysis using many large processors is the most obvious example. Other examples, however, include denial of service intrusions in which system resources begin to degrade as a result of the malicious activity. In theory and sometimes in practice, an intrusion detection system can detect this CPU resource degradation so that steps can be taken to avoid the situation. Common resources to be considered as intrusion indicators include system processes, system processors, memory and file size, file system usage, and network utilization. This is an area in which network management systems (the remote monitoring (RMON) management information base (MIB) in particular) can be useful in intrusion detection support.

*Service mix attributes.* One way to characterize the identity of a user or system is by the types of services that are invoked and used during a typical session. If a company sets up external access for its traveling employees, for instance, then it may be possible to characterize the types of services that will be used. File transfer, email, and other types of activities would be expected, for instance. If other service mixes are observed such as Telnet sessions to unexpected locations, then the intrusion detection system might become suspicious of an intrusion.

*User and system profiles.* User profiles are a more general notion than service mixes. A user or system profile would certainly take typical service mixes into account; but additional attributes would be included as well. Typical times of peak and minimal usage, typical lengths of sessions, and typical locations of entry (e.g., geography of dial access vehicles) are good indicators to use in building a user or service profile. Obviously, users or systems might not always exhibit the same behavior, and this is one of the great challenges in intrusion detection.

## CASE STUDY: TOLL FRAUD

The problem of toll fraud is interesting for intrusion detection because the case can be made that this type of intrusion has prompted more security investment by organizations than any other. The financial implication of toll fraud to service providers may explain why this may be so. Consider that some organizations like AT&T Wireless have even begun to refer to their toll fraud operations as revenue security. It is therefore instructive to examine toll fraud techniques as a case study in intrusions that produce observable, unexpected attributes in calling patterns of telephony customers.

Although there are many types of toll fraud, here is one of the most common intrusion techniques: A target organization is selected by a malicious adversary and is then subjected to a series of voice mailbox guesses. This guessing can be aided by the use of known private branch exchange (PBX) manufacturer default settings, the presumption of bad password choices by users, and the use of social engineering targeted at employees and organizational help desks. Once a mailbox has inevitably been cracked, the features of the local telephony will dictate the extent of subsequent activity. The more features in the local telephony environment, the better for the cracker.

Suppose, for this example, that the cracked organization allows outbound dial for employees with valid mailbox passwords. This is considered pay dirt for the cracker who can then share this number with his or her friends on cracker bulletin boards. Once the word gets out that outbound dial is available from this cracked mailbox, phone calls will typically start to emanate from the target mailbox to countries that the cracked organization might not typically call. This may be because content operators (e.g., providing recorded adult content) have been invited into this country to collect long distance toll for the local telephone company.

In any event, toll fraud intrusion detection systems would detect this intrusion because the calling pattern would not match the normal pattern of the cracked organization, unless, of course, the cracked organization regularly calls these countries. (By the way, this situation in which an organization regularly makes crazy calls all over the world at all sorts of unusual hours represents a really tough problem for toll fraud detection schemes.) Assuming the toll fraud has been detected, the service provider would typically contact the cracked organization and security steps would be taken to terminate the toll fraud and hopefully rectify the situation. Most likely, the cracked PBX would be reset with new passwords and services might be adjusted. The whole scheme is depicted in Figure 4-14.

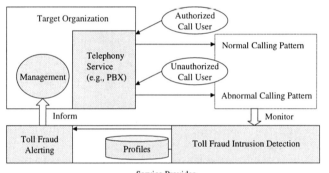

**Figure 4-14**. Depiction of (One Type of) Toll Fraud Intrusion

As telephony services continue to expand with more complex features, the toll fraud problem is likely to get much worse. Profiling and toll fraud intrusion detection systems will have to evolve with this inevitably expanding threat.

A key point worth pondering with respect to toll fraud, however, is the privacy implications of this sort of service provider monitoring. It is hard to imagine the PBX operator at a corporation complaining about the service provider monitoring telephony behavior when a problem is detected. All of the general notions that people make with respect to privacy and monitoring seem to not apply in the toll fraud scenario. This is a point that most people find rather fascinating and it has sparked more then one lively debate.

## CASE STUDY: ODS SECURESWITCH

Optical Data Systems (ODS) Incorporated (http://www.ods.com/) is a growing provider of enterprise and network solutions for companies and for the Federal government. One of their products, the ODS SecureSwitch, provides a good example of a technique for detecting intrusions via unexplained attributes in a system. In particular, the SecureSwitch provides detection of anomalies using traditional SNMP, RMON, and RMON II information gathered from agents on a target network. It is one of the few systems available today that harnesses the true power of network management techniques and protocols with emerging intrusion detection capability. This is surprising since network management tools are so prevalent in environments that are interested in network security solutions.

The product also provides more traditional attack signature-based intrusion detection capabilities through the ISS RealSecure intrusion detection system. The RealSecure engine is not totally integrated into the product from a correlation processing perspective, but this functionality can be created in a network correlation laboratory. ODS recently announced a deal with SAIC regarding integration of the CMDS product into the SecureSwitch. ODS also provides integrated firewall filtering using Checkpoint Firewall-1. In our remaining remarks in this brief section, we focus on the SNMP-orientation of the product.

The ODS system operates as a LAN switch, providing layer 2 functionality for an Intranet or enterprise network. It discovers devices on the network and queries for any available network management information. This discovery feature needs to be used carefully, especially in environments where the intrusion detection system is required for stealth operation. It also needs to be tested to ensure that the discovery does not degrade any on-going network operations. Using security knowledge and system profile-based information, the SecureSwitch can identify security problems in the network. Guessable SNMP community names used by devices on the network are an example of the type of vulnerability that can be detected.

Some issues worth noting with respect to the use of ODS system for intrusion detection are as follows:

- This SNMP-based technique is interesting because it really plays on the notion of comparing expected, normal network behavior with presumed insecure settings using nothing more than available network management information. Such information is powerful however, as it will help in identifying anomalies in performance and activity patterns.
- As RMON and RMON2 tools and methods improve, ODS users will gain the benefits. This is called a technology piggybacking and is a situation most vendors strive to obtain.
- The trend in the ODS product toward a faster hardware data capture facility for monitoring a network may be the way all intrusion detection vendors eventually must go. The notorious problems associated with dropped packets in a software capture library routine (e.g., *libpcap*) may force this trend to occur more rapidly.

In summary, the ODS focus on using network management information to detect anomalies is a concept we believe will become more and more common. It plays off tested concepts in network management and is reminiscent of toll fraud schemes such as the one described above.

## UNEXPLAINED PROBLEMS AS AN INTRUSION INDICATOR

A common indication of intrusion involves some unexplained problem that could be detected virtually anywhere in the target system or in the target system environment. This is not an easy indicator of intrusion because it is not easy to characterize. The concept here is that an intruder might design an intrusion with side effects that produce visible evidence that something has occurred. Some examples of these types of unexplained problems include the following:

- Unexplained system hardware/software problems (e.g., servers down, system processes not running). More security administrators are getting comfortable with the notion that malicious intent is sometimes at the root of such problems.

- Unexplained system resource problems (e.g., overflowing file systems, heavy CPU usage). This is another area in which security administrators are beginning to suspect cracking activity more and more.

- Unexplained system performance problems (e.g., Internet gateway service, server response times). Performance problems will only be detected in denial-of-service or computation-intensive attacks.

- Unexplained user process behavior (e.g., unexpected access to system resources). This one is often seen in cracking activity, where unusual programs that might be mapping resources or scanning systems are run.

- Unexplained audit log behavior (e.g., audit logs that shrink in size, which never makes sense). Practical accounts of law enforcers catching crackers have usually involved some sort of detected oddities in audit systems.

## CASE STUDY: STOLL FINDS AN ACCOUNTING ERROR

On an afternoon in October of 1987, a huge crowd was forming in one of the large ballrooms at the National Computer Security Center (NCSC) security conference in Baltimore, Maryland. A curious and somewhat unusual-looking man by the name of Cliff Stoll was inside giving a talk. He was a hugely entertaining speaker, standing on the desk and then jumping off, only to race down an aisle waving his hands, screaming and laughing as he went. I thought he was great.

It so happens that during this period of time, Stoll was working at the Lawrence Berkeley Labs and was in the process of chasing a cracker. He was at this particular conference to share some suggestions on catching crackers with the rest of us. While he didn't share any of the real specifics of what was happening to his network, his advice turned out to be well founded. Later, after the cracker was caught, Stoll wrote about his experiences extensively.

The genesis of the problem was a seventy-five cent computer usage accounting error that Stoll, a part-time system administrator, was having trouble resolving. The accounting error seemed innocent enough at first, but it soon pointed to some strange behavior. Through a series of inquisitive actions and stubborn resolve, Stoll traced the unexplained error to an unknown user account and then through a complex maze of intrusions and incidents to a West German cracker.

One cannot help but wonder how many times this sort of little error is brushed off and never investigated in other network environments. Would you, for example, worry about a 75-cent shortfall in monthly bills of nearly three thousand dollars? I think that one of the lessons to be learned from Cliff Stoll is that network and system administration are non-trivial activities—ones that can provide intellectual satisfaction even for a research astronomer. The whole incident is chronicled in his delightful 1989 book, "The Cuckoo's Egg." The story serves as an excellent case study in the use of an unexplained error as an intrusion indicator.

## OUT OF BAND KNOWLEDGE AS AN INTRUSION INDICATOR

An intrusion indicator that has nothing to do with computing or networking tools involves obtaining information from out of band sources about some past, present, or future cracking activity. The idea here is that many crackers like to share information about their often impressive exploits. Some useful forums and resources for gaining out of band knowledge about specific intrusions include the following:

*Magazines.* By far the best is *2600 Magazine.* The writing in this quarterly journal is crisp and clear, most of the information is technically accurate, and the topical focus is always up-to-date. My favorite section in the magazine is the reader letters section in which the details of different hacks and cracks are reported by readers from all around the world. Every issue contains loads of specific information about specific hacking activity. For instance, telephone numbers with attached modems are regularly reported as a service (*service?*) to *2600 Magazine* readers. (A second magazine called *Blacklisted! 411 Magazine* is also available. The focus is more on phone phreaking.) Intrusion detection researchers and engineers should consider this magazine required reading as it provides invaluable insights into the techniques being used by best-in-the-world hackers and crackers.

*Books.* A huge assortment of intrusion-related books have been published in the past decade. Here is a list of some of the best ones:

- *The Fugitive Game,* Jonathan Littman, (Little, Brown, and Company). I think Littman's writing style is excellent. I simply could not put this book down.
- *The Watchman: The Twisted Life and Crimes of Serial Hacker Kevin Poulsen,* Jonathan Littman (Little, Brown, and Company. 1996). This one is great too. It's written in the present tense which adds to the urgency of the story.
- *Takedown,* Tsutomu Shimomura and John Markoff (Hyperion Press, 1996). This book includes more technical detail than some people might be comfortable with. For technical folk, it's an absolute delight.
- *The Cuckoo's Egg,* Clifford Stoll (Doubleday, 1989). Perhaps the best of its kind. I'm still waiting for them to make a movie.
- *The Hacker Crackdown,* Bruce Sterling (Penguin Books, 1994). An early book by a skilled writer. This should be on your bookshelf.
- *Masters of Deception,* Joshua Quittner and Katie Hafner (Harper Collins, 1995). This book details a couple of young hacking groups. By the way, Quittner is the guy who cleverly reserved the McDonald's domain before the hamburger king. He was actually using ronald@mcdonalds.com for a time. He eventually settled with them, requesting a donation to a charity for payment.
- *At Large,* David Freedman and Charles Mann (Simon and Schuster, 1997). This is an intriguing, true crime, hacking thriller that you will not be able to put down.

*Web/Usenet.* Some of the best information on hacking, cracking, and intrusions is available on the Internet via the Web or Usenet. By the time this book reaches your hands, it is possible that newer, better repositories exist that I don't know of as of the time of this writing. Nevertheless, here are some of the best URLs and Usenet groups that have excellent material on these topics:

- http://www.2600.com. The official site of *2600 Magazine.*
- http://www.l0pht.com. A hacking site that regularly provides invaluable information on some clever and ingenious intrusion techniques.

- anarchy-online.com. A computer bulletin board type resource that is very non mainstream.
- http://all.net. Fred Cohen's site has lots of useful information on system intrusions, defenses, security technology, and other useful topics.
    *Conferences and meetings.* Conferences in the area of security, hacking, intrusions, and intrusion detection can be categorized into two types: a) mainstream conferences sponsored by professional organizations, governments, or industry groups, and b) non-mainstream conferences sponsored by hacking/cracking groups or organizations. The best of these from both types are listed below.
- *Hackers On Planet Earth (HOPE) Conference.* This conference is one of the best hacking conferences and is well-attended by hackers, crackers, security experts, and law enforcement groups.
- *2600 Meetings.* 2600 Magazine encourages and helps advertise a series of birds-of-a-feather meetings for hackers held on the first Friday of the month from 5PM to 8PM local time in specified locations. In the New York City area, meetings are held in the Citicorp Center in the lobby near the payphones located at 153 East 53rd Street between Lexington and 3rd Avenues. In case you were wondering, the New Delhi meetings are held at the Priya Cinema Complex near the Allen Solly Showroom; in Buenos Aires, the meetings are in the bar at San Jose 05; in Adelaide, Australia, outside the Café Celsius near the Academy Cinema; and so on. By my count, meetings are held in seventeen countries.
- *DEF CON Conference.* This is a big hacker conference that attracts a huge crowd. I'm surprised this conference doesn't attract more mainstream press than it does.
- *National Information System Security Conference.* This conference has a history with the National Computer Security Center and the National Institute of Standards and Technology. It still seems to attract lots of government people and the technical talks range from interesting to terrible. My group at AT&T goes to this conference regularly, but sometimes I wonder if this isn't because the Orioles have such a nice stadium nearby.
- *RSA Data Security Conference.* If you are interested in cryptography, then this is a must-attend event held every February in Northern California. It includes excellent, invited presentations and the information is always current and important.


## SUSPICIOUS TRAFFIC CONTENT AS AN INTRUSION INDICATOR

A final intrusion indicator that we will mention here involves suspicious traffic content. The idea is simple: the actual content being transferred over a network will provide evidence of possible intrusions. Some obvious issues that emerge with respect to this content indicator are discussed below.

*Suspicious content with respect to a specific destination or source.* Sometimes it may be the case that certain content into or out of some specified source or destination would be considered suspicious. Foreign language content, for instance, might be considered strange in some environments. Casual chat information that might be non-work related could be an indicator of an intrusion in some cases as well. Some governments might be interested in the transfer of cryptographic intellectual property as well.

*Suspicious content with respect to any environment.* There are certainly cases where certain types of content being sent between endpoints would always be considered suspicious. Examples include plans for constructing weapons, discussions that include particularly rough language, or sessions that involve the transfer of illegal material. These types of indicators could be expected to emerge as off-the-shelf kits for intrusion detection systems once standard application programmer interfaces (APIs) are included in commercial systems.

*Legal issues in monitoring content.* While our treatment here is more on technical approaches than on social and policy-based issues, we must acknowledge that the debate continues with respect to the legality of monitoring content. The situation is similar to that of telephony wiretapping in which court orders are required before content (i.e., speech) can be monitored.

## BIBLIOGRAPHIC NOTES

The Cheswick and Bellovin quote is from their firewall book [CB94]. The Garfinkel and Spafford quote is from their invaluable UNIX Security text [GS96]. The paper by Lindqvist and Jonsson [LJ97] was used in the taxonomy section. Cheswick and Bellovin's book [CB94] was used for the Berford example. John Howard's Ph.D. thesis [HO97] was used for one section. An article in 2600 Magazine (Winter 1995/1996 issue) was used for the SYN Flood log from the Shimomura incident. Materials provided by ODS Systems were used in the section on the SecureSwitch.

# CHAPTER 5:
# INTERNET IDENTITY AND ANONYMITY

*There are countless justifications for sending email anonymously, just as there are for sending anonymous paper mail or making anonymous calls.*

Larry Hughes

*We believe that some tracing ability, however imperfect, is better than none at all.*
Stuart Staniford-Chen and L. Todd Heberlein

## WHAT IS AN INTERNET IDENTITY?

Before we consider the notion of identity on the Internet, let's take a moment to examine how we determine the identity of an individual in everyday life:

- We can use our senses of sight, sound, smell, and touch. This is the most familiar approach to determining identity; we see someone and either recognize them or not. By the way, infants recognize their mothers best by smell, as opposed to sight, sound, or touch.
- We are introduced to someone by a trusted individual. The degree of our confidence in someone's identity is directly proportional to the degree of trustworthiness in the individual doing the introducing. What this stilted explanation means is that if someone you trust introduces you to Ernie and Bert, then you are likely to believe that they are really Ernie and Bert. If someone you don't trust does the introducing, then you are less confident.
- We are presented with trusted credentials (e.g., birth certificate, passport). This is common in any setting where visual identification or third party identification is simply not feasible. More and more trusted credentials include some sort of photograph.
- We use the situation and setting to establish identity. Information about an individual's identity can be combined with their location, their activity, and their surroundings. For example, seeing someone who looks like a famous New York Yankee baseball player produces a different feeling if you are at a ballet ("I'll bet that's not him") than if you are in the South Bronx outside Yankee Stadium ("I'll bet that's him").

Intrusion detection systems must determine identity based on information available from the target system and any other information that may be correlated with the target system. Since the target systems we focus on here are Internet-based, it helps to revisit some basic facts about Internet packet traffic. Recall, in particular, that Internet activity consists of IP packets arranged into streams that are routed in a connectionless manner between clients and servers. This packet view of the Internet is important to keep in mind because it will help us deal with the issue of Internet identity.

Suppose, for instance, that an arbitrary packet is selected at random from some arbitrary Internet location. Perhaps a network device such as a router or switch is used to pick off this packet as it progresses between different locations on the Internet. In our presumed scenario, nothing is known about the packet other than its header information and its payload. If either is encrypted, then this will further complicate any tracing activity.

Nevertheless, the following question arises with respect to this arbitrary packet: *Is it possible to associate the packet with a human initiator?* Another way to view the question is whether one can properly assign responsibility to arbitrary Internet activity without any other information about the packet (see Figure 5-1).

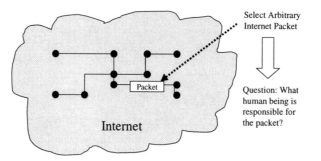

**Figure 5-1**. Question of Associating Responsibility to Internet Packets

As we will demonstrate, this question is basic to intrusion detection because it helps define the potential opportunities and limitations for any intrusion detection system. In considering the question, recall that Internet packets are stamped with originator information in the form of a source IP address. As a result, the most obvious initial answer most people provide to the question posed above is that the source IP address should point to some network interface, from which it should not be too hard to establish human responsibility. In fact, if the session involves interactive activity, as in a typical dial connection to the Internet, then assigning responsibility to client initiated packets should be easy (one might think).

---

*Source IP Address and Identity*

A common illusion is that source IP addresses link packets to their human initiator. For one thing, in ISP dial access, addresses are typically assigned dynamically from a pool of ISP allocated addresses at that dial access location. Furthermore, many TCP/IP LANs use protocols for dynamic address assignment which produces uncertainty about who in a workgroup has which IP address. Finally, many scheduled sessions doing routine EDI or network management don't have a human initiator, other than the administrator.

---

If a packet comes from some source IP address that is associated with a server or automated system as was just suggested above, then one would think that the owner or designer of that system can ultimately be assigned responsibility. For instance, stray packets from a Web site could be blamed on the owner of the Web site.

As it turns out, tracing identity on the Internet is not always so straightforward. In fact, we will show that in some cases it will be impossible to associate responsibility to Internet activity without diverting to trace back techniques that may have nothing to do with computers or networks. It is also important to note that this basic difficulty in performing effective trace back is one of the great advantages of the Internet from a personal privacy perspective.

## WHO NEEDS TO KNOW INTERNET IDENTITIES?

To begin, it helps to acknowledge the entities that may be interested in identifying Internet identity. We consider it beyond the scope of this book to consider suitability of motive in wanting to determine identity and we certainly acknowledge the potential for misuse of identity determination in ways that may conflict with basic human rights to freedom and privacy. Nevertheless, those authorized entities properly desiring to know the identity of initiators of Internet activity are discussed briefly below with some mention as to their likely motivation.

*Normal users.* Any normal user on the Internet or any monitored server might be interested in finding out what types of information are being kept for security reasons. This is particularly true for individuals doing embarrassing things on the Internet (e.g., posting to strange news groups). Privacy policies from service providers generally define what they do and don't examine, store, and maintain about user identity.

*Internet service providers.* Service providers like to establish identity when issues of billing or potentially malicious actions occur. For instance, if a Web site is the source of some potential attack like repeated pings, SYN flooding, or password guessing, then that site's service provider might want to determine the identity of the reported initiator for response procedures. This would be done by examining source IP addresses, correlating these with account information, and then trying to trace the account to a human owner of the account. It's worth noting that for toll fraud and other telephony cracking, this concept applies to the telephony provider.

---

*A Simple Question for your ISP*

You should ask your ISP whether they monitor anything other than IP source and destination addresses for Internet traffic. If the answer is anything other than no, then you should ask for some justification. Most ISPs will not provide such monitoring of traffic as it traverses their infrastructure. In fact, the legality of such monitoring is pretty muddy. An obvious exception is any traffic destined for the ISP's infrastructure, as one might find in a malicious attack on that ISP's servers or network elements. This is typically examined and processed using intrusion detection technology.

---

*Resource owners.* Organizations and companies who are Internet connected want to have the capability to establish identities for many different reasons. Some would like to use identity as the basis of marketing analysis at their Web site, some would like to use it as the basis of security protections (e.g., intrusion detection), some would like to use it to determine what their employees are doing, and so on. It's worth mentioning that a recent MacWorld survey revealed that 30% of companies with 1000 or more employees routinely monitor the activities of their employees by reading files and email. Being able to establish correct identity of a monitored target is therefore required.

*Law enforcement.* It should not take much imagination to consider why law enforcement would be interested in identifying the identity of individuals on the Internet.

Intrusion detection systems for law enforcement are intended to provide early indications and warnings of crimes as well as a means for initiating response to these crimes.

*Defenders of national infrastructures.* It should also be obvious that national cyber-defense efforts require the ability to properly identify the source of Internet activity. Intrusion detection systems for national defense would be used for indications and warnings of national attack as well as a means for initiating response to these national emergencies.


## A PRIMER ON INTERNET NAMING AND ADDRESSING FOR INTRUSION DETECTION

In an Internet environment, identity considerations must start with the naming and addressing scheme inherent in TCP/IP and the Internet. In this section, we provide a brief primer on how names and addresses are created, how subnets works, and where readers can turn for additional information. We provide just enough information here for readers to follow the intrusion detection concepts. Readers who want more should consult the bibliographic notes at the end of the chapter; readers familiar with IP addressing may wish to skip to the next section.

*Basics of IP Addressing.* In the current version of the Internet Protocol (IP), 32-bit addresses are used to define the network interface or *location* from which packets emanate or to which they are directed (IP Version 6 extends the address length from 32 bits to 128 bits). This is an important consideration because it implies that IP addresses are not associated with computers, but with their possibly multiple network interfaces.

IP addresses and domain names are assigned uniquely by the Internet Network Information Center (INTERNIC) upon request. This implies that a legal IP address should be traceable to some allocation from INTERNIC. It is worth recognizing, however, that most individuals and organizations on the Internet allow their Internet service provider to take care of this allocation for them. This should come as no surprises since most users couldn't care less what their IP address is and prefer that such details be dealt with by the provider. Thus, in most instances, dial access service providers have a pool of available IP addresses that are assigned dynamically to customers. This implies that a dial access user's address will be different for each different session.

You should also recognize that illegal IP addresses abound on the Internet. Some organizations utilize IP addresses not allocated from the INTERNIC in their enterprise and use network address translation (NAT) schemes at their firewall to hide this fact. NAT schemes generally work well, but it's not unheard of for unassigned IP source packets to leak out through some means such as an unknown router or some dual-homed system performing dial. Others simply assign IP addresses mischievously without any authority to do so. Still others use addresses beginning with '10' as their internal scheme. So you cannot examine a given packet found on the Internet and just assume that the source IP address was properly assigned and administered.

An IP address consists of a network identification portion to identify a network, and a host identification portion to identify a location within a network. Three main classes of IP address are worth noting here. Class A addresses are reserved for very big networks. They have an 8-bit network identifier that starts with a '0'. These addresses are no longer available, so don't bother trying to get one. Class B addresses are the most common for companies, universities, and reasonably sized organizations. They have a 16-bit network identifier that starts with '10'. Class C addresses are for more modest work groups and organizations. They have a 24-bit network identifier that starts with a '110'. Figure 5-2 depicts the bit ordering specification of these three types of address classes.

CLASS A   0NNNNNNN HHHHHHHHHHHHHHHHHHHHHHHH
CLASS B   10NNNNNNNNNNNNNN HHHHHHHHHHHHHHHH
CLASS C   110NNNNNNNNNNNNNNNNNNNNN HHHHHHHH
N: Network identifier bits; H: Host identifier bits

**Figure 5-2**. IP Address Formats for Classes A, B, and C

Note that each IP address is 32-bits long and includes both a network portion and a host portion (these are separated by a space in Figure 5-2). Actually, in most depictions of IP addresses, the separation comes after each 8-bit octet to ease the transition to the more natural dotted decimal notation that most Internet users are accustomed to using. In dotted decimal notation, each eight bits of the IP address, termed an octet, is translated to the base ten equivalent. This implies that the IP address:

10000111 00001000 00000001 00001000

would be expressed in dotted decimal notation as follows:

135.8.1.8

*Basics of IP Address Subnetting.* Subnetting is a way for network administrators to take their IP address allotment from INTERNIC and break the host bit portion into different networks for internal routing purposes. The host bits are interpreted as either actual host bits or subnet bits using an associated *subnet mask* that maps out this interpretation.

Suppose, for example, that an organization is given a single Class C network address from INTERNIC, but that there are two physical networks to and from which internal routing must take place. This would be accomplished via subnetting within the organization. The Internet would see the Class C network address at the advertised server, router, or firewall gateway; the associated host bits would be subnetted to the two internal networks.

*Internet Naming.* Host names on the Internet are defined in the context of a hierarchy implemented by the Internet Domain Name System (DNS). Figure 5-3 specifies the current Internet top-level domain names.

| | |
|---|---|
| COM | commercial organization (most companies have this as their domain) |
| EDU | educational institution (intrusions often originate from these domains) |
| GOV | government organization (often targeted by intruders) |
| INT | international group |
| MIL | military organization (often targeted by intruders) |
| NET | major network support center (becoming more popular as a domain name) |
| ORG | some other organization |
| 'country' | location/country code |

**Figure 5-3**. Top Level Internet Domains

Domain names on the Internet are organized into multiple level identifiers that generally, but not always, follow the official Internet domain system. In this system, top-level Internet domains are intended to specify the type of organization for which the domain name is provided. An obvious implication here is that an Internet host name of stevens-tech.edu would be interpreted correctly as an educational institution. Furthermore, whitehouse.gov would be interpreted as a government organization and please_send_your_money.com as a commercial group. From an intrusion detection perspective, the advantage of this interpretation should be obvious.

It's worth noting that names can consist of multiple domain levels. For example, the domain register.please_send_your_money.com might be considered a lowest level domain, please_send_your_money.com as a second level domain, and com as a top level domain. The convention is to write local domain labels first followed by increasingly more general domain labels.

Intrusion detection system designers must keep in mind that new domain naming conventions are starting to be used. This is less important for our purposes than the simple recognition that the use of domain names for intrusion detection will get more complex with *any* new scheme. Once the scheme becomes routinely used and deployed, then intrusion detection systems will obviously need to be configured to recognize new domains.

## WHY IS HIDING ON THE INTERNET SO EASY?

With such a well-conceived addressing scheme as is found on the Internet, one might presume that hiding identity on the Internet would be impossible. Consider, for example, that TCP/IP packets all come stamped with source and destination IP addresses to ensure proper routing. One would expect that intrusion detection systems should therefore follow the method of tracing IP addresses to their INTERNIC-assigned organization. From this organization, the assigned individual would then be identified.

As it turns out, many factors can be cited that make it quite possible to hide identity on the Internet. In the discussion below, we outline six particularly important ones.

*Non-existent source IP addresses.* It is possible for packets to travel across the maze of routers on the Internet toward a specified destination IP address even if the source IP address is non-existent (see Figure 5-4).

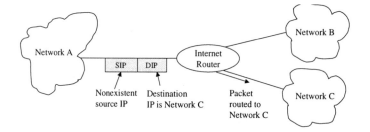

**Figure 5-4**. Packet with Valid Destination but Non-existent Source Address

Obviously, depending on upper layer protocols such as TCP, the presence of non-existent source IP addresses may become evident at some point in the protocol.

Nevertheless, certain attacks such as the SYN flood attack can be initiated with source IP addresses that expose nothing about the actual source of the attack. This is different in telephony where end-to-end point codes are more trustworthy.

---

*US Mail and the Internet Protocol (IP)*

Students routinely find it useful to compare the connectionless US Mail approach with IP or any other connectionless packet protocol. It is easy to see in the US Mail analogy, for example, how a missing or false source address on a package or letter probably will not affect its delivery to the receiver. If a problem ensues, then notification to the sender will not be feasible, of course. IP has the same properties.

---

*Changing of source IP addresses.* Once a user has the appropriate access privileges on an Internet connected computer, it becomes quite easy to change IP address. For most organizational users with workstations who gain their Internet access via an Ethernet local area network (LAN) with a dedicated connection through the organizational gateway, this changing is particularly easy—especially if the change is to an address already on the LAN. For dial access users through an ISP, the challenge is to gain access to an Internet connected machine on which privileges can be obtained or cracked so that the IP address can be easily forged. All this implies that an intrusion detection system cannot rely solely on IP addresses to determine who is initiating the activity.

*ISP dynamic allocation to dial users.* Dial access users are allocated IP addresses at network components often referred to as *edge vehicles*. These edge vehicles exist, depending on the ISP topology and approach, in convenient locations for the target user community. Large ISPs have them all over the country or world; smaller ISPs cluster them in a target community or area. Users then dial into the ISP at whatever edge vehicle is convenient or available and an IP address is dynamically allocated for the session. This address will be different among edge vehicles and across sessions (see Figure 5-5).

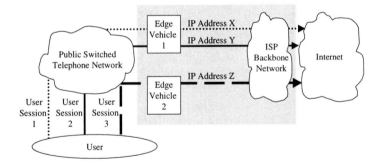

**Figure 5-5**. ISP Dynamic IP Address Allocation to Dial Users

Once again, the implication here is that intrusion detection systems cannot rely on IP addresses for identifying who the individual is that is initiating the traffic. In the case of dial access, it may be possible to identify the ISP of the initiator, from which subsequent techniques for trace back can be initiated (see below). Note that if the billing process at the ISP is sloppy and allows for misrepresentation of identity (e.g., signing up with account user names of William Jefferson Clinton or Bill Gates), then this will further assist in the hiding.

---

> *What about the ISP telephony logs?*
>
> Yes, ISPs certainly can log incoming telephone numbers and map them to IP addresses. This information is subject to legal protections and the privacy policy of the ISP. Only under written court order from a government law enforcement agency would this information ever be disclosed.

*Anonymous entry points.* Many means exist for gaining anonymous entry to the Internet. Publicly available computers with access from libraries, Internet cafes, and other locations (e.g., airports, train station terminals) provide a means for anyone to browse the Internet and perform other types of actions. This makes it difficult, if impossible, for intrusion detection systems to accurately determine the person or group initiating some intrusion.

*Anonymizing intermediate points.* An additional problem for intrusion detection systems is that many anonymizing intermediate sites exist on the Internet. An anonymizing site works by scrubbing all information about a given user before relaying service requests to the Internet. The most common applications for anonymizing browsing are email and Web browsing. More detailed information on anonymizers is provided below.

*Daisy-chaining of network attacks.* The idea here is that if an individual has the ability to steal an account on a remote system, then that account can be used to steal another account on another system. It isn't hard to imagine the arbitrary length daisy chain of stolen accounts that can result. This implies that even if an attack is traced to a particular account, this discovery may only be the beginning of the actual trace. Such uncertainty is particularly depressing because it highlights the weakest link problem in network security. An infrastructure is only as secure as the weakest systems that it includes.

*Cryptographic protocols for anonymity.* An additional consideration worth mentioning with respect to hiding identity is that cryptographic protocols are being designed for commerce that provide good anonymity. We focus below on Chaum's blinding techniques for digital cash as a case study; readers interested in these protocols are referred to Bruce Schneier's *Applied Cryptography* (Wiley and Sons, 1996) for more detail.

*Advice from a hacker.* In a recent 2600 Magazine issue, a convicted hacker by the name of Agent Steal (real name: Justin Peterson) offered some excellent advice for other hackers on how to maintain anonymity on the Internet. Here is a brief summary of his tips:

- Never tell other hackers or crackers your name, address, or phone number (advice he admits to having not followed himself).
- Never set up phone numbers in your real name.
- Never dial directly into anything being hacked or cracked.
- Never transmit personal data on hacked systems.
- Keep separate computers or networks used for work or personal objectives.
- Always examine and edit logs the minute you gain access to a system (he suggests looking for email daemons on administrative accounts that might be sending out copies of the logs).
- Always set up accounts on different systems with different login identifiers.
- Never go to hacker and cracker conferences.
- Don't use Internet relay chat (IRC) (he claims to have only used it rarely while hacking).

As you can see, each of these tips will greatly assist in achieving anonymity on the Internet. Most of the advice is centered on reducing the degree to which intrusion detection correlation processing can be performed on your various activities on different systems.

## CASE STUDY: ANONYMIZING INTERNET SITES

Anonymizing servers on the Internet are designed to privatize your service requests—particularly email and Web browsing. Actually, these sites are special cases of a service known as a *proxy*. Proxy servers typically sit between Intranet users and the public Internet. They accept requests from users and relay the requests along to the target destination, which may involve additional proxies. If you study firewalls, then you will learn all about proxies.

An advantage of using proxies is that the potential exists for the destination to only see information that the proxy decides to offer. This is why so many companies use proxy servers at their gateway for Internet browsing. Sites will not see internal IP addresses, but rather the address and information from the company proxy. This network address translation (NAT) has useful security implications. It also cause big problems for intrusion detection systems trying to share information (as in the CIDF). By the way, encrypted electronic commerce schemes are also complicated by NAT.

On the Internet, two major types of anonymizing service have become popular: *anonymous remailers* and *anonymizing proxies*. Both introduce challenges for intrusion detection systems; they are discussed in some detail below.

*Anonymous remailers.* The way an anonymous remailer works is that the user typically follows some specified syntactic convention to specify a receiving destination and to include the text of the email message. This is sent to the anonymous remailer which then strips off any information associated with the sender other than the text of the message. The email is then forwarded to the receiving destination with an anonymous source specification. This process is depicted in Figure 5-6.

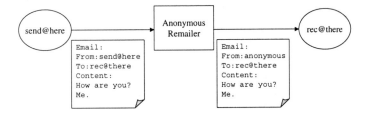

**Figure 5-6.** Anonymous Remailing Process

It is worth noting that most anonymous remailers are free. To date, this has been a result of obvious problems billing users for usage as well as the tendency among many remail providers to view this as a service that ought to be free. As more anonymous methods of payment emerge (see case study below on Chaum's blinding factors), remailers for pay are likely to emerge. In fact, Internet service providers offering anonymous remailing and other services are likely to find this to be a successful endeavor.

---

*Information on remailers*

Readers interested in finding available remailers on the Internet should visit Raph Levien's site at www.cs.berkeley.edu/~raph/remailer-list.html. There is also a Usenet group called ALT.PRIVACY. ANON-SERVER that may be a source of locating remailers.

---

Issues related to the use of anonymous remailers include degrees of confidence in the confidentiality of remailer logs, the use of encryption with anonymous remailing, and the potential that a remailer could be a trap (see Chapter 7). Readers are encouraged to experiment with anonymous remailers as it provides useful insight into the challenges they present for intrusion detection.

It's worth mentioning that anonymous remailers provide a much more desirable means for professors to obtain feedback from students. I've been using remailers for years to correspond with students in my courses and I've found the quality of comments to be much better than those silly paper forms used for so long. If you teach, then I suggest that your students give you feedback in this way.

*Anonymizing proxies.* As was discussed earlier, anonymizing proxies accept client requests and relay them to target destinations. Responses from these destinations are handled according to the proxy specification—the most common being a simple relay semantics (e.g., as in an organizational gateway proxy). The most popular anonymizing proxy site on the Internet is the Anonymizer located at http://www.anonymizer.com/open.html.

Anonymizing proxies such as the Anonymizer are intended to deal with the privacy issue of destination sites capturing information about users. For example, if you visit the Anonymizer on the Internet, it will provide you with a description of several easily deducible facts about your identity and environment. Take a moment and try it. You will find that some of these reported facts about your identity include:

- Your organizational affiliation and/or ISP. Note that if you use a service provider that resells backbone service from another provider, you will likely be tagged as belonging to the backbone service. This is a crude form of network discovery for you to use with your provider.

- Your general location.

- Your computer and operating system.

- Your Web browser (type and version). I've read in some informal mailing list traffic that an awful lot of Internet users are still using Netscape's earliest browser. I don't know if this is true, but it wouldn't surprise me.

- The title of the Web page you just left. That one might not be your favorite piece of information to share with other sites.

Those readers who find the availability of this information to be disconcerting may wish to make use of an anonymizing service. When they do, the challenge of intrusion detection for services rendering through an anonymizing proxy is increased.

From an intrusion detection perspective, this anonymizing is only relevant if the target being pursued has included browsing as part of their activity. For instance, if evidence exists that a drug trafficker is using electronic means to sell drugs on the Internet, then law enforcers would be interested in their browsing habits. Sites visited might provide some hints as to the source and nature of the trafficking business. All of this, obviously, would have to be done under court order. In any event, the point here is that anonymous browsing would greatly complicate this tracing activity. You may or may not like this; we merely report the facts here.

## CASE STUDY: BLIND SIGNATURE-BASED ELECTRONIC CASH

In this section, we shift gears somewhat and examine one specific cryptographic protocol that has some important consequences for intrusion detection. The protocol is David Chaum's blinding factor protocol, and some of its properties are as follows:

- It allows use of anonymous, untraceable cash. This is motivated by the untraceable nature of real, unmarked cash.
- It involves trusted third party distribution with full repudiation protection for the bank. Note that repudiation in this context means being able to claim ignorance. The bank can issue a note and if prompted for information about where the note was spent, it can repudiate any claims that it was involved in any way beyond blindly signing the note. This is a potential nightmare for law enforcement.
- It utilizes strong cryptography to ensure privacy. Note that privacy has to do with ensuring confidentiality of information.

All of these properties make intrusion detection in an electronic commerce environment more difficult because the Chaum protocol assists in the hiding of identity.

The way the protocol works is best explained in the context of a simple digital signature scheme in a bank. Suppose that a bank decides to issue electronic cash by allowing customers to send real money for a note that is digitally signed from the bank. The customer can then go out and buy things using this cash note and the merchant will not know who purchased the goods (see Figure 5-9).

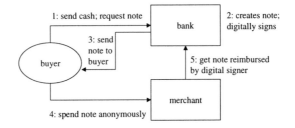

**Figure 5-9**. Bank Issuing Digitally Signed Cash Notes

Alert readers will note of course that this scheme is fine so long as the bank can be fully trusted. Obviously, the bank will know how the customer is spending the money because it must deal with the merchant who wants to cash the received note. Chaum's blinding factor protocol introduces an absolutely ingenious means for hiding identity information from the bank.

The way the protocol works is that the buyer creates a large number of notes (e.g., 1000) with random, unrelated serial numbers. The notes are all for some specified amount that the buyer wants in the cash note from the bank (e.g., $100). These notes are then blinded via some process such as multiplication by a random number or encryption with a key. The blinded notes are sent to the bank, which then requests all but one of the blinding factors.

The buyer sends all these blinding factors which the bank uses to unblind and read all but one of the blinded notes. Once the bank is satisfied that all the notes are requesting the same amount, it signs the unblinded note and sends it to the buyer (see Figure 5-10).

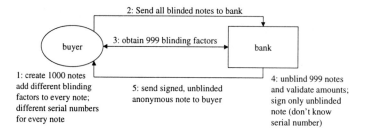

**Figure 5-10**. Chaum's Blinding Cash Note Protocol

This is a powerful concept because the buyer now has a note signed from a bank for a specified amount. The buyer can purchase things *totally* anonymously because when the merchant goes to cash in the note, the bank has no idea who created and spent the note as long as certain conditions are true:

- There is sufficient banking going on to obscure the relationship between notes and the cashing in of a note by merchants; for example, if the bank only signs one note, then it shouldn't be too tough to tell who the note came from.
- There is sufficient diversity in the amounts being requested; if all but one of the bank's customers request amounts in the hundreds of dollars, but one requests amounts in the thousands, then this hides anonymity; note that banks can easily avoid this problem by issuing blocks of notes in one common denomination.

The implication of Chaum's protocol for intrusion detection should be obvious. If an intrusion detection system detects a potential attack that involves the use of blinded notes, the bank will not be able to locate the identity of the requester (unless the two conditions mentioned above are compromised). This mirrors the use of anonymous cash in society. It has its advantages and disadvantages.

---

*Cryptography and Intrusion Detection*
One of the basic purposes of cryptography is to make it hard for third-parties to get information about data transmitted between end-points. Since intrusion detection often requires obtaining precisely this type of information between end-points, you can see how the two technologies would be somewhat at odds.

---

## INTERNET IDENTITY TRACE-BACK

Now that we have made the case that hiding identity on the Internet is possible and sometimes easy, we examine the opposing issue: tracing back identity on the Internet. This notion of tracing identity on the Internet involves deriving information that is available about the *real* source or destination of Internet protocol packets. This obtained information can be partitioned into the following two types:

- *In-band information.* This involves any information that can be derived directly from the computing and networking activity in question. For example, Internet packets could have a source IP address allocated by a service provider to a particular individual. Additionally, a Web site might make available a public key certificate that has been validated by a third party certificate authority. Caller identification in telephony is another example of in-band information.
- *Out-of-band information.* This involves any information derived indirectly from non-computing or networking sources. An example might be any information about the real identity of a person who has changed their name or lied about who they are on an application. Another example might be information that results from physical surveillance by a law enforcement organization on a suspect. Sometimes in our discussions below, we will refer to the combination of out-of-band and in-band information as all-band information.

A simple depiction of the in-band and out-of-band trace back challenge in the presence of a sequence of identity changes is shown in Figure 5-11.

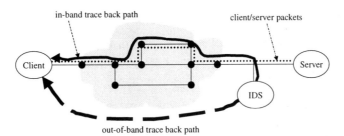

**Figure 5-11**. Depiction of In-Band and Out-of-Band Trace Back

The picture in Figure 5-11 assumes that a client is initiating a session to a server. An intrusion detection system, denoted IDS, is shown to be monitoring packets at some intermediate point in the infrastructure. The picture implies that trace back methods by the IDS can follow in-band paths through the same communications medium in which the potential intruder is sending and receiving messages. These methods are discussed below. Additionally, more creative approaches can be used to bypass the challenges inherent in the in-band approach by creating out-of-band traces. Techniques for out-of-band trace back are discussed below.

## TECHNIQUES FOR TRACING IDENTITY

How do you trace activity to its source? In many real life non-computing aspects of our daily life, we have techniques and even entire disciplines devoted to the collection of information about events so that they can be traced, interpreted, processed, and acted upon. Here are some examples:

- Detectives in law enforcement and private investigators work a crime scene by collecting evidence and then interpreting this information to try to trace back what happened.

- Lawyers argue in courts of law that the evidence should be interpreted in a manner that supports whatever trace back theory their client will benefit from most ("From the evidence, it should be obvious that my client didn't do it, but that the *babysitter* in fact did it!"). This illustrates the somewhat uncertain and probabilistic nature of tracing back activity based on evidence.

- Scientists frequently initiate experiments that result in observations about cause and effect. The challenge for such scientists is to trace a path of activity that will explain the results of their experiments. The inevitable arguments that arise among differing theories further illustrate this problem of reconstructing events based on observable evidence.

It's time to get more specific about how in-band and out-of-band trace back techniques work in computing and networking environments. The reader is warned that trace back is an immature technology and much of the material presented below is based on research experiments, conjecture, and still-to-be-implemented design approaches. This should not diminish the importance of this discussion. It is our opinion that the future of intrusion detection rests largely on the degree to which effective trace back techniques can be demonstrated in practice.

We organize our discussion in this section around a collection of different techniques that are related only in that they attempt to determine Internet identities. We specify each technique and describe how it can be used, whether it is in-band or out-of-band, and whether the technique has been actually used in live situations.

*Internet trace back workbench.* Many different tools exist in a typical Internet environment that support *attempts* at tracing identity. Some of the tools that provide information for intrusion detection systems to gain information about identity are discussed below:

- *Finger.* The *finger* program allows one to query information about a specific user on the Internet. Details on the *finger* program are provided in a section later in this chapter.

- *Ph.* The *ph* command, short for phone book, is used by some companies,  organizations, schools, and sites as a simple directory service. It must be noted, however, that enterprise directory commands like *ph* generally only offer a means for identifying individuals after you have some idea of their general affiliation (e.g., ISP, workplace).

- *Ping.* The *ping* command provides a basic test tool for Internet processing. What happens when you *ping* a host on the Internet is that an Internet Control Message Protocol (ICMP) echo request message is sent to the specified target IP address. When the target system receives the echo request message, it responds with an ICMP echo response message. Some more sophisticated versions of *ping* exist that allow for series of echo requests to be sent along with the ability to capture statistics on lost packets. The *ping* command provides intrusion detection systems with the ability to test for connectivity between systems.

- *Traceroute.* The *traceroute* program is more verbose in its reporting than *ping* in that it provides details of path hops between the source and destination hosts. The way it works is that the IP protocol 'time-to-live' field is used via attempts to solicit ICMP TIME_EXCEEDED responses from each hop along the routed path between a source and destination. If you've never seen *traceroute* work, you might consider visiting one of the Web-based traceroute gateways at http://www.beach.net/traceroute.html or http://www.llv.com/~lasvegas/traceroute.cgi. You can use these gateways to locate the host associated with an IP address that you might have (e.g., from a Usenet posting you're interested in finding the source of). Figure 5-12 shows the different uses of *traceroute* and *ping*.

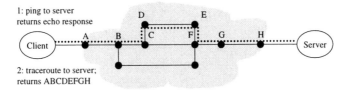

**Figure 5-12**. Traceroute and Ping Usage for Trace Information

It's worth noting that an interesting tool for locating who is using a particular IP address is called the 'IP Address to Hostname and Vice Versa' utility. You can find it at http://cello.cs.uiuc.edu/cgi-bin/slamm/ip2name.

- *Rusers*. The *rusers* command can be used to get information about users on a specified network. For instance, if you know a particular domain, you might try the *rusers* command on that domain to get information about active users. An example use of this command might be in conjunction with attempts to locate the true identity of someone hiding in an Internet relay chat (IRC) session in which IP addresses are not necessarily hidden.

- *Nslookup*. The *nslookup* program is a name server utility that allows you to look up an ISP's numeric address or who provides service to the ISP's site. A Web-based front-end to *nslookup* is located at http://ldhp715. immt.pwr.wroc.pl/util/nslookup.html and http://www.uia.ac.be/ds/nslookup.html.

- *Whois*. The *whois* service is centrally located at http://rs.internic.net/ and provides domain registration information about Internet sites. Information provided via *whois* includes domain addresses, technical contacts, phone numbers, and addresses. Web-based *whois* gateways exist at http://rs.internic.net/cgi-bin/whois and http://www. magibox.net/~unabest/finger/index.html.

    *Telephone records*. A second type of resource for performing trace back involves the use of telephony-based information. In particular, when Internet users make use of telephony to gain access to the Internet—as in all dial access situations—trace back efforts can make use of the caller and called phone records kept for billing and other purposes by the telephony provider. This type of trace back raises several technical, legal, and policy-based issues including the following:

- *Customer privacy*. Many ISPs make great attempts to respect the privacy of their customers. This is essential in today's Internet environment as no ISP would ever maintain customers if it were using call records in a cavalier manner. Obviously, legal issues in various countries abound here to protect customer privacy and to prevent the misuse of this information.

- *Accuracy of call records*. Call records are generally more accurate from an end-point confidence perspective than IP address session information. Making a local phone call in the United States from your home to your ISP dial access edge vehicle, for example, will result in the U.S. local exchange company (LEC) generating a call record of the time and duration of the call. Deleting this record from the LEC database would require a special type of access, not normally obtainable by crackers (except in the most special cases—

see the Bibliography, for example, for a reference to Jonathan Littman's outstanding book on serial hacker Kevin Poulsen).

- *Caller ID.* If your LEC supports caller identification functionality, then this provides some degree of trace back in special situations (e.g., if you are running a bulletin board). It is not difficult to imagine simple trap situations where caller ID would be combined with a honey pot bulletin board to attract and trace certain types of crackers, criminals, and other types of users. More detailed information on Caller ID is provided in a later section.

- *Opportunity for call records.* Between most users and their dial access connectivity, several opportunities exist for obtaining call records. Some examples of these include the LEC, the long distance company, any on-premise private branch exchange (PBX) components, and any other types of computer telephony support (e.g., Centrex).

It goes without saying that as the Internet becomes more integrated into the global telecommunications infrastructure, the delineation between telephony and data networking will become less obvious. When voice over the Internet, for example, finally becomes economically feasible for service providers and more reasonable from an infrastructure capacity perspective, then the distinction between voice and data becomes even more blurred.

The implication of this infrastructure evolution for trace back support to intrusion detection systems is that existing out-of-band techniques will become more in-band. This is likely to make trace back easier, but it remains to be seen. Cryptographic techniques such as tunneling could be a major source of trouble for anyone trying to perform in-band trace back on the Internet.

*Internet directories.* The essence of any directory service is to provide a logically centralized information source for users. Internet directories abound with information about individuals, groups, organizations, services, systems, and networks that may be useful in trace back situations. Some of the better Internet directories for performing searches include the following:

- http://www.worldpages.com/
- http://www.four11.com/
- http://bigfoot.com/

*Internet search tools.* Search tools also provide excellent sources of information tracing. As we listed earlier in the book, some of the better search tools include the following:

- http://www.altavista.digital.com/
- http://www.dejanews.com/
- http://www.excite.com/
- http://www.hotbot.com/
- http://www.infoseek.com/

One thing you might try for fun is typing your own name into these different search tools. You might be surprised at what you find. If you want to try something slightly more devious, try typing '/etc/passwd' into the search tool.

*Reverse cracking.* A somewhat controversial technique for trace back involves so-called *reverse cracking.* The only reference to this technique that I've ever seen in print was in a paper by L. Todd Heberlein and Stuart Staniford-Chen where they suggest that a U.S. Air Force group claimed to have done this (see bibliographic notes at end of chapter). Other than this, the only time I've ever heard the topic discussed and debated was in informal discussions, email discussions, and Internet forums. The most common viewpoint with respect to this technique is that the government probably does it, or so goes this popular viewpoint, and that such behavior is to be condemned.

Regardless of whether anyone is actually doing this or not, it helps to explore exactly what the technique comprises. The basic idea is that if a server is compromised and intrusion detection techniques are to be used to determine the source, then one might make use of a simple observation: If a cracker managed to gain access to the compromised server via some multiple hop route, then security vulnerabilities must have existed at these hops for the cracker to have woven a path to unauthorized access.

In reverse hacking, this observation is used to reverse the direction of the access path from the compromised site. That is, the intrusion detection system would target the same vulnerabilities used by the cracker in order to locate the cracker. (See Figure 5-13).

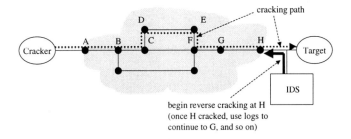

**Figure 5-13.** Reverse Cracking Heuristic

While reverse cracking may seem technically reasonable in principle, the truth is that in practice this will not work in most circumstances. In particular, many of the anonymous functions cited earlier such as blinding factors and anonymous remailers will serve as barriers to this type of trace back. In any event, whether you like it or not, additional research in this area should be expected.

*Trace back traps.* One of the best ways to trace back identity on the Internet involves the use of traps, also known as honey pots and lures. The method uses the trap to attempt to obtain information such as your name or phone number directly from you which might subvert any approaches used to ensure an anonymous access path. We devote Chapter 7 to the topic of traps and will therefore defer our discussion on this deception-based approach. Nevertheless, it must be acknowledged here that this may be one of the best techniques, especially for out-of-band trace back.

## CASE STUDY: UNIX FINGER PROGRAM

The popular *finger* program is an Internet utility that provides information about system users. *Finger* clients are available for most operating systems including most UNIX systems and Windows NT. The way *finger* works is that an Internet-connected system may or may not be running a *finger* server program called *fingerd* that is listening for *finger* client requests on port 79. If the server is running, then it will be listed in the file */etc/inetd.conf* on the server system. Removing *fingerd* from this file disables *finger* requests into the server.

The information that *fingerd* provides to a requesting user is based on the server configuration settings as well as some decisions made by individual users on the server system. One example is the restriction some administrators place on finger requests so that only specified users can be directly probed, as opposed to entire systems of unspecified users. In addition, certain versions of *fingerd* are available that provide enhanced security features for more discerning administrators.

Users also have some control over the information provided by the *fingerd* program. On most systems, they can create files called *.plan* files that specify the information to be provided if they are the target of a *finger* request. This information can be virtually anything, which might cause the creative juices to flow in certain mischievous individuals. In any event, the baseline information that is available via the *finger* program is described below.

- *Directory information.* Initiating the request *'finger person@host.com'* will specify the directory where the user *'person'* resides.
- *Environment information.* On a UNIX system, the specified user's shell program will be reported via *finger.*
- *Last login information.* The date of the specified user's last login will be reported; this is a great hint for those searching for unused or rarely used accounts.
- *Mail information.* Mail that is queued and mail that is unread is reported; this also provides a hint about account use.
- *Other subtle hints.* Sometimes special information like version and type of operating system being used can be interpreted from the way *fingerd* reports and formats information.

As you might expect, if this *finger* information is available, it may be very useful in the tracing of a reported identity on the Internet. This is one of the main reasons gateway administrators generally disable incoming *finger* program requests. In fact, *finger* gateways provide a useful means for honey pots and purposely deceptive information about users, if the security administrators are so inclined to behave in this manner. One cannot help but sigh at the implications of all this deception. We must acknowledge, however, that this is a fact of performing proper security protection on the Internet.

## CASE STUDY: INTERNET COOKIES

The idea of an Internet cookie seems innocent enough when you first consider their purpose. The basic notion is that a Web server sends a bit of information to a browsing client that would be written to the user's hard drive in a special cookies file. The purpose of this is to build customer profiles, enable certain types of commerce applications (e.g., such as virtual shopping carts), and support various types of statistical analysis for marketing and other purposes. Another major use of cookies is for saving authentication information to support single sign-on in environments where multiple Web pages are being visited. In Netscape browsing environments, cookies are stored in an HTTP cookie file called cookies.txt which can be opened with a text editor.

The reason we include cookies in our discussion on trace back is that cookies could be used theoretically as a means for tracing identity. Certainly the repeat patterns of a browsing user could be determined via this technique. This information could be useful in correlating activity between different sessions that an intrusion detection system may suspect are initiated by the same user.

The key issue with respect to trace back and cookies is that this persistent state information is intended to be created and used by the *same Web site*. That is, an origin server sends state information (i.e., a cookie) to the user, and the user returns the state information only back to the origin server. Several comments are worth noting here:

- The use of cookies as a means for creating single site audit trails has been documented (see RFC2109) and may raise privacy concerns among users; multiple site audit trails as a means for performing trace back is a largely unexplored topic.

- Cookie information in transit is clear text, as opposed to encrypted text, and could be captured by an intrusion detection system for trace-back (subject to legal and policy considerations).

- Under the current method of cookie provision and acceptance, users will always have the option of being vigilant and avoiding this type of trace back if it is even feasible by careful administration of client side state information from servers.

As the development of a public key infrastructure (PKI) continues, one would hope that public key certificates would replace cookies for many types of applications, especially those in which sites are authenticating users for single sign-on. However, as the PKI is so slow to emerge and as legacy applications proliferate that rely on cookies, one cannot help but presume that cookies will be with us for a very long time. In any event, they will certainly play a role in the Internet identity tracing equation.

## CASE STUDY: CALLER IDENTIFICATION

One of the more controversial features in modern telephony is the Calling Number Identification (CNID) feature, more commonly referred to as Caller-ID. It turns out that Caller-ID, while a relatively recent phenomenon, is actually based on Automatic Number Identification (ANI) data that has been used by telephone companies for some time. ANI is used to determine the account to which a call is to be billed. It has had other obvious uses such as 911 emergency identification, law enforcement use in authorized wire taps, and telephone company operator usage to improve customer service.

The way CNID works is that when you pick up the phone and dial, your ANI is passed from switch to switch along its way to the destination number. At each of these intermediate hops, the ANI is typically available for use. There are some exceptions, particularly in more complex arrangements such as international calling with certain countries. Nevertheless, CNID information can be passed to the destination party in a protocol that provides a 1200 baud bit stream of information in between the first and second ring signals on the line. The formatted protocol for simple CNID in single message format looks something like this:

```
RING
MM-DD  HH-MM  Caller-ID
RING
```

The notation we use above for describing this protocol should be obvious enough. Continuing our discussion, you might find the following Caller-ID transmission in a typical arrangement:

```
RING
02-22  5:42  123456789
RING
```

In the multiple message format, additional directory information is provided as part of the Caller-ID stream. The formatted protocol would look as follows:

```
RING
Time: MM-DD  HH:MM
Caller Number: Caller_ID
Caller Name: Caller_Name
RING
```

An example of this type of more detailed Caller ID transmission is shown below:

```
RING
Time: 02:22  05:42
Caller Number: 123456789
Caller Name: JoeSchmoe
RING
```

As you might expect, additional examples abound for the variety of different scenarios that might arise as callers might or might not impose line blocking. For instance, before making a call, you have the option of pressing *67 to inform the local switch to set the privacy bit on the CNID information passed. As a result, the CNID is available to the switch, but the privacy bit imposes a blocking of transmission to the destination station.

Clearly, Caller ID has caused a debate among technology and privacy interest groups. Some of the issues that have been discussed on-line and in public forums are summarized below:

- While forgery is viewed as infeasible from the calling station, there have been some reports of improperly designed infrastructure devices that can be exploited to cause incorrect ANI. Furthermore, break-ins to telephone companies could result in the CNID scheme being compromised at a switch.

- Suggestions that Caller ID be used to authenticate users for services like bulletin boards have prompted the development of software and freeware by some vendors to assist in this endeavor. While this scheme certainly works, it will not be a uniform scheme when calling individuals impose per call blocking. Service providers and bulletin board operators are advised (by this author) to use a legitimate authentication package rather than Caller ID.

- To trace back the identity of individuals, one should certainly use CNID if it is available. Some cautions must be acknowledged, however. If the malicious attacker, perhaps dialing into your system, is truly naïve, then Caller ID might work. If the calling individual is more versed in technology, then the privacy option will more than likely be set. Even more devious, however, would be the malicious cracker using incorrect ANI, perhaps through some toll fraud scheme, with the privacy intentionally not set to cause some sort of diversion. So trace back engineers must be aware of these possibilities.

- You can buy products all over the place to help you do Caller ID in conjunction with your service provider. Lucent Technologies, for example, makes a great device called the Lucent 485 Caller ID Unit that you can buy for about fifty bucks. It remembers up to 99 CNIDs, which is pretty good for that price. If you need more, then you're going to have to spend more money.

## BIBLIOGRAPHIC NOTES

The first quote is from Larry Hughes book [HU95] and the second quote is from the IEEE paper on thumbprinting [SH95]. The Web site of the Electronic Privacy Information Center (http://epic.org) had some useful information. Comer's book on TCP/IP [CO95] is an excellent resource for TCP/IP information; it was consulted in the preparation of the IP addressing primer in this chapter. Andre Bacard's Anonymous Remailer FAQ (which I found at http://electron. rutgers.edu/~gambino/anon_servers/anonfaq) helped with the material on anonymous proxies and servers. Michael Banks' book on Web psychos, stalkers, and pranksters [BA97] was helpful in various places throughout this chapter. One of my favorite books (and one that I've made many graduate students purchase) is called *Maximum Security* [AN97], written by an anonymous author. I used material from this book in the trace back section. The Cookie Central Web site (http://www. cookiecentral.com) was interesting and helpful in the preparation of this chapter. RFC2109 (http://www.internic.net) is a readable specification of persistent state information (i.e., cookies). I found some really cool sites on Caller ID. Look at the Web pages at http://www.cpsr.org/ and http://www. telepath.com/bennett/page5.html, which contains a link to Padgett Peterson's great FAQ on Caller ID. I consistently found myself wasting time reading and not writing because these pages were so interesting. So be careful before you start browsing this stuff. Make sure you have some serious time to kill.

# CHAPTER 6:
# INTRUSION CORRRELATION

*An intrusion detection system should provide all pertinent connection and session data in real time so the security team can immediately analyze the event.*

Lee Sutterfield

*A rule of thumb: Don't lump concerns together that were perfectly separated to start with.*

Edsger Dijkstra

## WHAT IS MEANT BY INTRUSION CORRELATION?

If you talk to the experts about the real challenges inherent in detecting intrusions on the Internet, eventually the conversation gets around to the topic of correlation. Here are some familiar examples of what we mean by correlation in our everyday lives:

- You see a young man in your neighborhood shooting baskets in his driveway night after night; years later, you find out that he is an all-state basketball player and in your mind, you correlate the two pieces of information.

- A loud siren goes off in the streets of an American city during a period of national peace. Most people in the city shrug and ignore the siren. If this same siren were to go off just as an armed conflict had begun, then people would correlate this information and perhaps treat the siren more seriously.

- A maintenance request for a broken soft drink machine comes in from a college dormitory. The service people assume the students broke the machine, especially if it was from any college I ever went to. If the *same* maintenance report for the *same* vending machine comes in from a religious convent or place of worship, then the service people probably make different assumptions about the cause of the problem.

- A friend smokes incessantly; inevitably, you get the phone call that this friend has taken ill or died of emphysema, cancer, or some other disease. You do the sad medical correlation in your mind.

- You are waiting outside the Lincoln Tunnel in traffic wondering what's going on as you attempt to drive into Manhattan. Your radio reports that the President is arriving in New York for a fund-raiser. You correlate the two events and turn off your engine.

- You are working the Sunday evening shift in the network operations center of a major voice telecommunications company. The Super Bowl, a major American football event, has just begun and you notice that voice traffic on your network has suddenly decreased dramatically. When the game is interrupted for half-time festivities, you notice a significant surge in traffic. The correlation between these incidents is obvious.

- In a more computing context, a series of UNIX *syslog* messages on one machine suggests strange behavior (e.g., someone is doing a port scan). If this problem were only seen on one machine, then the security manager might shrug and decide to ignore the problem as a spurious anomaly. If the problem is seen on lots of machines on the overall enterprise network, then the action might be different. The UNIX security manager might correlate knowledge of these distributed events and perform the necessary intrusion correlation to determine an appropriate response. Phone calls or email to the other security managers or to clearinghouses like CERT might be used to gain additional information for correlation.

For our computing and networking-oriented discussions in this chapter, we introduce the following definition:

---

*Definition of Intrusion Correlation*

*Intrusion correlation* refers to the <u>interpretation</u>, <u>combination</u>, and <u>analysis</u> of information from <u>all available sources</u> about target system activity for the purposes of intrusion detection and response.

---

As usual, let's go through what we mean by the underlined words and phrases in the definition:

"*Interpretation*". This word always causes problems. For logicians and theoretical computer scientists, it means associating some syntactic construct with an underlying semantic concept. For the purposes of intrusion detection, we presume it to mean the subjective identification of some *meaning* to some available information ("Hmmm," ponders the network manager, "I think I know what this audit record means").

"*Combination*". This implies that information is combined from different sources or collection points. The manner in which the combination is performed will differ from one correlation implementation to another.

"*Analysis*". This is an over-used term (my apologies). It would be tough to talk about correlation, however, without including mention of analysis. The idea here is that human intelligence, with the assistance of automated tools can provide a resultant analysis process that can be quite powerful.

"*All Available Sources*". This means what it says. Correlation of information is better and more accurate when it involves lots of different information from lots of different sources.

A couple of notes on correlation must be made at this point. First, we will not limit intrusion correlation to computer and network based information. This implies that any type of information useful to the intrusion detection manager can be taken into account. This information can thus include out-of-band intelligence, world events, and even the subjective suspicions of a network security manager. In fact, in any practical intrusion processing center, one will find that out-of-band information is often the most powerful indicator of an on-going incident.

Second, we will not limit intrusion correlation to executable processes run on a computer or across a network. While this will certainly constitute a major portion of the correlation processing one expects in an intrusion detection system, human beings interpreting available information will also provide an important component in intrusion correlation. The notion of an intrusion detection infrastructure with automated and manual processes provides a useful view of how intrusion correlation is likely to be carried out in practice. Figure 6-1 depicts the high-level architectural strategy that an intrusion detection system must follow for intrusion correlation.

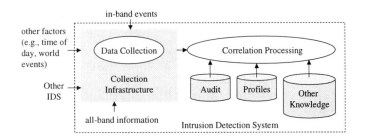

**Figure 6-1.** Basic High-Level Intrusion Correlation Strategy

Note in Figure 6-1 the different in-band (i.e., Internet and TCP/IP data networking) and out-of-band (e.g., human discussion, world events, telephony information, subjective suspicions) information sources that must be taken into account. Note also that the diagram is in two dimensions and that the time dimension, roughly from left to right, is not easily drawn in a picture. This should not diminish the critical importance of time in the correlation of information for intrusion detection. As we continue in our discussions on correlation, we will have more to say about the importance of minimizing time in correlating information.

## A PRIMER ON STATISTICAL CORRELATION

Those readers with advanced degrees in statistics or related branches of higher mathematics can and should hop over this section. For the rest of you, this section outlines some of the real basics of correlation in the statistical sense. Only the trivial basics are included, but even these provide some useful insights into the task of correlating computing and networking data. If you think you want more on this topic, then I suggest a couple of statistics books in the bibliographic notes.

Statisticians generally frame the correlation problem in terms of *variables*. The key notion of a variable is that it can be associated with a distinct value from some defined domain. Thus, if we model a universe (mathematicians like to do that) as consisting of a collection of variables, then at any instant each variable will have a certain value. Computer scientists use this approach to model variable attributes in computer and network systems. Statistical correlation focuses on the following variable-related concepts:

- *Change.* This usually means positive increase or negative decrease in variable values. Obviously, if the possible values in a variable domain are not ordered, then increase and decrease will have no meaning. For situations where variables take on numeric values, an increase or decrease can be easily measured and compared with other changes.

- *Trends.* This involves any patterns that can be detected in the changes in variable values. These trends can be absolutely anything that has some meaning; in fact, correlation will require creativity on the part of the analyst or tool developer to identify such trends. The existence of a trend in the mathematical sense usually corresponds to the identification of some function or relation that can be written down. In computing and networking, trends might not be as well-defined ("Every time that system goes down," the network managers mutters, "I get this funny feeling").

- *Calculations.* Statisticians like to look at data and perform calculations on the data. One prominent calculation involves computing the so-called *mean* in a set of data. The intuitive notion of a mean is that it serves as a balance point for the data. Another calculation involves a so-called *standard deviation*. This is an average distance between successive values in a set of numbers.

As an example of how variables and trends are used in simple math, suppose that we identify two variables $x$ and $y$ that will contain positive integer values at any instant. Let's sample some of the possible values of $x$ and $y$ in the following simple table:

| x | y |
|---|---|
| 1 | 2 |
| 2 | 3 |
| 3 | 4 |
| 4 | 5 |

On observation, we notice the obvious relationship for these values and we presume the relationship to be one of *positive correlation* between $x$ and $y$ defined by the simple function $y = x + 1$. That is, as $x$ increases from 1 to 2 to 3 and so on, $y$ experiences an increase from 2 to 3 to 4 and so on. Since the relationship is linear, we sometimes refer to this as a *perfect positive correlation*. As an exercise, create a negative correlation between two variables where an increase in one correlates with a decrease in another.

Statisticians note that if we jumble the values of x and y, the correlation might disappear. Interestingly, if we do this, note that the mean and standard deviations of the numbers would be the same. This highlights the manner in which certain calculations will have a direct effect on correlation whereas others might have a more indirect effect. In particular, consider that a measured difference in two values in a set will be interpreted differently for different standard deviations. For instance, suppose that a student scored ten points higher than everyone else in the class, but where the standard deviation was twenty. This might be less impressive than scoring five points higher than everyone else with a standard deviation of less than one.

To account for this sensitivity in data change, the notion of a *z-score* was invented. The z-score is the distance between values divided by the standard deviation. It therefore provides a numeric means for highlighting the effects of standard deviations. Furthermore, by multiplying the z-scores of two variables, we produce a result that has been called the correlation coefficient. Have I lost you yet?

---

### A Word on Statistics and Correlation

I should first expose my bias. I believe that computer scientists and engineers do not study mathematics properly in school and are typically ill-prepared to tackle problems that use non-trivial mathematical concepts. That said, I will also suggest that you do not really need to get into the muddy details of statistical correlation to appreciate what needs to be done. I think that *very simple relationships* will likely provide security engineers with enough information to initiate response. If the correlation results are too complex, then the results may not be trusted. So don't get too crazy with the statistics.

---

If you don't agree with my advice and you really want to dig into statistical correlation, then the following couple of issues are likely to be important:

- *Predictive techniques.* One reason we bother to look for trends is that it allows prediction (just ask your weatherman). So a reasonable avenue of research would involve building up a large knowledge base of predictions and results, just like we have in the meteorology business. Issues of how to represent the real factors influencing both predictions and results are unclear at this time. Perhaps languages for representing information about trends could be designed and integrated with existing database technology. This would be a nontrivial activity, so good luck.

- *Curve-fitting.* You probably remember from high school trying to fit a curve or line onto a bunch of points. You might also remember that if the points are scattered and unrelated enough, the punt solution of just swiping a horizontal line through them all is actually the best technique. Because display of data in security network operations environments is likely to take on a great significance in the next few years, displaying data over a best-fit curve is a useful area in which to study. In addition, provision of active displays that allow drill-down capability for analysts examining a curve would be attractive. Linking displays with database algorithms that generate alarms when certain patterns emerge is also considered an attractive avenue of research.

## WHAT TYPES OF INTRUSION CORRELATION EXIST?

By now it should be evident that correlation is fundamental to the processing of information in intrusion detection systems. For Internet computing and networking environments, the types of intrusion correlation that must be performed include at least the following three types:

- *Single session* versus *multiple session network correlation.* In this case, sessions are considered TCP/IP data network sessions between defined endpoints. A single session requires that correlation be performed on the series of client and server requests and responses in the data stream, whereas multiple sessions require more involved treatment. The important conceptual notion of *association* (recall from Chapter 3) will be used to illustrate a design approach to session-based correlation. Obviously, this sort of thing is easier with protocols like TCP that have a more mature notion of session than protocols such as UDP.

- *Real time* versus *after-the-fact correlation.* In this case, real time is a requirement that minimizes the response duration after incidents are detected. After-the-fact correlation processing is often done by security analysts after the damage has occurred. This allows analysts to determine or approximate the strategy used by the attacker. Most intrusion detection system vendors are trying desperately to improve the real time correlation and processing capabilities in their products.

- *In-band* versus *all-band correlation.* In this case, in-band refers to the Internet and TCP/IP environments and out-of-band refers to all other frameworks including the physical and paper worlds. Thus, correlation of different process characteristics on a UNIX system would be considered an in-band situation, whereas taking into account non-computing issues would make it all-band. This type of correlation implies the presence of an infrastructure to handle the non-computing and networking information that must be included in the intrusion correlation.

These different types of intrusion correlation are examined in detail in this chapter. It is important to keep in mind that the different correlation approaches presented are not mutually exclusive. In fact, as we will show, most intrusion detection systems makes use of each of these techniques to a degree.

## CORRELATION PHILOSOPHY: SMALL HEURISTIC APPROACHS

Before we begin our discussion on correlation processing, it is instructive to comment on our basic philosophy. Correlation processing has not been the focus of much research in computer and network security. We believe this stems from its lack of clear definition. It also stems from the tendency to equate complex statistical analysis with correlation—an equating we believe to be misleading.

Our pedagogical approach to this topic is to illustrate and explain the various approaches to correlation processing as a series of separate, *small* algorithmic heuristics. For those of you who are programmers, you might view each of these heuristics as a correlation tool in your intrusion correlation manager's toolbox. Some of these heuristics will involve automated processing, some will require manual action, and some will require thinking and subjective interpretation.

The point is that a subset—possibly all, possible none—of the heuristics available for correlation will work in any given intrusion instance (see Figure 6-2).

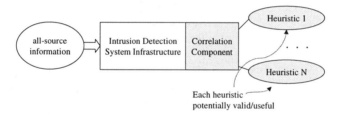

**Figure 6-2**. Correlation Using Small Heuristic Approaches

The term *separation of concerns* is often used by computing scientists to describe the notion of focusing one's attention on a small task before considering its context in a larger one. Our contention is that correlation is best viewed as a large challenge that is best achieved via a series of much smaller ones. In fact, most correlation environments utilize the notion of an 'analysis tool kit' comprised of a collection of tools that perform smaller tasks in order to accomplish the larger task of correlation.

## INTRUSION CORRELATION WITHIN SINGLE SESSIONS

We begin our correlation discussion by focusing on intrusion detection systems that are targeting TCP/IP-based data networks. In this case, data network sessions will be viewed as corresponding to a connection-oriented TCP interaction and a connectionless orientation of IP interaction between defined source and destination endpoints. This has always struck me as a useful pedagogical approach; certainly protocols such as UDP do not fit this simple model; but it seems easier to provide a uniform framework onto which the special cases can be applied rather than the reverse. The parameters of the session in our model correspond to the so-called full association in TCP/IP in which the source and destination IP addresses, source and destination ports, and protocol are defined.

The correlation problem will be different for single sessions in which packets are transferred between the defined session endpoints, and multiple sessions that will involve different endpoint pairs. In the single session case, the correlation is between packets, whereas the multiple case could involve many different endpoint pairs.

Also, in single session correlation, a bi-directional stream of packets is examined and processed solely with respect to temporal and contextual considerations. The context associated with a session can include information from any reasonable source (e.g., information about either end point in a session, information about the environment in which the session is taking place). This greatly simplifies the correlation problem as it allows separating one's concern and focusing on a specific endpoint pair.

A high-level depiction of the single session correlation processing approach with its emphasis on time and context concerns is represented in the picture in Figure 6-3.

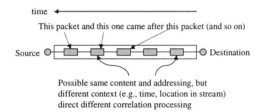

**Figure 6-3**. Single Session Correlation

Before we examine time and context considerations in the next sections, it is instructive to acknowledge several technical factors that will have an effect on whether intrusion correlation can be properly performed on single streams of data at a single sensor. These different factors are discussed below.

*Cryptographic protocols between endpoints.* If single key or public key-based cryptographic protocols are employed at either end of a session, then the opportunity for correlation processing based on content and addressing is greatly diminished. This statement highlights the technical basis for the on-going debate in the telecommunications industry regarding encryption policy. This does not, however, imply that correlation cannot be performed when sessions are encrypted. In particular, techniques are available including the following:

- *Covert channel identification.* When any feature of a network channel *not* designated as an overt channel for providing communications is in fact used to communicate information, then we say that a covert channel has been created. In cryptography, it is possible to detect covert channels in successive blocks of bulk encrypted data. This can be avoided by chaining the cryptography for successive blocks of data.

- *Session traps.* This could involve spoofing one end of a session key exchange in order to identify and understand the communications intended for the encrypted channel.

- *Brute force or heuristic cryptanalysis.* This is the traditional way to break crypto. It involves brute force searches through a key space or heuristic searches for keys or clear text patterns usually based on some mathematical knowledge.

- *End-point key management surveillance.* This is the classic attempt to crack the end-point of an encrypted channel. Security experts agree that this is the most vulnerable place for encrypted data. It is also therefore an attractive place for potential surveillance and correlation.

Figure 6-4 depicts these techniques for processing of encrypted sessions.

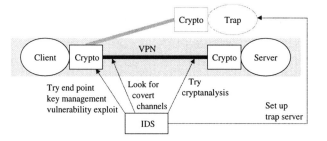

**Figure 6-4**. Intrusion Processing Opportunities for Encrypted Sessions

It seems ironic that the very security flaws that the security community has been ranting about for years (e.g., computer security weaknesses in protecting keys, information flow vulnerabilities that result in covert channels) may provide an opportunity at the end-points of a session for obtaining information for authorized (e.g., law enforcement, national cyber-defense) session decryption.

*Capacity and speed of the session transport networks.* It stand to reason that an intrusion detection system can only target environments where the available information for correlation can be tractably processed. If more information is available than can be handled—as in a network intrusion detection system targeting a network with too great a transfer capacity—then the intrusion detection system has a problem. Nevertheless, some options do exist. For example, the intrusion detection system can employ a sampling approach where statistical processing would be required to generalize the samples to the full environment. Sample rates and sample amounts would be determined based on local requirements. Alternatively, the intrusion detection system can make use of large buffers to try to store information for later correlation processing. In either of these cases, the obvious preference would be for sufficient processing capability to be present in the intrusion detection system to handle the available information load.

## PACKET HEURISTICS FOR SINGLE SESSION PROCESSING

In this section, we explore some techniques for correlation of packets in a single data network session. These heuristics will rely on the sequential nature of a bi-directional packet stream in a session. Note that the temporal ordering of packet transmission may differ from the sequential ordering created by an application such as TCP. In particular, we examine heuristic algorithmic sketches for the following:

- *Association Processing*. Recall from Chapter 3 the notion of an association for correlation processing. Associations are structures that provide dynamic context information about streams of activity.
- *Time-to-Store*. This involves determining appropriate lengths of time for storing associations. Time-to-store considerations are fundamental to dynamic processing in intrusion detection systems.

- *Bi-directional Build.* This involves rebuilding bi-directional session packets based on available information.

Each of these three heuristics is intended to provide insights into the internals of an intrusion detection system targeting single sessions in a TCP/IP data network. Intrusion detection designers and researchers must consider these issues in the creation of more effective systems for detecting intrusions.

*Association Processing.* This heuristic is central to correlation processing. The idea is that a captured packet will be processed according to its context in the single session. Note that we use packets as the unit of processing for convenience. The heuristics remain the same if the unit of processing is a message, word, or byte. A given packet P might therefore be processed using approach A if one instance of P is detected in a given sampling size, versus being processed using approach B if multiple instances are detected in the sample. Another example is that a packet P might be processed one way if it follows packet P' and another way if it follows some different packet P''.

Recall from Chapter 3 that we introduced an algorithm for creating associations based on dynamic behavior. The presumption here is that such an association building function would be present in the correlation toolbox. A high-level sketch of an association processing algorithm is provided below:

```
1       repeat
2               target_system_feed (packet)
3               case
4                       association_A (packet) → response_A
5                       association_B (packet) → response_B
6                       . . .
7               esac
8       forever
```

**Figure 6-5.** Association Processing Algorithmic Sketch

Annotation of the algorithm in Figure 6-5:
- Line 2: Note our reuse of the information feed function.
- Line 3: To simplify matters, we impose a trivial case semantics in which each association is examined until a match is found. Once one is found, the case statement is exited. If one is never found, then the case falls through and exits. By the way, simultaneous evaluation of all conditions (as in Dijkstra's notation) avoids any response denial or bias toward the earlier association rules.
- Line 4-5: If an association is matched, then the specified response is performed. This is a classic rule-based system approach.

The very simple idea being expressed here is that response activities would be based on predetermined decisions about the dynamic associations that are being maintained. The responses that are followed as a result of association processing can involve any of the following activities:
- *Updates to association information.* If an existing association is being kept (e.g., counting the number of instances of some event), then an obtained packet in a session could cause an update to this metric.

- *Creation of some new association information.* If no existing association is relevant to this packet, but some predetermined context knowledge suggests that a new association be created, then this would be a valid response.
- *Intrusion detection alerting.* If the obtained packet causes a condition to become true and an alert to an administrator or security officer is warranted, then this can be the response action.

*Time-to-Store.* Another temporal correlation heuristic that we will investigate for single sessions is the time-to-store concept. When packets in a session stream are captured for correlation analysis and deemed to have some security relevance, then (as we have already proposed in the association processing heuristic above) some means must be present for maintaining information about these packets.

The time-to-store heuristic proposes a basic strategy for determining appropriate times for maintaining dynamic associations about target system activity. A possible algorithm that triggers re-examination of each context upon packet receipt is sketched below. Note in the algorithm that we must assume that the variable 'associations' is the set of all association information structures being maintained by the intrusion detection system at a given time. Obviously, if the set is empty, then the loop index will by definition not be positive. We must also assume that the variable 'timeout' is based on some predetermined clock decrement for each association. This can be a problem if the associations are being developed, stored, and maintained in different locations with different physical and logical clocks.

```
1       repeat
2               target_system_feed (info)
3               for all (a in associations) do
4                   if unrelated (a, info) and timeout (a) then
5                           remove a from associations
6                   fi
7               od
8       forever
```

**Figure 6-6**. Time to Store Association Algorithmic Sketch

Annotation of the algorithm in Figure 6-6:
- Line 3: A loop is indexed by every element in the association. The order here is abstracted by using a set construct. Some implementations might prefer to use a prioritized sequence of associations on which to search.
- Line 4: Associations are examined to see if they are unrelated to the information being extracted from the target session. In addition, each association is being timed to ensure that it does not continually report unrelated without being removed. Some issues with respect to this line of code include serious performance challenges in implementation (perhaps with few associations, fast implementation platforms such as hardware, and low information feed capacities), as well as the need for off-line, concurrent timing decrements in the timeout function.
- Line 5: Garbage collection for associations is done here.

The purpose of the time to store algorithm is to highlight and address the basic problem in intrusion detection correlation processing of storing and maintaining dynamic information. As this information is gathered and stored, basic questions of how much to store, where to store it, and how long to keep it must be addressed by designers of intrusion detection systems.

The predetermination of how long to keep associations must take into account the following factors:

- The amount of time that has passed influences how long an association is kept. If more time has passed, then the likelihood that an association can be removed is greater.

- The degree to which the association remains relevant must be considered. If the session that an association targets has been destroyed, then the association may no longer be valid.

- One must consider the degree to which later response activities will require this association for correlation. This will determine if an association should generate an audit record.

    *Bi-directional Build.* When intrusion detection systems capture single session target system activity on network links that include bi-directional information transfer, rebuilding the session for analysis may require attention to the following concerns:

- Source and destination information provides the basic sorting of direction for session interpretation and correlation.

- The direction of packets should be correlated with source and destination information to ensure proper consistency.

- Where acknowledgement packets can be differentiated from initial packets as in TCP-based services, this can be used to correlate packets into sessions.

- Where acknowledgement information is not present, time out conditions can often be used by intrusion detection systems to correlate requests from associated responses for specified source and destination end points.

## CASE STUDY: SYSTEM CALL TRACE CORRELATION

Andrew Kosoresow, Steven Hofmeyr, and others from the University of New Mexico and MIT have been experimenting with a promising technique for characterizing normal system call traces for Internet services such as *sendmail.* These normal system call trace characterizations—which can be viewed as session profiles—provide a means for examining live session traffic or examining audit records of session traffic to determine if an anomaly exists.

The basic idea is that in a normal trace of UNIX system calls one can establish patterns that are considered normal. The researchers utilize mathematical structures called *finite automata* (also known as state machines) as their means for representing this behavior. As traces of real session behavior are examined and compared against these automata-based session profiles differences can be identified.

The processing heuristic used in this method is that for a given system call S, there is a set of acceptable system calls that could have occurred just before S, and just before that, and so on. Similarly, a set of acceptable system calls are identified that could have occurred just after S, and just after that, and so on. The notion *before* and *after* branches of system calls can be depicted as shown in Figure 6-7.

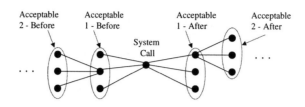

**Figure 6-7**. Before and After Acceptable System Calls

One small problem with this approach is that certain traces of systems calls that stay within the set of acceptable next steps may not correspond to any meaningful traces. Nevertheless, the claim is made by these researchers that the method does work in identifying patterns of unacceptable system calls.

As suggested above, the specification approach they use for defining system call behavior for a given function or service involves the use of a finite automaton. The automaton has a reachable start state and a collection of transitions that define the closure of reachable states. A final state is identified from the set of reachable states. The automaton for the *sendmail* function is shown in Figure 6-8 (where each reachable state corresponds to one of the system calls).

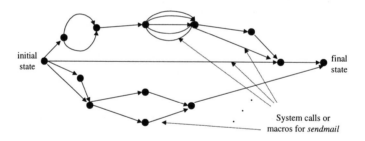

**Figure 6-8**. Normal *Sendmail* Behavior Automaton

Some of the more important research results from this work include the following:

- The claim is made that system call trace anomalies for various attacks tend to clump together; this suggests that small window sizes are needed for monitoring changes from expected acceptable system calls (as in Figure 6-7). This is an important claim because the primary criticism of this line of research is that huge, unmanageable, combinatorial explosions might emerge for real pattern anomalies.

- Techniques for reducing the size of the traces using encoding schemes for system calls seem to have been successful for the cases examined in the context of this research.

- Experiments were done with *sendmail*, *lpr*, and *syslog* traces; obviously more experiments should be done. This would appear to be a fruitful area of research for graduate students in the ensuring years.

Readers interested in more details on this technique are advised to consult the reference listed at the end of the chapter.

## CASE STUDY: NIDES/STATS STATISTICAL COMPONENT

One of the great strengths in the SRI intrusion detection research platforms including NIDES and Emerald is the wealth of statistical techniques used to correlate available information into information about intrusion. The first-ever statistical component was reported by SRI researchers to have been used to store IBM mainframe System Management Facility (SMF) records in the 1980's. This component was extended to analyze and search for anomalies in conjunction with Dorothy Denning's IDES model (recall our discussion in Chapter 2).

As this statistical component evolved into what eventually became known as the NIDES statistical profile-based anomaly detection subsystem (NIDES/stats), several important advances were reported in the area of statistical correlation. Interested readers should look at some of the SRI references mentioned in the Bibliography. Most of the real advances in statistical processing of intrusion related information have been somehow linked to the work that has been on-going at SRI. In particular, the following techniques are a small subset of the correlation advances that have been investigated and reported from SRI researchers:

*Profile-based statistical scores for users.* The idea here is that user behavior is characterized in a profile and audit trail information is used to gather evidence of actual user behavior. Using multivariate statistical scoring approaches, scores are assigned to user sessions to specify the degree to which the user behaves as expected. Multivariate statistical techniques allows correlation of many different statistical parameters. Note that in standard deviation approaches, a confidence range is produced using one parameter to measure observed behavior. Multivariate techniques generalize this to multiple parameters. A problem with multivariate approaches is that the multivariate cross product on three variables with 100 categories each results in a matrix with one million possibilities. That may be more than can be dealt with manually, but perhaps computing methods can make this approach more manageable. The question of what happens when hundreds of variables are involved remains to be seen.

*Profile-based statistical scores for applications.* SRI worked with Trusted Information Systems (TIS) in 1995 to extend their multivariate, profile-based statistical scoring to individual applications. This work is important as it creates a means for detecting anomalies in applications that may be caused by on-line intruders, Trojan horses, viruses, and others dynamic security vulnerabilities. By the way, the report that summarizes this work is challenging to read and understand.

*Statistical half-lives for detected events.* An interesting concept in NIDES/stats involves assigning half-lives to detected events as part of the dynamic profiling. When a given event is detected at some instant, the presumption is that the likelihood of that event occurring at that instant is 100% (by definition). As time progresses, this likelihood will reduce if no additional instances are detected. This type of decay for half-lives should be consistent with your intuition about statistics and probability of events.

For example, if the specified half life for an event E is one day, then after the event is detected on day 1, the decay progresses on subsequent days if no additional E events are detected (see Figure 6-9).

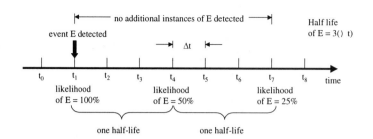

**Figure 6-9**. Half Life Decay for Detected Event

If an E event is detected at some point, then the statistical component can either reset the likelihood to 100% at that instant and begin decaying until additional instances are detected, or it can recompute the half life based on the dynamic behavior to that point.

*Comparison criteria for statistical approaches to intrusion detection.* Harold Javits and Alfonso Valdes from SRI propose a useful comparison criteria for different statistical approaches to intrusion detection. The criteria is specified as a series of questions including the following:

- Does the method allow for profiles of individuals users?
- Does the method allow for profiles to periodically update without human intervention?
- Does the method allow for multivariate processing?
- Does the method allow real time evaluation of audit records?
- Does the method require assumptions about the distributions of intrusive behavior?
- Does the method require the existence of simulated or actual intrusions?
- Does the method develop its assessment based on differences between individual users?

## MULTIPLE SESSION CORRELATION

In data network-based intrusion detection, the likelihood that the target network system will include multiple, interleaved sessions is virtually 100%. This does not imply that separation of concerns will not dictate focusing on one session in intrusion correlation, as was discussed earlier. Nevertheless, at some point in the detection of intrusions, correlation of information about multiple sessions must be examined.

In this regard, it must be acknowledged that *everything said in the previous section about single sessions also applies to multiple session correlation.* This should not come as a surprise since single session correlation is only a special case of the more general multiple session problem. So all of the heuristics presented with respect to packet correlation using associations, time to store considerations, and bi-directional builds, must be done similarly in a multiple session context.

Unfortunately, multiple session correlation methods where more than one session are being considered introduce several additional correlation-related problems that are discussed in this section. This should not come as a surprise since the generalization of any Internet method from single to multiple sessions generally introduces considerable complexity. A general schema for multiple session correlation approach is depicted with three sample sessions in Figure 6-10.

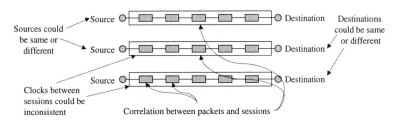

**Figure 6-10**. Multiple Session Correlation

Some technical issues that arise in the context of multiple session correlation include the following:

- *Remote sessions.* A potential problem exists in gathering information from sessions that are remote. Obviously, this implies that a centralized data collection facility would not be feasible, unless it included remote adjunct collection resources. It also raises questions of capacity required for delivering remote information to a central facility. In fact, this question of whether to perform processing locally and carry back alarms and results-oriented information versus performing processing centrally using remotely directed feeds is a major issue in practical intrusion detection infrastructures.

- *Same source or destination end points.* The possibility exists that different source and destination end points that might be reported as having different identities are actually the same. This could be established by examining behavioral patterns, out of band connection information (e.g., telephony-based), or Internet traps (see Chapter 7). This is a key point because it illustrates the problems that Internet spoofing introduce to multiple session correlation—problems rarely seen in voice contexts.

- *Time inconsistencies.* If differences exist in the reported times between sessions, then correlating events may be complicated. For example, if an event occurs at some specified time in a given session, and this is to be time-correlated with an event in another session (i.e., determine which occurred first), then the mutual synchronization of clocks is required. Many researchers in intrusion detection today claim that large-scale time synchronization is impossible; my suspicion is that using events to synchronize at key times may be enough to create orderings that accomplish what is needed. Several years ago, Leslie Lamport published a paper called "Time, Clocks, and the Ordering of Events in a Distributed System" in the Communications of the ACM. That paper describes how to do this time-based ordering when remote systems are involved. I think more intrusion detection researchers should read that paper (see Bibliographic notes at end of chapter for citation).

- *Patterns in unrelated sessions.* A basic challenge in correlation involves determining if similar patterns exist in presumably unrelated sessions. This can involve complex models of processing, thumbprints of sessions (see next section), or other means.

- *Connecting unrelated sessions.* An additional challenge in intrusion correlation involves determining if different sessions are in some way connected. This is particularly challenging when trace-back techniques are being invoked to figure out the source of a given intrusion.

## CASE STUDY: CORRELATION OF SESSION THUMBPRINTS

Stuart Staniford-Chen and L. Todd Heberlein from the University of California at Davis have reported recently on techniques for thumbprinting different data network sessions to try to piece together patterns. In their method, a thumbprint is defined as "a small quantity which effectively summarizes a certain section of a connection." One might consider it as a unique checksum or hash on certain attributes of the connection.

The heuristic involved in thumbprinting is that if an intrusion occurs, security analysts or automated systems might piece together thumbprint information from multiple sessions to correlation what might be going on. One view of the use of thumbprints is depicted in Figure 6-11.

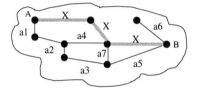

**Figure 6-11.** Thumbprints to Correlate a Connection from Multiple Sessions

In the example above, the picture intends to suggest that multiple thumbprints that may be measured for a variety of sessions around a given network could result in a clear correlation. In the case shown, the thumbprints denoted by the chain of X's in the path between points A and B might suggest a connection. As a simple example of how this might occur, suppose that one element in the thumbprint is any large file transfers. If a large file transfer takes some path from A to B, then it might leave a distinct effect on the trail of thumbprints in the path chosen.

In practice, this notion is greatly complicated by several factors including the following:

- *Thumbprint construction.* An algorithm based on available factors is required to construct the thumbprint; the researchers from Davis have been relying on content after reconstruction up to the transport layer. I would imagine that significant trade-offs must exist between complexity in the thumbprint and real-time performance.
- *Thumbprint comparison algorithm.* A comparison algorithm is required for the various thumbprints (the example in Figure 6-10 exaggerates the simplicity of identifying streams of connected thumbprints). A further trade-off would seem to occur in calculating thumbprints to result in easily compared values (e.g., integers) versus saving computation and producing results that require more effort to compare.
- *Thumbprint analysis.* A calculus of thumbprinting is needed so that addition of thumbprints would give information about successive connections, subtraction of thumbprints would isolate connections, and so on. This requires more research into the way thumbprints are constructed in the first place.
- *Clock skews on different systems.* As was suggested in the previous section, these researchers report that clock skews are a source of error with their technique. Alert readers will note this recurring problem of clock synchronization in intrusion correlation.

- *Propagation delays.* Slightly different data may be used for thumbprinting as propagation of session information moves through a connection. The faster thumbprints can be constructed and compared, the less a problem this becomes.

Readers interested in more information on this technique are advised to consult the paper by Staniford-Chen and Heberlein referenced at the end of the chapter. I would expect thumbprinting to become standard components of intrusion detection systems. In fact, as network management systems continue to rely on SNMP, RMON, and RMON II-based MIBs, it wouldn't seem too far fetched to expect such network management systems to include simple thumbprints based on already collected and processed information. Numbers of packets, for example, could be used as a crude thumbprint in an RMON-monitored LAN already.

## CASE STUDY: GRIDS GRAPH PROCESSING

As should be evident by now, the University of California at Davis under the direction of Karl Levitt and Matt Bishop has become one of the leading academic institutions working in the area of intrusion detection. Their staff is deeply involved in intrusion detection research and development and their graduate students are involved in many interesting projects. In this section, we provide a brief overview of a research platform called GrIDS that is being used as the basis for much intrusion detection research at Davis. We include the discussion at this point in our chapter because the essence of GrIDS is correlation of multiple sessions.

The way GrIDS works is that as network activity is monitored, security critical information is reported to the intrusion detection system which creates structures called *activity graphs* that are based on the activity being reported. It's worth noting that activity graphs are the GrIDS implementation of the association concept described above.

As time passes, related activity causes the activity graphs to be enhanced with additional branches; however, if no related activity is reported for a given activity graph, then the graph is discarded. Note also that this is the GrIDS implementation of the time-to-store algorithm presented earlier in the chapter.

A useful example of this operation was included in a paper given at the National Information Systems Security Conference in 1996. The example suggests that GrIDS is monitoring a network for worm propagation; if a worm begins on some host A, and then initiates network connections to hosts B and C, then GrIDS will construct a simple activity graph as shown in Figure 6-12.

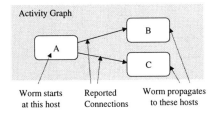

**Figure 6-12.** GrIDS Activity Graph for Worm with Two Connections

If no connections are made from either hosts B or C during some specified duration, then GrIDS would discard the graph shown in Figure 6-12. If, however, the worm spreads from B to hosts D and C, then the activity graph would be updated as shown in Figure 6-13.

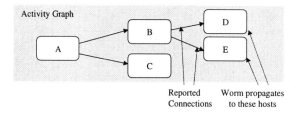

**Figure 6-13**. Update of Activity Graph Based on Additional Connections

As you might imagine, this sort of operation can result in very large activity graphs. Furthermore, GrIDS must have some means for interpreting these activity graphs of multiple sessions so that response actions can be taken. In particular, the following are some of the challenges inherent in this type of intrusion detection approach.

- *Intrusion detection.* A detection heuristic is required to recognize the tree structures shown in Figure 6-12 and 6-13 as worms; these heuristics must be present for any sort of intrusion (e.g., TCP port scans and *ping* sweeps) that GrIDS purports to detect.
- *Graph correlation.* Correlation is not always easiest based on connections; other information such as ports or types of operating systems can be used to connect multiple sessions as well.
- *Architecture.* GrIDS must have an architecture that supports the building of graphs, the building of attack rule sets, the aggregation of information, and the interpretation of graphs as attacks. (Readers interested in this system are referred to the referenced paper at the end of the chapter.)

## REAL TIME VERSUS AFTER-THE-FACT CORRELATION

The issue of whether the correlation of information is being done in real time versus after-the-fact is key to proper correlation algorithmic design. The basic difference is that in real time correlation, the processing algorithms cannot "look forward" whereas after-the-fact correlation could have all the information about an incident. This allows after-the-fact algorithms, common in audit trail analysis tools, to consider time as an index into a complete historical record of all activities.

In this section, we briefly examine the processing and algorithmic implications of this limitation on real time correlation. In particular, some of the technical and infrastructure issues that arise in real-time correlation of intrusion information include the following:

- *Problem of manual human time.* One of the advantages of automation in intrusion processing is that information can be processed quickly. If human beings must be involved in the processing, then this will invariably introduce great time delays. Infrastructures for intrusion correlation that include computing systems, networks, and human beings thus try to automate as much of the processing as possible. Anyone doing intrusion detection in the context of a real infrastructure knows, however, that you can't automate everything.

- *Reliance on audit trails.* If intrusion correlation is dependent on audit trails for information, then the time involved in making the audit trails available will effect timeliness of detection. Traditionally, audit trail processing has been categorized as a batch mode intrusion detection method, which implies a large time duration between an incident occurring and it's detection via the intrusion processing. Research continues on methods for making audit trail analysis more efficient; it will always remain, however, fundamentally a batch technique.

- *Situational dynamics.* A key issue in the real time processing of intrusion information is whether the incident in question is still occurring. If the situation has long since passed, or if that is the prevailing view by the correlation analysts, then real time tools become less important than having a thorough tool set for analyzing available information. If the incident is still occurring, then real time processing becomes more important.

- *Processing power.* In some instance, raw horsepower will help direct whether the intrusion detection system can manage to perform real time processing. This is particularly true in on-the-fly network intrusion detection with large target transfer capacities. It is worth noting that most intrusion detection system vendors are obsessed with this idea of adding horsepower to their engines. In the vast majority of cases, this is to increase the degree to which high capacity broadband data can be collected. In the future, my prediction is that considerable attention will be placed on adding processing horsepower to perform complex correlation algorithmic analyses.

## CORRELATING IN-BAND AND ALL-BAND INFORMATION

Recall from Chapter 1 that we define the notion of *in-band* to consist of the computing and networking activity that is inherent to the target system. Since our primary concern in this book is on TCP/IP-based processing, then clearly in-band activity will be packet networking transmission over public and private TCP/IP networks.

We will then define all-band to constitute all activity that is either in-band or out-of-band. Thus, if a user initiates some Internet service command (e.g., by clicking on a Web hyperlink), this is considered in-band activity for use in the intrusion detection. If that same user is stealing cable television, has a police record for physical crimes, and was seen going into a foreign embassy, then this information is considered all-band. More specifically, we can characterize the two types of information as follows:

- *In-Band Information*: Any information contained in one of the potentially-many headers or trailers inherent in a computing application running in a TCP/IP context over some lower level transmission medium. In addition, the payloads included in this network transmission is considered in-band. Information that is encoded on the network in some available resource (e.g., the network time) is also included in-band. As a useful shorthand concept, if a computer system or network element can obtain some information item X without human intervention or data entry, then that information item X is considered in-band.

- *All-Band Information*: This includes all in-band information plus any other information that might be considered in the correlation. This can be virtually anything from breaking world news to opinions of network administrators. A problem with all-band information is that it introduces more opportunities for inaccurate data to influence an intrusion processing scenario.

As we will show, the challenge of all-band correlation is to ensure proper levels of trust, accuracy, and priority, as information becomes available from multiple sources. Some of the challenges that emerge in the correlation of all-band information for intrusion processing include the following:

*Common formats for all-band information.* When in-band information becomes available for correlation, it can generally be represented in the framework of the relevant target system protocols and services. For example, if audit information about a target system is available, then the audit records are already represented in a format conducive to processing and correlation. If, on the other hand, information become available from out-of-band sources such as a news report, technical article, or phone message, then this information by definition is not represented in a common format for correlation.

A basic challenge in any intrusion detection correlation infrastructure is how to represent this information for processing. Two main approaches exist:

- *Spoofing an In-Band Component.* All-band information can be forced into an available format. For example, WheelGroup NetRanger (now Cisco NetRanger) messages to the Director might be spoofed from a component other than an NSX sensor. Thus, a workstation could be developed to allow operators to enter out-of-band information that could result in an NSX-like message to the Director. Types of out-of-band information that could be spoofed into the Director could include telephony-based data, local physical and facility-based intrusion data, or other local information.

- *Special All-Band Information Format.* All-band information could be represented in its own special format; this would require adjunct processing capability in the intrusion detection system to account for the new format and semantics. This is clearly a research topic and is not something available in any current intrusion detection product.

*Different confidence levels for all-band information.* When out of band information becomes available, a common problem for infrastructure managers is the degree of confidence to assign this information. This will require attention to factors such as:

- The source of the information; if the source is not trustworthy, then the information should not be considered trustworthy.

- The means by which the information was obtained; any law enforcement deals that may have been involved in the obtaining of information should seriously compromise the integrity of the information.

- The timeliness of the information; old information may be too stale to be of much real use.

*Subjective interpretation by human beings.* Any time human beings are involved in the processing of all-source information, one has to recognize the subjectiveness inherent in human thinking and actions. Some issues that arise include the following:

- Biases in intrusion processing managers toward certain information sources
- Biases in intrusion processing managers against certain types of information
- Lapses in vigilance by individuals during critical information exchange

## CASE STUDY: ALL-BAND AIR FORCE INFORMATION WARFARE CENTER (AFIWC) INTRUSION DETECTION PROCESSING

The United States Air Force has been a leader in applying intrusion detection technology to problems of large-scale network infrastructure. As such, it has set up a basic organization in its Air Force Information Warfare Center (AFIWC) that serves as an exemplary case study in organizational structure. The material presented here is taken directly from the Air Force Web site.

In particular, the AFIWC is charted to develop, maintain, and deploy information warfare (IW) and command and control warfare (C2W) capabilities to support operations, campaign planning, acquisition, and testing. As you might imagine, to support these types of activities, an infrastructure is required to correlate available intrusion-related information about IW/C2W. This centralized, time-sensitive correlation is done for the Air Force at AFIWC.

Some elements of AFIWC's organization that serve in its function and mission include the following:

- *Well-defined organizational reporting.* As in most military organizations, AFIWC has a clearly defined reporting structure as a subordinate unit of the Air Intelligence Agency (AIA); the AIA is a Field Operating Agency (FOA) subordinate to the Assistant Chief of Staff, Intelligence (ACS/I). So as you can see, if decisions must be made based on correlated information, clear chains of responsibility are defined. This is critical for an intrusion detection and correlation infrastructure to work in times of intrusion-related stress.

- *Well-defined responsibilities.* The AFIWC has a defined set of IW/C2W-related responsibilities to its organization, as well as to other related groups such as the U.S. Army, Navy, Marines, Joint organizations, and agencies. This also serves to assist during times of intrusion-related stress.

- *Organizational planning.* The Air Force has recognized the importance of proper organizational set-up for an intrusion detection infrastructure; as such, the AFIWC went through a formal eleven-step strategic planning process which resulted in six strategic goals for the AFIWC in the areas of operations, organization, people, information, technology, and training.

- *Tool support.* AFIWC includes tools in areas ranging from intrusion detection (Distributed Intrusion Detection System – DIDS and the Automated Security Incident Measurement – ASIM) to risk management (Air Force Automated Risk Management Systems – AFARMS). One of the great challenges that the Air Force faces in the ensuing years is how to integrate the use of these powerful tools into a correlation and response infrastructure dominated by human beings, organizational processes, and Air Force policy.

## CASE STUDY: CORRELATION DECISIONS IN A HYPOTHETICAL INTRUSION DETECTION INFRASTRUCTURE

To further demonstrate how an intrusion detection and correlation infrastructure must operate, in this section we create a hypothetical environment in which sensors are distributed and correlation is performed in a centralized processing location. This arrangement, which is depicted at a high level in Figure 6-14, is typical of most large

Intranets that include intrusion detection at Internet choke points and critical internal processing locations.

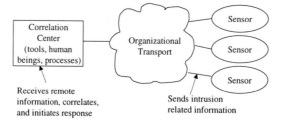

**Figure 6-14.** Hypothetical Detection and Correlation Infrastructure

In our example, let's assume that network intrusion data in the form or incident alarms that characterize information about an intrusion incident is continually sent from the remote sensors to the centralized correlation center. We can further assume that it is provided whenever some intrusion-related event is detected locally. If we suppose that this information gets appended to a log at the correlation center, then the local correlation managers have the following challenges:

*Detection of the remotely sent information.* To do this properly, requires constant vigilance as well as tool support. A typical UNIX-based tool that can be used to detect changes to an audit log is the well-known *tail –f* utility that detects and reports changes to a specified file (i.e., the audit log). This information must be processed, however, and in our example, we presume that operational support by human beings is present twenty-four hours a day, seven days a week. Thus, we know that our hypothetical correlation center must have local audit processing tools, as well as human beings present at all times.

*Correlation with other in-band information.* Once the data has been sent to the correlation center, processing must take place to determine the relation of this information to other in-band information. For example, if the intrusion detection system in place supports a notion of dynamic association (e.g., in GrIDS this would be a dynamic activity graph, in NetRanger, this would be an internal cache, and so on), then the association would have to be updated accordingly. Other in-band processing based on time, related events, port numbers, and end-point source and destination relations would be done as well. This implies that the correlation center must have the requisite intrusion processing tools to perform centralized processing of data.

*Correlation with all available information.* To support all-band correlation, the processing tools and human beings in the center must have access to relevant information sources including:

• *News reporting from relevant sources.* This could include television news, printed news, and other sources. Visitors to the AT&T Network Operations Center, for example, always find it interesting that a large television monitor displays a live Cable News Network (CNN) feed to operators in the center.

• *Intrusion-related information from relevant sources.* This could include other networks not within the control or responsibility of the correlation center. If the information is represented in a different format, then this must be dealt with during correlation.

- *Organizational reporting from within the organization hierarchy.* An example of this would be any company-reports that would be relevant to the correlation center.

*Initiation of response.* This key function of the correlation center is often forgotten until a time of intrusion stress. The idea is that the correlation center must have the appropriate functions, reporting, and authority to properly initiate response actions based on correlated information.

## BIBLIOGRAPHIC NOTES

The Sutterfield quote is from [SU97]. The Dijkstra quote is from his classic *A Discipline of Programming* (Prentice-Hall, 1976). (By the way, when my graduate students in computer sciences ask me for career advice (e.g., how to get a better job, how to perform better on the job), I generally recommend that they spend some time reading Dijkstra's works and then trying to apply what they read to today's world of the Internet. Some students get the point immediately – but others find Dijkstra too restrictive. "Imagine," they often complain, "this guy says we should understand systems before we build them. If we did that, there'd be no Internet.") Leslie Lamport's "Time, Clocks, and the Ordering of Events in a Distributed System" is from Communications of the ACM, Vol XXX, 1978. This paper is one of the reasons I personally went into computer science – it is an amazing piece of work. I think computer science professionals should be required to familiarize themselves with Lamport's work. Unfortunately, we don't have good professional standards for computing; if we did, then I'd recommend required readings from Lamport. Some material from Cheswick and Bellovin [CB94] was used in this chapter. The system call trace technique is described in an *IEEE Software* paper by Kosoresow and Hofmeyr in [KH97] as well as an Oakland conference paper by Stephanie Forrest and others [FO96]. The thumbprint material is from an Oakland conference paper by Staniford-Chen and Heberlein [SH95]. The GrIDS information is from [ST96]. The Air Force Web page I found useful was at http://www.aia.af.mil/ aialink/homepages/afiwc/. The Emerald and NIDES/stats information is from [PN97].

# CHAPTER 7:
# INTERNET TRAPS

*With trap doors, bogus user accounts and passwords sound an alarm when someone attempts to use them.*

Teresa Lunt

1. *Place bait in Bait Pedal. Pull Back Bow and Hold Down with Thumb.*
2. *Engage Locking Bar on Curved Portion of Bait Pedal.*
3. *Place Trap (s) with Bait Pedal Facing Wall.*

Instructions on Mouse Trap Package

## WARNING FOR READERS ON INTERNET TRAPS

My eleventh grade high school English teacher taught me to avoid starting any piece of writing with a negative thought. In spite of this advice, I feel obliged to start this chapter with a serious warning about the use and deployment of the technology described in this chapter. So please be advised of the following:

- This chapter describes research and development into tools and methods for trapping intruders that should only be used by authorized groups for legal and authorized purposes. If you are ignorant or unsure of the legal and moral implications of unauthorized entrapment, then my advice is to obtain some competent legal assistance before you do anything.

- Our primary motivation in describing this line of research is for the purpose of protection. Infrastructure providers, for example, have every right to protect their computer and network resources; crackers entering a network and destroying resources after having been properly warned, may sometimes only be caught using some of the techniques described in this chapter. Hence, in a properly authorized environment, these trap-based tools may be an important component of the intrusion detection analyst's toolbox.

- We are fully aware of the potential misuse of trap techniques by malicious individuals. This does not diminish our enthusiasm for the development of these protection methods. Instead, it points to the importance of proper Internet and infrastructure security controls for ensuring authorized access. Public key-based certificates for authentication, secrecy, and digital signatures are examples of such infrastructure controls.

- By publishing the techniques here, we believe that we contribute to a greater community understanding of what types of trap-oriented security protections are available to the security manager. This results in these protective techniques becoming more readily available to everyone. It also helps to advance the state of the art in this important intrusion detection area.

## WHAT IS AN INTERNET TRAP?

Few researchers to date have approached the Internet trap problem with any real enthusiasm. One might speculate that the reason for this stems from the unknown legal and policy issues that remain with respect to this technology. It may also stem from the ideological conflicts that sometimes arise in the use and installation of deception-based Internet traps or sting operations to catch intruders. It may even stem from the great difficulty associated with proper implementation of the technique.

Nevertheless, some researchers and practitioners have reported some progress with traps during live incidents using homegrown tools. Almost none of these reported trap methods, however, were approached from an engineering perspective (i.e., with a set of requirements, a specification and design, development, and test). Instead, trap tools have been generally thrown together in the haste of the incident, often by administrators ignorant of proper software engineering techniques. Recall the landmark writings, referenced earlier, from pioneers such as Bill Cheswick, Steve Bellovin, Cliff Stoll, Tsutomo Shimomura, and others.

In this chapter, we define Internet-based intruder traps and introduce technical and procedural issues that will assist the intrusion detection system designer in the use of this indispensable functionality. We fully recognize that much of the material here is theoretical and has not been demonstrated in practice. This does not diminish our enthusiasm for the potential usefulness of Internet traps. To begin, we will need to properly define the concept. For the purposes of this chapter, we will define Internet intruder traps as follows:

---

*Definition of Internet Trap*

An *Internet trap* is a set of functional and procedural components that use legal and authorized deception to divert the activity of a potential intruder from real, valued assets to bogus assets (and vice versa) for the purpose of gathering intrusion-related information and initiating response.

---

Let's go through this rather involved definition and try to expand on the various terms used to define an Internet trap.

"*Set*". This little word packs a lot of punch. It implies that a trap will consist of a collection of elements that are not associated with any ordering relation, as in a sequence. The notion of a computing tool kit for traps comes to mind.

---

*Readers Interested in Set Theory*

The best book ever written on this topic is Paul Halmos' *Naïve Set Theory* (Springer-Verlag, 1990). It is a wonderful and tiny book that is deceptive because you can actually read and understand it. My Dad introduced me to this book many years ago (not everyone can be lucky enough to have a mathematician for a Dad). If you come into my office at AT&T you will find three copies of this book on the shelf. *Really*.

---

"*Functional and procedural components*". Our definition stipulates that catching intruders on the Internet with traps will require a mix of automated functionality and procedural methods. This should not come as a surprise because trace-back techniques required the same mix.

"*Legal and authorized deception*". Here's an interesting term. The somewhat controversial idea expressed here is that it is all right to deceive if the end is justified and the process is legal and authorized. You cannot break the law by entrapping people and you cannot violate local policy (e.g., a company security policy). Keep this in mind because most of the criticisms of Internet traps to catch intruders forget this important constraint.

"*Divert the activity*". Traps are all about diversion. The manner in which computing activity is diverted requires attention to application, server, and network issues. The most obvious approach utilizes network equipment at the switching or routing layer to move packets onto a diversionary network segment.

"*Potential intruder*". Don't forget that this is the reason for doing this work. Potential intruders can cause damage to resources; and, yes, we fully recognize the mischief one can get into if the interpretation of the word 'potential' is too liberal. The issue of probable cause in law enforcement will almost certainly find its way into the computing vernacular, if it has not already.

---

*Network Security and Legal Careers*

It's my contention that anyone with a graduate degree in computing with a concentration in network security can become extremely valuable by then going to a good law school. I believe that in the near future, attorneys with network security expertise will be in great demand.

---

"*Real, valued assets*". This is the stuff that the intruder presumably wants. An effective trap will not compromise these real assets in any way to the intruder. Instead, the trap will provide some degree of protection for valued assets either by proper diversion of the intruder's packets or by introduction of suitable protections around the real assets.

"*Bogus assets*". The artistry involved in a trap is creating bogus assets that look and feel like the real thing. This is difficult and considerably more research is required before plausible trap systems can be fielded for use in live environments.

"*Vice versa*". What we mean here is that a trap ought to have the ability—limited in most cases—to return an intruder from bogus assets to real, valued ones if the activity being monitored suggests that the intruder is actually benign. This restoration is extremely challenging if the potential intruder makes substantive changes to the environment while being presented with bogus assets.

"*Gathering intrusion-related information*". The trap is there so you can gather information. If you are in law enforcement, then you're looking for evidence of a crime. If you are protecting your infrastructure from harm, then you may be trying to figure out how malicious the intruder really is. By the way, if you are doing the trap for any reason other than the two just cited, then perhaps you need to revisit the legal and authorization issues.

"*Initiating response*". In a mouse trap, the response is death for the rodent. In an Internet intruder trap, the response could be a stern response warning, if you have any idea where to send it, bait information for subsequent tagging of the intruder ("If you want the drugs you ordered, then please bring the money to 1313 Mockingbird Lane tonight at midnight"), or some other tactic.

It is worth noting here that another name commonly associated with traps is *honey pot*. In our discussions in this chapter, we distinguish between traps and honey pots in that traps constitute the diversion functionality (i.e., the mouse trap) whereas honey pots are the interesting resources that keep the intruder interested (i.e., the cheese). In practice, honey pots will be designed with interesting-looking files, suggestive directories, and realistic network views. This may be the most challenging aspect to Internet trap design.

The basic concept in an Internet trap involves an intruder interacting with a set of real resources subject to activity monitoring by an intrusion detection system. After sufficient evidence of intrusion becomes available based on the monitoring, the intruder is diverted to a set of bogus trap resources. A model of this trap interaction and operation is depicted schematically in Figure 7-1.

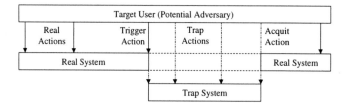

**Figure 7-1**. Internet Trap Model

Note in the model that a trigger action from the intruder causes the diversion from real to trap resources. This trigger could be a specific marked action (e.g., rm *.* on a UNIX system) or it could be an iteration on some event that passes a threshold (e.g., the third wrong password guess). In either case, the trigger could theoretically be deterministic or non-deterministic. The non-determinism could be injected into traps that deal with particularly savvy intruders who might suspect that they understand the trigger mechanisms. The uncertainty associated with the non-deterministic functionality would surely improve the effectiveness of the trap.

Note also in the diagram the inclusion of a second trigger called an acquit action that causes a return from the trap resources to the real resources. This is included in the model as a balance to the first trigger action. It would be used only after sufficient evidence is obtained during the trap interaction that the intruder is actually an authorized, non-malicious user. To be honest, I've never seen this type of acquit action implemented in any nontrivial environment.

Some technical considerations that arise with respect to this Internet trap model include the following:

- *Detection of intrusive activity*. Identification of intrusion patterns via monitoring will rely on the use of virtually every intrusion detection technique discussed in this book. The diversion to trap resources can be viewed as a response action.

- *Detection of trigger actions*. Trigger definition is important as it defines the boundary between real and trap assets. Intruders would like to know the trigger mechanism in order to carefully avoid it. These are almost like mines in a mine field, but the intent is not for random harm to innocent bystanders, but rather directed, focused effects on those exhibiting behavior that suggests intrusion.

- *Reversing decision about intrusive activity*. This notion of returning a user to real assets after a period of interaction with trap resources will only work in a subset of cases. In particular, the technique only works if the user interacting with the trap resources utilizes a subset of trap resource commands that can be reconstructed and applied to real resources.

- *Remaining stealth throughout the process.* No trap ever worked that was obvious to the intruder, unless the purpose of the trap is preventive. So if the trap is intended to actually catch intruders, then stealth design is imperative. It would be best if the trap were embedded into the normal functional and procedural environment so that any effects it might have on that environment's operation would become normal.

## PACKET DIVERSION VIEW OF INTERNET TRAPS

For on-the-fly intrusion detection targeting data network transmission, internet traps can be viewed in the context of Internet packet diversion. To see this, first recall that a dormant Internet trap does nothing while users access actual resources in a manner that is considered acceptable. A possible design view of this dormant trap concept for packet diversion is depicted in Figure 7-2.

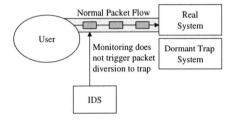

**Figure 7-2**. Dormant Intrusion Detection Trap

After intrusion detection monitoring provides sufficient evidence of intrusive activity, the dormant trap in Figure 7-2 can be activated and used as the target of diverted Internet packets. A depiction of this diversion of user traffic from a system with real assets to a previously dormant Internet trap is shown in Figure 7-3.

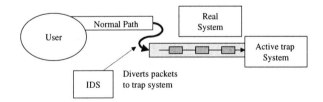

**Figure 7-3**. Intrusion Detection Trap in Use

As one might expect, such diversion introduces technical problems of dealing with and explaining inevitable packet loss during diversion, dealing with real time issues especially for interactive user sessions, and ensuring that target systems include suitable resources to keep intruders interested. All of these issues must be addressed in the practical design and implementation of an Internet intruder trap.

### FOUR TYPES OF INTERNET TRAPS

Creating a taxonomy of Internet traps will help depict some of the design decisions that must be made during trap design. In this section, we create a taxonomy based roughly on the "size" of the trap environment and the "size" of the real environment (explained below). In particular, Internet intruder traps can be viewed as consisting of one of four different basic architectural approaches (depicted in the diagram in Figure 7-4):

- *Real Environment with Trap Elements.* This is the most commonly found trap architecture. It involves interaction between the potential intruder and the real environment, but with certain embedded trap elements. An example of this is a real UNIX environment with a phony password file. When a normal user requests a copy of the password file, which presumably would never be considered a reasonable occurrence, the system would provide the phony password file which would either contain bogus accounts or would contain at least one marked account which would be used by the trap system to key on subsequent attempts to gain access.

- *Small environment to large trap.* In this approach, the real environment might be considered "small" in the sense that it does not include many critical or particularly interesting resources. A trap system might be included that suggests "large" honey pots with interesting files, directories, and network connections for intruders. The notion of a Pandora's Box comes to mind in this small-to-large trap approach.

- *Mirrored environment and trap.* This method involves the creation of a trap that mirrors the real environment to the greatest degree possible. A switch could be involved in which the trap serves as a hot standby system. Upon intrusion trigger events, the diversion of user activity to the hot standby trap could be automatic.

- *Large environment to small trap.* In this case, a large and potentially interesting environment would be associated with a smaller trap. This large-to-small approach would be considered reasonable in cases where creation of a comparable trap would be too involved or expensive. Care would have to be taken to provide suitable explanations as to why the environment is degraded (e.g., mail in administrator's mailboxes complaining that certain subsystems are down).

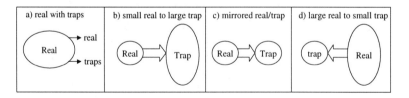

**Figure 7-4**. Types of Trap Architectural Approaches

As was suggested earlier, these four architectures are based on largely theoretical concerns. To date, the real environment with trap resources is the only type of method that has had any real practical application. As trap engineering matures in the context of intrusion detection, hopefully additional experience will be gained using the other approaches. The mirrored trap, in particular, seems promising as it is not significantly different in principle from availability-oriented hot standby cut-over systems.

### CASE STUDY: MULTILEVEL SECURE UNIX INTRUDER TRAP

As an example of a real environment with trap elements, the first of the four design approaches described above, let's examine the intruder trap being built at AT&T Laboratories in my group. We started with the UNIX System V/MLS operating system that we developed and certified at the Orange Book B1 level in the late 1980's. After several years of good use, our secure operating system seemed destined for eventual retirement as the UNIX market changed so dramatically, with an obvious de-emphasis on multilevel secure controls. Recently, however, we've rediscovered and resurrected the system as an attractive basis for our intruder trap design and development research.

Features in System V/MLS considered attractive for intruder trap design include the following:

- Security labels define the views that users will see. That is, users at the Secret level will see a Secret view of the system, users at the Unclassified level will see an Unclassified view, and so on. The implications of this for trap design should be obvious — we manipulate the underlying label of a user based on the activity patterns exhibited. I'm surprised that more people have not harnessed the power of multilevel views for intruder traps. The secure database community, in particular, could find some interesting new applications for their systems in this area.

- Auditing is built into the kernel. This greatly reduces the manner in which users might tamper with or view the processes associated with auditing. In fact, we can even leave an obviously broken *syslog* on our trap system to fool potential intruders into believing that they are not being audited. This importance of this type of system-level auditing really becomes obvious in the context of intruder trap design.

- Hidden multilevel secure subdirectories are built into the system. These are used in directories such as /tmp that maintain information for processes at different levels. The way these subdirectories work is that users at the Secret level writing to /tmp will actually write to a hidden subdirectory called /tmp/Secret. Similarly, users at the Unclassified level will write to the hidden /tmp/Unclassified, and so on. This hidden subdirectory view is shown in Figure 7-5 below.

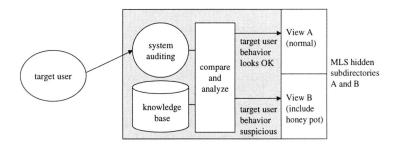

**Figure 7-5**. UNIX System V/MLS Hidden Subdirectories

The operational concept associated with this trap is as follows: Potential intruders would gain access to system resources under the surveillance of the system audit trail. If their behavior matches a profile of suspicious behavior and a sufficient trigger is present to cause a context switch, then that user's security label would be changed. As much environment cleansing would be done to hide this context switch from the user. Continued monitoring would be done, perhaps with focus on some honey pot resources embedded in this system view. If the intruder grabs the bait, then a response would be initiated. We are currently experimenting with how to restore the user to the previous view if the honey pot bait is not taken.

An additional strategy we've been experimenting with on our trap platform involves dropping bait passwords in our bogus password file. These bait passwords are ones that are easily crackable. Users coming back in with any of our baited passwords have their label set to a view with honey pots. They will also see bogus honey pot information set in the associated hidden subdirectories.

## DESIGN TIPS FOR INTERNET TRAPS

In the analysis, design, and implementation of an Internet trap, certain technical considerations will arise that require engineering attention. Some of these considerations are discussed below as a collection of design tips for Internet trap engineers.

*Ensure proper honey pot design.* Recall that a honey pot involves the inclusion of resources that would be considered of great interest to a potential intruder. The design of honey pots to keep these intruders interested involves several different design concerns. Among these are the following:

- *Advisory notices for honey pots.* If the honey pot is only entered via warning messages that explicitly specify who can and who cannot enter the site, then this often meets the primary legal challenge. Administrators must be careful, however, because additional legal requirements on consent and privacy must be met as well.

- *Keep the intruder in mind.* The honey pot must be created with the intruder in mind. If, for example, a Web administrator for a military site decides to create a honey pot; the likelihood is high that intruders visiting this site would be looking for military-related information that might be considered of a confidential nature. Thus, the administrator would be advised to include military-looking resources as bait to the intruder.

- *Don't be too obvious.* If the honey pot includes resources that are too obvious in their openness or availability, then this may raise suspicions. Password files, for example, are best provided with encrypted passwords that will result in at least one dictionary entry becoming available after the off-line *crack* attack.

- *Software hacking tools are always attractive.* Don't forget that if you are looking for crackers coming into your system, you can be pretty sure that they will be interested in any hacking tools that might be available. Provocative names for directories filled with executables with equally provocative names are generally going to be of interest.

To date, honey pots have been largely trivial research tools used to gather information and experiment with techniques. As this technology matures, a knowledge base of honey pot design methods and principles should emerge and will hopefully be reported in the security literature.

*Include trap preparation and baiting.* An additional concern in the design of an Internet trap involves any preparation or baiting that might accompany intrusion monitoring (see Figure 7-6).

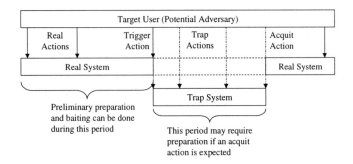

**Figure 7-6**. Trap Preparation and Baiting Period

The preparation period in a trap might be done before interaction with the trap resources has been initiated, or it could be done as part of the initial trap interaction. It is also important to note that if restoration is expected via an acquit action, then some preparation might be required during the trap interaction period. The idea here is that as part of the creation of a realistic trap environment, certain preparatory actions might be taken to ensure a more believable trap. Among these are the following:

- *Administrator correspondence.* An effective means for preparing a trap involves placing spoofed administrator correspondence messages in a real system. These might include notices that certain resources are to be unavailable for some period; this is especially useful for "large real to small trap" design methods. For example, if a trap system is to be created with most of the available subsystems missing, then plausible explanations are required to ensure that intruders are not tipped off to the trap.

- *Rigged mail.* If the trap is to direct intruders to certain honey pot resources, email is an excellent way to direct intruders to the bait. Mailboxes of administrators or prominent users are the best choices for placing such rigged mail messages.

- *Rigged scan points.* It's well-known that crackers use scanning tools to find open doors into enterprise networks. For instance, war dialing is common in the cracker's methods for gaining entry. Port scanning to find programs that might be listening for inbound access are also common. From a trap perspective, one obvious technique that arises involves leaving phone numbers with associated modem-connected machines ready to detect inbound war dialing. My group at AT&T has been exploring this line of research recently, and we've written Linux-based code using the *mgetty* program to monitor incoming dial and direct intruders to a honey pot on the dialed machine. Similarly, Fred Cohen is exporting a deception tool kit at his Web site (see http://all.net/) that ensures that scanners will find something interesting. The hope is that they will then find and enter the open port, resulting in their being caught in the deceptive environment.

- *System messages.* Any sort of system-generated message that might assist in the explanation of the trap environment should be considered. Audit log messages are good examples of plausible system events that will help to create a more believable message. Thus, a useful intrusion detection system trap tool would create audit messages designed by an administrator and stuffed into an audit trail. We are fully aware of the potential problems this might cause if it ever got into the wrong hands.

*Include out of band traps for trace back.* A third design tip worth mentioning involves the interaction between Internet traps and trace-back techniques. Recall from Chapter 5 that identity trace-back represents a particularly difficult problem; we approached the problem by partitioning trace-back into in-band and all-band techniques. Internet traps—it turns out—provide an effective means for tracing identity with minimal effort.

The basic concept is that the trap should lure the intruder into compromising identity via an environment that creates *incentives.* These incentives should be plausible and should be designed to meet the presumed characteristics of the intruder. For example, Web site promises of great management tips to help one's corporate career may not be particularly enticing to an intruder. On the other hand, promises of cracking tools and information about system vulnerabilities may be considerably more plausible and enticing to the potential intruder (see Figure 7-7).

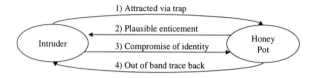

**Figure 7-7.** Concept of Plausible and Enticing Traps for Trace-Back

*Don't forget legal and policy considerations.* We have already mentioned banner messages for entry to sites that might include traps. Additional legal and policy considerations that must be considered include the following:

- *Consent.* Do you have consent to monitor the traffic, systems, or individuals that the intrusion detection system targets? If you don't then you've got yourself a problem.
- *Local policy.* Are you certain that your intrusion detection system and trap do not constitute a violation of local, organizational policy? If you're not certain, then you'd better find out before any thoughts of deployment ever enter your mind.
- *Benign user protection.* Have you made certain that your Internet trap does not damage, block, or compromise the resources of unsuspecting benign users who might fall into the trap? This is required for long-term viability of traps in real infrastructure elements.
- *Legal response.* Are you certain that any response activities initiated by the trap are fully legal and cooperative with local, state (for U.S.), and federal (for U.S.) laws? Again, this is something you need to become familiar with.
- *Ethics.* Are the actions initiated by your intrusion detection system and Internet trap consistent with professional code of ethics, as in the Institute for Electrical and Electronic Engineering (IEEE) or Association for Computing Machinery (ACM) ethics policies? If they are not, then you might reconsider the suitability of your activities.

The only safe approach that we know of in this area is to obtain legal assistance through your organization before embarking on any intrusion detection-related Internet trap method. A good rule of thumb is that intrusion detection and traps can generally be used to protect direct attacks aimed at infrastructure components that you own and operate, but you have to be careful with this view. Determination as to who owns what in the era of the Internet is not straightforward.

## CASE STUDY: WEB SPOOFING TRAPS

Perhaps the simplest yet most powerful Internet trap involves the use of a Web page with hyperlinks that redirect users from an expected link to a trap link. This trap link can then lead the potential intruder into a virtual Web that the intrusion detection system creates and uses for purposes of monitoring and response. The technique is obviously controversial, as it has traditionally been viewed as a malicious attack rather than a legitimate intrusion detection method. The reader is again advised that we do not condone the use of this technique for any purpose other than research or for legal and legitimate application by authorized groups with proper legal justification and authority.

In a recent paper by Edward Felten and others from Princeton (see the Bibliographic notes at the end of the chapter), this technique is described and referred to as Web spoofing. What we've done here is to take their proposed attack method and turn it into a trap technique. The result is a simple transformation of the technique from offense to defense with minimal change. It allows shadow copies of Web accesses to be funneled through a trap machine. As a result, the trap machine can monitor all activities, including passwords and other sensitive data.

This type of trap approach requires little more than access to sufficient Web-connected resources and some knowledge of the hypertext transfer protocol (HTTP) and the hypertext markup language (HTML). The first stage of the trap involves gaining access to a target Web page and rewriting all of the universal resource locators (URLs) to pass through the trap machine. This is done by pre-pending the trap machine URL to all the legitimate URL links on the target page.

For instance, let's assume that the trap machine where we wish to perform monitoring of Web browsing is located at the following location:

http://www.internettrappage.com/

Let's assume further than the target normal page includes a link to the following:

http://www.cert.org/

What would happen is that this normal URL link would be rewritten on the target normal page as follows:

http://www.internettrappage.com/http://www.cert.org/

Visitors to the target normal page would thus request access to the CERT page through the trap machine. Monitoring would be done on the trap machine and the browsing victim would not know what is happening (except for some browser-based issues addressed below).

This simple technique would thus provide the trap with a "man in the middle" opportunity to filter, monitor, and block connections between the client browser and the target page (in this case CERT). Furthermore, any forms-based interfaces would be easily watched and cryptographic protocols such as secure sockets layer (SSL) would only serve to prevent listening between the client and the trap. Figure 7-8 shows the trap technique.

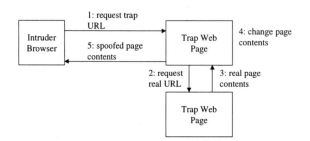

**Figure 7-8.** Web Spoofing Process

This technique does introduce certain browser-based issues that must be addressed before it can work properly. Some of these are listed below:

- *Browser status line.* The status of pending Web protocol transactions is typically displayed at the bottom of the user's browser. This implies that when the user's mouse is passed over the hyperlink on the target machine, the spoofed URL would be displayed. In addition, during the HTTP handshake, the spoofed URL would be displayed. Felton, et al. recommend using JavaScript programs in the trap to write to the status line and participate in the spoof.

- *Location line.* Similarly, the URL location of the server is displayed at the browser; this could also be dealt with via JavaScript programs.

- *User typed URLs.* If users opt to type in a URL as opposed to clicking on a URL, this would circumvent the trap. The proposed technique for dealing with this involves JavaScript programs that hide the real location line and replace it with a fake location line. User-typed URLs would be rewritten at the trap.

---

*What is JavaScript?*

For those of you who like to write hypertext-markup language (HTML) code, you probably already know all about JavaScript. For the rest of you, you should know that JavaScript (different than Java) is a browser-interpreted language that is written in-line with your HTML to accomplish some basic tasks not easily accomplished any other way. Browsers can be configured to avoid any incoming JavaScript. To use the monitoring technique described above, browsers would have to tampered with to ensure that JavaScript can always be read and interpreted. The best approach would be to adjust the browser so that only JavaScript from the trap system is allowed in. Now that Netscape provides source code, this might be reasonably accomplished.

---

- *Viewing document source.* If the user tries to look at the HTML source, a JavaScript program could spoof the toolbar and display the original HTML when the user clicks on the "view document source" key.

- *Trap location.* Since the trap must be installed in a specific machine, the stealth nature of the trap may be in question. This is a problem that may require just acknowledging that the trap is part of an organization's Intranet. In fact, one would expect that any organization choosing this path would make their policy known to all employees in advance of any employee browsing activity.

An important final point with respect to this technique must be made. Remember that the purpose of intrusion detection is to detect and respond to incoming attacks on infrastructure. This Web spoofing technique begins to cross the fine-line of defensive techniques into privacy-compromising methods that may do more harm than good. Clearly, if an intruder is being pursued and it has been determined that this intruder is using the victim's network for browsing, then the spoof method described above is a suitable and justified approach. Using such techniques to simply monitor for unreasonable purposes is obviously discouraged.

## CASE STUDY: INTERNET LIGHTNING ROD

Fred Cohen describes an interesting defensive security technique on his Web site (see http://all.net/) that is related to honey pot technology. The technique—known as an *Internet lightning rod*—is intended to divert cracker energy from real Internet sites to the lightning rod site. Presumably, a good lightning rod would include enough interesting resources to keep intruders interested, but without any real risk of loss to the sponsoring or any other organization. One might argue that the Web, with its rich plethora of interesting resources and information, serves as somewhat of a lightning rod for hackers who desire to find information.

The all.net lightning rod apparently served as a live system for almost two years, during which time Cohen and his associates performed research on defensive techniques. Through a variety of attack encouragement methods, including intentionally angering known hacking and cracking groups, Cohen's lightning rod served as a effective honey pot.

The implementation of a lightning rod involves several technical concerns including the following:

- *Method of shunting packets.* Packets coming into a defined perimeter choke point (e.g., a router or firewall) can be routed based on source information and purported content (e.g., port numbers) to either a real system or a lightning rod system. This shunting of undesirable traffic can be implemented in hardware with a router or firewall, or it can be implemented in software using a rule base or TCP wrapper.

- *Proximity of rod and real asset.* Cohen comments on the dangers of placing an Internet lightning rod close to a real asset. Obviously, if the rod is imperfect in its shunting implementation, then real damage could occur. On the other hand, proximity to live resources increases the value of the system to potential intruders.

- *Attracting hackers and crackers.* Attracting hackers and crackers is a dubious activity as it could bring real damage to an individual or group. As such, it violates many principles of security including low posture and modest profiles. Nevertheless, Internet lightning rods must be prominent and must take steps to attract real hackers and crackers to come and visit.

For more information on Cohen's lightning rod, visit his site for access to his technical account and analysis of the all.net experiment. My suspicion is that lightning rod techniques are not useful for most organizations. For example, it is hard to imagine recommending to an Intranet manager that to improve the local security posture, a diversionary lightning rod site be set up. However, for the alternate site to be set up as an intruder trap to detect cracking activity, rather than to divert it from the real systems, seems reasonable.

### CASE STUDY: CABLE COMPANY TRAPS FOR SERVICE THIEVES

A classic problem in the cable television industry is a lack of in-band techniques for detecting theft of service. The most common type of attack by service thieves involves an illegal tampering with the company-provided set-top box in order to descramble premium channels that have not been paid for. This is typically accomplished by purchasing a test kit from an electronics magazine to replace the EEPROM on the set top box board with a ROM chip. The cost of such chips is usually in the $10 to $15 range. Their use has the effect of descrambling everything coming in and the cable companies cannot detect the switch without gaining physical access to the box. So if you're ripping off cable, you'd better not let the cable repair person into the house.

An ingenious trap method has been experimented with by cable companies, however, that serves to locate a subset of service thieves. The way the trap works is that the company broadcasts a channel or signal that is blocked to all paying customers. This means that no paying customer should ever see the channel or signal. It might be a banner message across the screen or it might be an actual new channel with an appropriate message on the screen.

The presumption, however, is that anyone descrambling everything using the ROM chip will get this blocked channel or signal. They will see the banner across the screen or they will actually get the new channel. By including enticing content in that channel or signal, the company might succeed in getting the thief to compromise their identity. Some content enticements that might be considered include telephone numbers advertising vacation giveaways, where operators would then request telephone and address information from the caller. The basic concept of this technique is depicted in Figure 7-9.

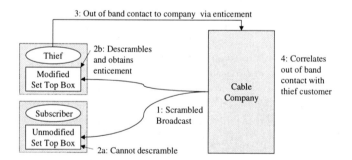

**Figure 7-9**. Cable Company Out of Band Content Enticement Trap Method

Peter Neumann from SRI International reports in his Internet risks forum on a real instance of this technique used by Continental Cablevision of Hartford. What they did was the following (in Neumann's words):

*(The company) offered viewers free t-shirts during the broadcast of the Holyfield-Bowe fight on November 14, 1992. However, the offer and its free telephone number were seen by only those people using illegal decoders; 140 freeloaders called the 800 number within minutes of the ad's broadcast.*

*Continental sent the callers t-shirts by certified, return-receipt mail, with a follow-up letter
reprimanding them of the (U.S.) federal law (fines up to $10,000) and demanding a $2000 fine.*

As this out-of-band trap technique becomes more accepted in the cable industry, it
may be installed into more cable enterprises. It is worth mentioning that most future cable
service architectures include the use of set-top boxes that are actually Internet computers
with IP addresses that will allow the use of remote content monitoring, which is likely to be
very unpopular with many customers. Monitoring policies will then become a marketing and
perhaps legal issue that each cable provider will have to address with their customers.

The lesson learned here for data network intrusion detection is interesting indeed.
Consider, for example, that intruders coming anonymously into a network for access to
interesting resources could be given access to the network equivalent of banners or new
channels. They could, for example, see a view of the environment that normal users would
never see. In this view, enticing content would hopefully lure the intruders into
compromising their identity through out of band means.

## CASE STUDY: BERFORD INCIDENT

We've mentioned the Berford incident at AT&T several times throughout this book.
Specifically, Bill Cheswick and Steve Bellovin have reported extensively on an interesting
case in which an intruder visited the AT&T gateway and tried some attack methods. During
this incident, several Internet traps were used. We briefly summarize a couple of them here.

*Bogus password file.* A phony copy of the gateway UNIX password file was sent to the
Berford cracker. This included several prominent, easy to guess, user ids including *dmr* for
Dennis Ritchie, one of the inventors of UNIX and *ches* for Bill Cheswick, who is very
prominent in the security community. Although in this case, the bogus passwords were not
sent with the intention of monitoring subsequent login activity, it very well could have.

*Internet jail.* Several people from AT&T got involved in the incident; in particular, a
small group set up an Internet jail using a UNIX *chroot* environment to contain Berford's
actions. This could have been implemented with a separate machine but Cheswick claims
that one was not available at the time. The jail was really just a sacrificial lamb used for
monitoring. A bogus file system was created with some enticing entries, and the UNIX
environment had to be tweaked to ensure believability. The claim was made that the jail
seemed to be good enough and that the intruder seemed to simply shrug off any oddities in
the gateway. Perhaps this last point provides an interesting lesson for designers of Internet
traps for intrusion detection: environmental irregularity probably makes it easier to create
effective traps. I don't think this point can be stressed enough. Flaky server behavior
provides an excellent smoke screen for intruder trap functionality.

## BIBLIOGRAPHIC NOTES

The mouse traps are from the Woodstream Company, an EKCO Group Company in Lititz,
Pa. Their Victor traps are still the best mouse traps ever designed. The cable anecdote is from Peter
Neumann's excellent book *Computer-Related Risks* (Addison-Wesley, 1995). Web spoofing is described
in [FE97]. The Teresa Lunt quote is from [LU88]. Fred Cohen's Web site (http://www.all.net)
includes an excellent number of resources and papers on intrusion detection and related topics. I got

the Internet lightning rod information from his site. The cable set top box attack is described in *2600 Magazine* (Volume 12, Number 2, Summer, 1995). The Berford stuff is from [CB94]. The UNIX System V/MLS information is from an AT&T technical report entitled "Two Techniques for Trapping Intruders in a Multilevel Secure UNIX Environment," by myself, Joe Pepin, and Paul Ramstedt. The paper has been submitted for publication.

# CHAPTER 8:
# INCIDENT RESPONSE

*Your response plan needs to specify what kind of situation warrants disconnecting or shutting down, and who can make the decision to do that.*
Brent Chapman and Elizabeth Zwicky

*After tracing an intruder, tell your tale to others — let the rest of the world learn from your sorrows.*
Cliff Stoll

## WHAT IS INCIDENT RESPONSE?

The majority of this book has focused on techniques for intrusion detection, processing, and correlation, with only superficial mention of the processes required to coordinate these activities in live settings. In this chapter, we investigate more thoroughly the types of procedures, techniques, processes, and tools that are required for effective *incident response*. In our everyday lives, many incident response situations exist that provide some insight into the types of issues we will address in this chapter:

- When someone is injured or sick, a call is placed to activate emergency medical response. This requires a carefully designed infrastructure for reporting problems, assisting callers with cardiopulmonary resuscitation (CPR), contacting an emergency medical team, and providing information to the emergency response team (e.g., location of the victim, description of the victim's problem).
- When something goes wrong in your car, an indicator light is illuminated on the dashboard to suggest a course of action (e.g., "Service Engine Soon" or "Refill Washer Fluid"). This is a form of automated incident reporting with operator initiated response activities.
- If your credit card is being used in a manner that is uncharacteristic of your normal usage (e.g., you don't usually buy fifty suits from a shop in Caracas), then the credit card company will typically initiate a phone call to you to find out if your card has been stolen.

Each of these examples provides some insight into the salient aspects of incident response. For the purposes of our discussion, we will define incident response in the context of Internet-based computing and networking as shown below.

---

*Definition of Incident Response*
*Incident response* consists of the <u>real-time</u> <u>decisions and actions</u> of <u>asset managers</u> that are intended to <u>minimize incident-related effects on their assets</u> and to <u>mitigate residual security risk</u> based on <u>available evidence from the incident</u>.

---

Examination of the underlined words in this rather involved definition will help to explain what we mean by incident response.

*"Real-time"*. Timeliness in incident response is important. We generally do not include leisurely post-mortem analyses after an incident has occurred as being included in incident response. However, this should not preclude incident response activities if an incident is discovered to have occurred a long time ago.

*"Decisions and actions"*. Incident response is process that includes a collection of decisions about what to do as well as subsequent actions that implement the decisions. If you recall the emergency medical response example cited above, it should be clear how decisions drive actions in an incident response situation.

*"Asset managers"*. This general term is intended to mean anyone who owns, uses, relies on, has responsibility for, or cares about the asset in question. In reality, this could be virtually anyone—but then, virtually anyone could be part of an incident response scenario.

*"Minimize incident-related effects on their assets"*. This means doing whatever is necessary to stop, contain, or minimize any damage being done. Recall that threats to resources can be of a disclosure, integrity, blocking, or theft nature. Minimizing damage in each of these cases will be different. Once key information has been disclosed, for instance, it's tough to reverse. If access to a resource is being blocked, however, steps can be taken to remove the blockage and solve the problem.

*"Mitigate residual security risk"*. Incident response processes would include steps to close any vulnerabilities that might have been exploited. So, if an intruder came through network connection X, then the incident response process should be looking closely at network connection X to reduce its security risk.

*"Available evidence from the incident"*. The reliance on available evidence should be obvious. What is not so obvious is that evidence from previous incidents should be included as well. A problem is that corporations and organizations around the globe are rarely willing to share information about their security incidents for fear that it will negatively effect their sales and any trust their customers might have in their ability to protect resources.

As you might imagine, practical incident response will involve human processes, organizational structures, and other *soft* management structures. This does not imply, however, that *hard* concepts such as trace back tools, intrusion detection systems, Internet traps, and other functional techniques are not part of the incident response environment. In fact, the two sets of concerns play complementary roles in an effective incident response process (see Figure 8-1).

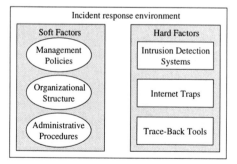

**Figure 8-1**. Hard and Soft Components in Incident Response

Incident response has not been the subject of great research interest in the security community. One reason for this lack of interest is the inclusion of the soft factors noted above. Researchers tend to avoid these types of factors as they are not conducive to clearly-defined experimentation, modeling, and investigations. This does not diminish their importance to practical incident response in a security environment. In fact, incident response practitioners will be the first to tell you how important the soft factors are in successful processes after an incident.

Another reason that incident response has received little attention is that it is perhaps the least glamorous aspect of the intrusion detection process. It rarely includes significant algorithmic development, often does ot require any clever networking utilities, and almost never requires deep research investigation to solve problems in the critical path. As such, few research grants, if any, are ever provided to teams trying to understand or improve the softer aspects of incident response capabilities. This is unfortunate, but is unlikely to change in the near future.

## INCIDENT RESPONSE PROCESS

In order to get ourselves started in understanding incident response, let's do some simple process modeling. Recall from our discussion in Chapter 1 that a generic incident response process can be characterized as shown in Figure 8-2 as consisting of a collection of normal and subverted system states, as well as a collection of dormant and active response states. To read the diagram, focus your attention on the Target System block and follow the first arrow upward.

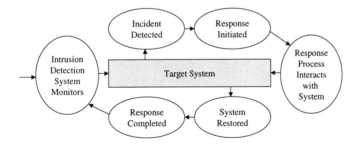

**Figure 8-2**. Generic Incident Response Process

The various elements of the generic process are discussed in more detail below.

*Intrusion detection system monitors.* The first component in the generic incident response process is the intrusion detection system. This highlights the fact that effective incident response is triggered by intrusion detection monitoring. This is not to imply that incident response can only be initiated in environments that are running intrusion detection systems. Obviously, this is not the case since intrusion detection is a relatively new technology and incident response has been around for some time (e.g., in service provision, this is a major area).

*Incident detected.* The second component of our model involves the detection of a security incident. We include this in our model to denote that the response process enters a state in which evidence has been obtained that some security related event may have occurred. An obvious question that emerges in this regard is how to differentiate a normal event from a security-relevant event. Some factors that influence this determination include the following:

- Security critical events are those that could produce a negative security effect on some critical resource.
- Security critical events might consist of predictable actions or sequences of actions that follow an understood pattern (e.g., an attack signature)
- Security critical events may result from correlation of information from all-band sources.
- Security critical events may result from well-known malicious sources of activity.

We mention this set of criteria for security critical events because they will drive the types of incidents that will initiate incident response.

*Response initiated.* In this third component, we enter a state in which a response to an incident is initiated. We can say that responses will be initiated in one of three possible ways (as shown in Figure 8-3):

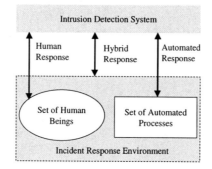

**Figure 8-3**. Three Types of Incident Response

- *Human initiated response.* A human initiated response involves information being passed from an intrusion detection system to a set of human beings who are charged with determining the proper actions. They may or may not make use of automated tools in this response, but human beings are in the critical response path and can either terminate or continue the response process.
- *Automatically initiated response.* An automatically initiated response involves automated processes or systems that accept information from the intrusion detection system and generate a sequence of response actions. The key element is that human beings are not in the critical response path; response is automated and humans are only involved in setting up or changing the automated configuration.
- *Coordinated human and automatic response.* This involves a hybrid approach in which humans and automated process receive intrusion detection system information as the basis for response. The implication is that these human beings and automated processes would be closely coupled and would cooperate in the most effective response approach. Most

large response infrastructures, as would be found in an Internet backbone service provider, follow this general model.

*Response process interacts.* This component illustrates a state in which response activities interact with their target environment. For instance, if the incident in question involves some asset being damaged, then the response action could be to fix the asset. This is especially tricky if the damaged asset is in some degraded state where a set of users continues to rely on the asset. Another possibility is that the interaction could involve manual or automatic reconfiguration of the intrusion detection system. For instance, if the incident provides information that is insufficient for the response environment, then the response action could be to adjust the intrusion detection monitors to gather additional information (see Figure 8-4).

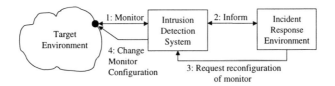

**Figure 8-4.** Dynamic Incident Response Reconfiguration of a Monitor

*System restored by response process.* In this component, the system is restored as a result of the incident response activities. In most environments, this step is considered the most important one in the incident response process. Consider, for example, the case in which a service provider is attacked and put out of service. The obsessive goal of the response team is first and foremost to restore service to customers. Other post-mortem analyses and response activities can come later. System restoration is not a flat notion of simply turning things back on, however. Instead, restoration corresponds to one of the three following cases:

- *Degraded restoration.* In this case, the system is restored after an incident, but some set of assets or system attributes remains in a degraded or damaged state. It may be that degraded restoration is an intermediate state in the incident response process that is used as a short-term bridge to a more acceptable restoration state (see Figure 8-5). Stepwise introduction of functionality as a means for preventing continued collapse often results in degraded restoration during an initial period. This is a common restoration technique when major Internet or data services are degraded.
- *Mirrored restoration.* This case corresponds to restoration of a system from its pre-incident state to exactly the same state after an incident. Rigorous back-up procedures are the best method for ensuring this type of restoration. Smaller systems can be restored in a mirrored sense more readily than larger systems. Every time you make a back-up copy of your hard drive, you are planning for this type of restoration.
- *Improved restoration.* This case is the best of all in that it allows the incident to provide information that can be used to prevent future occurrences of the incident in question. Many crackers try to justify their activities by claiming this as a goal: improved operations as a result of restoration after an attack. Intermediate steps through degraded or mirrored restoration states should be considered common in this scenario (as shown in Figure 8-5).

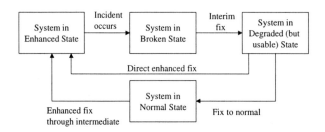

**Figure 8-5**. Restoration Process via Intermediate States

*Response completed.* In this component, the response is completed and the incident response environment presumably returns to a vigilant state, waiting for the next incident. In complex service provision environments, incident response may involve a weaving of response actions by different groups to different incidents. Thus, at any instant, the incident response progress for active incidents will be in different states.

## HOW DO VARIOUS FACTORS INFLUENCE INCIDENT RESPONSE?

As was suggested in Chapter 1, certain basic factors will influence and affect incident response. We can categorize these incident response factors into two groups: *active response factors* (or just active factors) and *passive observational factors* (or just passive factors). Active factors can be viewed as considerations that the incident response environment must take into account about the effects of a given response. For instance, the impact to system users of a particular response such as shutting down service must be examined.

Passive factors can be viewed as interpretations or decisions that must be made with respect to the intrusion detection information about the target system. For example, if the intrusion detection system provides raw information that defines an attack, one factor that an incident response environment must consider is the seriousness of the attack. This is not a question about an active response, but rather a question about the passively obtained information. Figure 8-6 depicts this difference in factors.

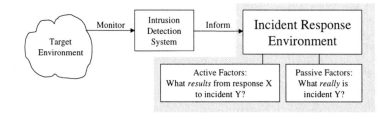

**Figure 8-6**. Active and Passive Response Factors

It is important to note that our distinction between active and passive factors is used to provide insight into the incident response process. That is, factors are generally of an observational or active nature. There are, however, many cases in which a given factor has elements of passive and active response. Determining the criticality of an incident, for example, will involve passive questions about what may have been affected, as well as active initiative to confirm this assessment.

It also must be noted that the number of active and passive factors that influence this process may be infinite; this is because incident response includes the subjective judgement of certain individuals (e.g., security officers, organizational officials, users, and so on). Since subjective judgement is certainly not a discrete, measurable entity, we cannot expect to identify every factor that could be involved. Response, for instance, could be based on the revenge motives of certain individuals, it could be based on complete ignorance on the part of a manager (not uncommon), it could be based on a misunderstanding between individuals or groups, and so on.

Nevertheless, in the next sections, we try to list some factors that may be of use in trying to make this difficult process more understandable and hopefully, more tractable.

## PASSIVE FACTORS INFLUENCING INCIDENT RESPONSE

Some commonly encountered passive observational factors that would be likely to influence incident response activities in a practical environment are listed below. Keep in mind that passive factors are represented as questions about the incident; they represent considerations that the incident response engineers or managers must take into account.

*What assets have been damaged by the incident?* Perhaps the most important passive factor to be considered is an assessment of which assets were affected by the incident. If these assets are of a critical nature, then this will certainly produce a different response process than if the affected assets have negligible value. Typical means by which one determines which assets are affected by a given incident include the following:

- Is the incident based on observable degradation in performance for some system asset (e.g., Internet gateway)?
- Does the organization have a set of obviously desirable and clearly identifiable assets (e.g., medical database)?

It must be acknowledged that you might not be able to answer this question easily. Determining which assets have been damaged is almost impossible, for instance, in cases where disclosure of information is involved. This is because when someone reads information, they may not leave any evidence because reads are non-destructive and may not result in the changing of any observable system attribute.

---

*Safely Examining a System after an Incident*

One topic that has been under-examined in the literature is how to safely examine a system after an incident. Poking around a cracked UNIX system, for example, might destroy important file or directory attributes. Some guidelines can be found for doing this sort of thing properly, but these guidelines are often in non-obvious places. Shimomura and Markoff's book *Takedown*, for instance, has some good anecdotal advice based on their experiences, but their book is certainly not a reference work that one would use to assist in an incident response setting. A good system forensics standard for post-attack analysis would be a welcome contribution.

*Has this incident occurred before?* Another passive factor is whether the incident may have occurred before. This may not be easy to determine as visible evidence can be different after multiple instances of the same incident.

*How did this incident occur?* The means by which an incident occurred is critical to selection of response. Perhaps the most fundamental issue in this regard is whether the incident was caused by a malicious or non-malicious source. Security experts agree that this is often impossible to determine.

*How trustworthy is the incident information source?* If information about the incident comes from a reliable, trusted source, then response activities might be more certain than if the source of the information is more dubious.

*Can the incident be correlated with other information?* Information correlation can be either in-band with other environmental computing or networking characteristics. It can also involve out-of-band information such as world events, time of day, or military intelligence.

*Was the incident detected as a result of a trap or tracing action?* Certain defensive actions such as traps or trace back methods are designed to obtain information about incidents. Therefore, when incidents are initiated as a result of these methods, the response process can often follow a well-defined plan.

## ACTIVE FACTORS INFLUENCING INCIDENT RESPONSE

Some commonly encountered active response factors that would be likely to influence incident response activities in a practical environment are listed below. Keep in mind for this case that active factors are represented as questions about the effects of response actions; they are considerations that the incident response engineer or manager must take into account before initiating repair, restoration, or other types of activities.

*What would be the effect of modifying target system functionality?* System functionality can be modified for response in a number of ways. Some common response modifications include the following:

- Shutting down all system operation. This is the most severe response modification and should only be used in the most extreme cases. It also may accomplish the denial of service task intended by the intruder.
- Cutting off all in-bound service. This is common in cases such as flooding spoofs where the source of the intrusion is unknown. This also produces a denial of service effect.
- Cutting off in-bound service access from the reported source address of the intrusion (see Figure 8-7).

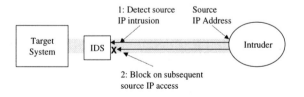

**Figure 8-7**. Incident Response by Cutting Off Source IP Address

This is the most common response technique found in current commercial intrusion detection systems. A problem with this technique is that the confidence in the correctness of source IP addresses is pretty shaky. This type of response provides crackers with a means for shutting off access from A to B by cracking B, perhaps via a SYN flood, with reported source IP address A.

*What would be the effect of initiating traps or trace back?* The effect of initiating active defensive strategies such as traps and trace backs requires some attention in the local incident response environment. Users may be affected by such techniques in markedly different manners. For instance, in some sensitive government environments, such techniques are considered acceptable and employees are notified that this is the case. In almost all other environments, this would be considered totally unacceptable.

*What would be the effect of doing nothing?* Most managers do not consider this important factor to be an explicit decision. Instead, due to uncertainty or the inability to make a decision on the part of many managers, nothing is often done in response to an incident. This may be appropriate in some cases, as long as the decision to not do anything is viewed as an explicit management technique. The problem is that doing nothing is rarely the best choice.

*Is the proposed response legal and within relevant policy?* This should be obvious. Unfortunately, the details are not obvious. Each country, region, organization, community, and workgroup has its own set of laws and policies. The only reasonable means to proceed after an incident is via a set of well-defined, written procedures that have been approved by management. An issue worth considering is that some management teams are ignorant of the legal and policy-related subtleties involved in certain response techniques.

*Who should be involved in the response?* Law enforcement is an example of a group that may or may not be involved in a given incident. Many organizations shy away from involving law enforcement because they fear bad press and increased expenditures as a result of such action. In addition, there are a number of clearinghouse organizations such as the Computer Emergency Response Team (CERT) who can help.

## CASE STUDY: REALSECURE AND FIREWALL-1 RESPONSE

The RealSecure intrusion detection system from Internet Security Systems (ISS) is a popular commercial product that has received considerable attention in the marketplace. This may be because the ISS SAFEsuite integrity scanning tool set is so popular and successful that security managers are comfortable turning to ISS for an intrusion detection solution. Another reason is that RealSecure is a good implementation with an excellent GUI and configuration system that includes both Unix and Windows NT runnable versions.

One of the interesting features in the RealSecure system is that the designers have managed to create an integrated configuration with Checkpoint Systems' Firewall-1, the industry leader in firewalls as of this writing. As a result, if the RealSecure engine detects suspicious activity on the network link being monitored, a message can be sent to the Firewall-1 to remove in-bound access privileges from the suspect source IP address. This is a form of automated response that many intrusion managers would consider acceptable for their Intranet. This concept is illustrated in Figure 8-8.

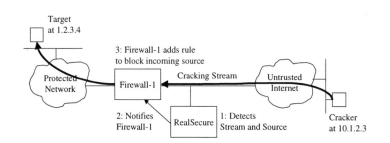

**Figure 8-8**. RealSecure Detection and Firewall-1 Source Blocking

Some issues with respect to this type of dynamic response reconfiguration of rule sets include the following:

- The approach is vulnerable to the above-stated denial of service attack in which an intruder shuts off access to system A from B. This is a heavily debated issue and as of this writing, it is unclear how problematic this feature really is in practice.
- Many vendors are trying to implement this functionality, perhaps in response to pressure from the marketing departments for each vendor. The NetRanger can now reconfigure a Cisco router, for example, in much the same manner as is shown in Figure 8-8. As the NetRanger functionality embeds itself into the Cisco product line, this capability is sure to improve.
- ODS Systems has an interesting implementation in which the RealSecure and Firewall-1 components can be housed in their SecureSwitch. This allows network security administrators to purchase one integrated component to get layer 2 switching with the type of functionality described above all in one box.
- Be sure to ask your vendor how this reconfiguration is implemented. Many vendors perform a telnet from the intrusion detection system to the component being reconfigured. If this is done, ask them to justify how this does not open a security hole in your perimeter network. They might have a hard time answering.

## TAXONOMY OF INCIDENT RESPONSE APPROACHES

In this section, we examine a taxonomy approach to incident response that I created recently with assistance from Michael Yalubovich, one of my students at the Stevens Institute. The taxonomy approach is presented here as a collection of representative factors that separate the various approaches to incident response. Only eight are used in this section to simplify matters and to focus the reader's attention on the proposed methodology. However, an obvious question is how many relevant factors can be identified, particularly in environments where some unique set of local circumstances must be considered.

Thus, in this section, we suggest a means whereby incident response approaches can be categorized and derived based on the relevant factors. As will be shown below, response approach factors correspond to management decisions that must be addressed in the process that follows a detected incident. In some cases, these decisions may require technical insights into the incident in question.

In the paragraphs below, eight representative factors are introduced and used to illustrate the basic concept being proposed here. Note that we blur the distinction between active and passive factors in our presentation. The reader might like to perform the mapping as an exercise. Note also that we include a mnemonic word in parentheses before the description of each factor below. We do so in order to more easily refer to the factor in later discussions.

*Factor 1 (Manual?) Will the incident be handled via manual or automated techniques?* Most reported incident response techniques to date have been manual. Administrators of firewalls, for instance, have reported means for responding to live incidents using ad hoc manual measures, as in the Berford case cited numerous times throughout this book. Nevertheless, promise does hold for automated response. In telephony, for example, toll fraud incidents are regularly handled using profile-based tools that detect unacceptable patterns of phone usage. Internet intrusion detection systems are now commercially available and they should be the key to the deployment of automated response in practice.

Managers must therefore decide whether automated techniques for response are feasible in their environment. When this is the case, they must determine whether proper tools exist that address the needs of their response environment. They must examine their budgets to determine if funds are available for obtaining the technology and technical support for automated response. They must also determine some means for estimating the confidence that should be afforded to automated response alarms and reported information.

If all of the above obligations are met, then automated response becomes an additional response technique for that manager. Since manual techniques will always be available by default, a relevant factor in any response activity becomes whether that response includes the use of automated tools.

*Factor 2 (Traps?) Will the incident be responded to using any honey pots, traps, or lures?* This area requires some care to ensure that legal requirements are met. Banner messages and warnings that potential intruders are entering the domain of a given organization are the types of protections that need to be considered here. For instance, recall from Chapter 7 that a trap can be used to detect a common type of probe attack known as war dialing. This trap involves setting up an isolated computer that can be dialed into via an obvious phone number. In most cases, the company PBX has been allocated a block of numbers within an easily determined area code and exchange (e.g., from a company employee business card). The trap is connected to a modem at one of the allocated numbers and anyone remotely dialing into this machine will signal to the network managers that something may be amiss.

*Factor 3 (Law?) Will the incident be responded to with the assistance of law enforcement groups?* This decision is often prompted by the criticality of the asset at risk, and hence, the seriousness of the incident. Many organizations shrug at the observance of an incident, noting that catching intruders is not the organizational mission. The Federal Bureau of Investigation (FBI) was recently quoted as suggesting that only 5% of attacks are ever detected and of these, only 15% involve response with the assistance of law enforcement.

*Factor 4 (Correlate?): Will the incident response involve correlation with other potential events?* Attacks on a computer network generally involve various stages of probing, gathering, and exploring. Since real time must pass between the various stages of an attack, temporal data must be stored and used to understand the attack behavior. An example is the potential correlation between an observed theft of access token information (e.g., the remote theft of the password file on a Unix machine) followed by unexpected access attempts with these stolen tokens (e.g., login attempts using the stolen passwords). Response techniques in this example could, for instance, predict future access attempts with stolen tokens and network traps could be set.

*Factor 5 (New?): Is the incident in question deemed to be new, or is it part of some other on-going incident?* If the incident is deemed to be unrelated to some on-going incident, then response techniques are more likely to adopt a "wait and see" attitude. This is especially true if the asset in question is not deemed so critical as to jeopardize something irreplaceable (e.g., human life, significant financial assets). However, if it is determined via correlation that an incident is related to some other on-going incident, then this should be taken more seriously. An obvious means by which this could be determined is if the two incidents involve the same set of techniques initiated from the same source IP address. Time is another factor that can be used to link events to on-going incidents.

*Factor 6 (Local?): Will the incident be handled "locally" or will some external group or authority direct the process?* The detection of an incident is generally done by personnel or tools that may be native or local to the asset at risk. On-premise firewalls, gateways, and administrators are examples of such local detection agents. Differences occur between local detection and detection by third party groups or authorities brought in by some outsourcing arrangement. One difference is often timeliness in response, since a notification step must increase the time to respond when third parties are used. This factor becomes blurry when the detection is done by a remote source (e.g., a centralized network operations center).

*Factor 7 (Sever?): Will the incident be handled by cutting off access to the resource at risk?* Most organizations that detect incidents will immediately cut off access to the resource at risk. Nasty-gram email from an administrator at the targeted site will often then be sent to the suspected source, followed by some hand-wringing on the part of local personnel that the incident does not recur and that the actual source of the incident was properly advised to not do this again. However, response techniques that allow access to continue, hopefully with monitoring, are sometimes more effective at gathering evidence for subsequent conviction.

*Factor 8 (Probes?): Will the incident be handled by initiating some new set of monitoring techniques or probes?* The incident response may include a new set of observation probes that will assist in detecting subsequent related events. This powerful technique must be done in the confines of legal requirements for monitoring (e.g., warrants may be needed for some types of probes).

It is worth reinforcing at this point that the above list of eight factors is by no means complete. In fact, it is our contention here that hundreds of relevant factors may be involved in a practical intrusion response setting. One should therefore expect combinatorial explosions, which may explain the relative lack of progress in incident response technology and process in recent years. This does not, however, imply that incident response should be ignored. It simply means that much more research and emphasis is needed in this area. A generally available repository of industry-validated response factors might be a good collective project for the government to suggest and fund.

## SCENARIOS RESULTING FROM THE PROPOSED TAXONOMY

By listing the eight sample factors identified in the previous section as the column headings to a matrix, and by interpreting the resultant binary combinations as the possible scenarios, a useful representation arises for deriving and depicting the resultant 256 incident response scenarios. This matrix may be viewed as a means for deriving scenarios for focused analysis. It also may provide an effective means for investigations such as those related to legal requirements that need accurate definitions of the differences between incident response cases. Figure 8-8 below depicts this matrix for a few representative incident response scenarios.

| Scenario | Manual? | Traps? | Law? | Correl.? | New? | Local? | Sever? | Probes? |
|----------|---------|--------|------|----------|------|--------|--------|---------|
| 00000000 | Yes | Yes | Yes | Yes | Yes | Yes | Yes | Yes |
| 00000001 | Yes | Yes | Yes | Yes | Yes | Yes | Yes | No |
| 00000010 | Yes | Yes | Yes | Yes | Yes | Yes | No | Yes |
| ... | ... | ... | ... | ... | ... | ... | ... | ... |
| 11111101 | No | No | No | No | No | No | Yes | No |
| 11111110 | No | No | No | No | No | No | No | Yes |
| 11111111 | No | No | No | No | No | No | No | No |

**Figure 8-8**. Some Incident Response Scenarios

Listing all of the scenarios here is not required here since any of the scenarios is easily derived. However, in the design of a practical incident response approach, each of these scenarios (as well as any more that may arise due to additional factors) must be explicitly considered. Some examples will illustrate the use of the scenarios in designing incident response.

*Example: Doing the minimum.* The case that corresponds to doing the minimum possible amount of work in responding to an incident is going to differ slightly between environments. This is because differences will exist in what is considered simple in a given response (e.g., one environment may have administrators available to perform some simple manual procedures, whereas other may not). In spite of these differences, one might target the following scenario (see Figure 8-9) as consisting of decisions that will minimize cost and resources needed to respond to the incident.

| Scenario | Manual? | Traps? | Law? | Correl.? | New? | Local? | Sever? | Probes? |
|----------|---------|--------|------|----------|------|--------|--------|---------|
| 01110011 | Yes | No | No | No | Yes | Yes | No | No |

**Figure 8-9**. Minimum Response Scenario

In the above example, the incident response involves manual techniques, thus not requiring the time and effort to develop or identify tools. No traps or correlations are done, and service is neither severed nor subjected to additional probes. Law enforcement is not notified, the incident is presumed to be new, and no third parties are used.

*Example: Taking more serious action.* When an organization decides to really take some action as a result of a noticed intrusion incident, additional cost and resources are going to be required. Generally, this type of approach can only be effectively followed in organizations for which security and incident response are valued and supported by management. Without such support, the investment of time, money, people, and other resources required for such action will never be achieved. This type of response can be seen in the following scenario (shown in Figure 8-10):

| Scenario | Manual? | Traps? | Law? | Correl.? | New? | Local? | Sever? | Probes? |
|----------|---------|--------|------|----------|------|--------|--------|---------|
| 10001110 | No | Yes | Yes | Yes | No | No | No | Yes |

**Figure 8-10**. Maximal Response Scenario

In this scenario, notice that the time and effort to install automated techniques have been invested, but that this does not preclude the need for manual techniques as well. Network or server-based intruder traps have been set, correlation with related events has been considered, law enforcement has been notified, third party assistance has been employed, new probes have been set, and access to resources at risk have *not* been terminated, which will require diligent monitoring.

*Example: ISP response to password fishing.* Internet service providers (ISPs) must deal with the ever-present annoyance of bogus requests to their users from malicious individuals requesting password information. This is usually done under the guise of some bogus network problem or process change that requires these target users to send in their passwords, usually for new ones or for service to be continued.

Response to such incidents can range from proactive and aggressive techniques to more passive response. The taxonomy presented here is useful in comparing these different strategies. Consider, for instance, the response scenario shown in Figure 8-11.

| Scenario | Manual? | Traps? | Law? | Correl.? | New? | Local? | Sever? | Probes? |
|---|---|---|---|---|---|---|---|---|
| 10001100 | Yes | No | No | No | Yes | Yes | No | No |

**Figure 8-11**. Sample Password Fishing Response

In this scenario, the ISP has taken a passive approach. Manual response has been performed, probably via manual notification of users to disregard the bogus message. No traps, new probes, or correlation have been done in response to the incident. Law enforcement has not been involved, and no service has been changed or severed as a result of the incident.

If this response is not deemed aggressive enough, perhaps if the incident is recurring or results in serious asset loss to some ISP customer, then the following more proactive scenario might be considered:

| Scenario | Manual? | Traps? | Law? | Correl.? | New? | Local? | Sever? | Probes? |
|---|---|---|---|---|---|---|---|---|
| 11110011 | Yes | Yes | Yes | Yes | No | No | Yes | Yes |

**Figure 8-12**. More Proactive Password Fishing Response Scenario

In this scenario, response is still considered manual, which may be reasonable as long as password fishing does not become unacceptably frequent. In this response, however, traps are placed for the password fisher. An example might be for the ISP to knowingly send the fisher the password to one of the accounts targeted in the attack. This would require the owner of the account to relinquish control of that account, hence the severing of service. The idea is that the fisher will then log into the account and can be monitored carefully by real-time probes.

Also in the scenario, notice that law enforcement is notified and that steps are taken to correlate this fishing incident with other incidents perhaps by visiting logs and archives. The incident is *not* just handled locally, which may reflect the involvement of third-parties such as anonymous remailers who are often involved in password fishing. And finally, new probes would be required to follow subsequent activity of the fisher with the newly found password supplied intentionally by the ISP.

## METHODOLOGICAL APPLICATION OF THE RESPONSE TAXONOMY

The taxonomy presented above makes for a neat categorization of incident response techniques, and certainly enhances understanding and provides useful insight. However, incident response in practical settings is anything but neat and cannot be handled by rote selection of entries in a taxonomy. In this section, some guidance is provided for practical use of the taxonomy is responding to real security incidents.

*Step 1: Select environment-specific response factors.* In the previous sections, eight response factors were presented to illustrate the concept. It is unlikely, however, that these will be the proper factors for a given environment. These factors will certainly differ, for instance, between data service providers, voice providers, electronic commerce merchants, individuals users, large companies, small companies, government organizations, law enforcement entities, and other types of groups that might need to respond to incidents. So the first step is to determine an appropriate set of response factors.

Techniques used by some organizations to determine these factors include establishing a local incident response database of previous activity to characterize the types of factors that have been significant in past incidents; establishing an incident response team to centralize the knowledge base around incidents for that organization; and making liberal use of incident-related-forums to try to correlate local incidents with those reported by other groups.

*Step 2: Create response taxonomy and annotate.* This implies that from the selected factors, a taxonomy is created such as above, and annotated with local information that will be useful during a real incident. An example of annotation for a given scenario might be lists of previously seen incidents that should be handled in the future with that scenario. Another example might be interpretations that should be associated with a given scenario or factor for some incident. For instance, in the password fishing example above, the manual versus automated factor might be annotated with the suggestion that automation will not be reasonable unless such incidents increase in frequency beyond some reasonable threshold.

*Step 3: During a live incident, use the taxonomy as a check.* This implies that response should follow local processes and should take into account any existing business requirements for expediency, management reporting, or legal restrictions. The suggestion, however, is that the taxonomy may provide useful insight into the response path being selected. For instance, a given response may appear proper; but examination of its location in the taxonomy may suggest that similar, but slightly different scenarios may be more appropriate. This is especially likely in serious incidents during which strict attention to all relevant factors may not occur due to the intense pressure that may surround the response environment.

*Step 4: Update the list of factors and the taxonomy.* The implication here is that as the types incidents noticed by an organization will inevitably evolve, the corresponding response factors should be tracked and updated as appropriate.

## CASE STUDY: CERT-CC INTRUDER DETECTION CHECKLIST

The Computer Emergency Response Team (CERT) runs a Coordination Center (CERT*/CC) that provides a useful set of procedures for recovering from a UNIX root compromise and for detecting whether or not an intruder has had access to your system.

Both are available at their Web site, and the intruder detection guidelines and checklist are summarized briefly below.

The purpose of the intruder detection checklist is to provide expert assistance to system administrators and managers dealing with the incident response problem. In particular, CERT*/CC outlines some steps that can be taken to look for several types of attacks. Companion technical documents are referenced on the Web site and are available from CERT via *ftp*.

The checklist consists of ten system administrative and management steps that can be described as follows:

- *Step 1: Examine log files.* On a UNIX system, this would include last logs, *syslog* output, and any other security logs (e.g., firewall logs, router logs). If you are running log file analysis tools such as *swatch*, then these tools should be used in the examination as well.

- *Step 2: Look for privileged programs.* On a UNIX system, unexpected *setuid* or *setgid* programs are often useful evidence that a cracker was present. As an illustration, the following UNIX command finds all *setuid* to root files on the entire file system:

  find / -user root —perm —4000 -print

- *Step 3: Look for system file tampering.* This involves checking the binaries of system files for changes. Comparison with trusted back-up copies or off-line stored checksums is an effective approach. If you aren't doing back-ups now (and testing your back-ups) then perhaps you should consider starting.

- *Step 4: Look for sniffer programs.* These tools, if present on your system, can be used for unauthorized monitoring of system activity. Most of the best crackers consider the installation of a sniffer in a target network to be the pinnacle of attacks. (I agree.)

- *Step 5: Examine UNIX cron and at program files.* Look for unexpected things like world-writeable files and programs referenced by these programs.

- *Step 6: Look for unauthorized services.* The UNIX dispatcher program *inetd* is a good place for crackers to leave additions or changes. You might check to see if legitimate services have been commented out in the configuration file.

- *Step 7: Look for password file changes.* Any modifications to this file could signal that an attacker was present. Unexpected new accounts would be a definite clue.

- *Step 8: Check system and network configurations.* A popular crack involves a '+' entry in the hosts files; these files should not be world writeable.

- *Step 9: Look for unusual files.* Files and directories with unusual names may signal that something is wrong; directories that start with a dot are not normally shown by the *ls* command. Crackers may have created such directories to store tools or files. The following UNIX command will look for file names starting with a dot:

  find / -name ".. " —print -xdev

- *Step 10: Look at multiple hosts.* If one server has been cracked, then there is a good possibility that others have as well. Examination of other hosts is therefore an important step. One problem that arises is that as more hosts are Windows NT-based, many of the heuristics developed for UNIX systems described above need to be developed for

Windows NT-based systems. These are slower to develop since Windows NT is a more recent phenomenon and since the operating system kernel is Microsoft proprietary.

## BIBLIOGRAPHIC NOTES

The Chapman and Zwicky quote is from their excellent book, *Building Internet Firewalls* (O'Reilly, 1996) [CZ96]. The Stoll quote is from his paper on what to feed a Trojan horse [ST87]. The CERT information is from their Web site at http://www.cert.org/. Sales literature from ODS Systems, ISS, and Firewall-1 was also used in one of the sections in this chapter. The FBI statistic was from a little blip I saw in *Information Security* magazine.

# APPENDIX A: ANNOTATED INTRUSION DETECTION BIBLIOGRAPHY

When I started writing this book in early 1997, most of the literature on intrusion detection consisted of research reports from the audit trail analysis community—SRI International being the most prominent source of information. Since then, I've found a flood of new information on the Web, in book stores, at conferences, and from vendors; as a result, this bibliography is only a snapshot of the literature that is probably available as you hold this book in your hands. I've done the best I can, but there's no way I could have gotten everything. (By the way, if you know of a book, report, paper, or article that should be included in this bibliography, please drop me some email at eamoroso@mail.att.net.)

I also believe that including Web URLs in any bibliography is not the right approach (a point you will see that I violate in a few places below); search tools provide the best available source for obtaining information on the Web. Some useful strings to try include 'intrusion detection', 'network security', and 'hacking internet security'. Of course, if you've read or thumbed through any of the chapters in the book, you know that I've included some URLs in the text, with the implicit caveat that URLs last only as long as their owner decides to pay their Web hosting bill.

*Security in Cyberspace,* Hearings Before the Permanent Subcommittee on Investigations of the Committee on Government Affairs – United States Senate, 104th Congress, 2nd Session, May 22, June 5, 25, and July 16, 199 (S. Hrg. 104-701) (ISBN 0-16-053913-7). My copy of this little report is worn out from extensive flipping. I'm not sure how easy it is to obtain, so I included the ISBN number. The accounts of the Rome Labs hack are useful.

*2600, The Hacker Quarterly,* Volumes 1 through 14, 2600 Enterprises Inc., 7 Strong's Lane, Setauket, NY 11733. (available at http:// www.2600.com). This may be the clearest, best-written technical journal I've ever seen. By way of contrast, stuffy security conference proceedings are often filled with papers that are intended to promote the author's scholarship more than anything else. You'll never see this sort of thing in 2600 Magazine. I am happy to admit that I've learned more from this journal about hacking than from any other publication I've ever seen. I think I have pretty close to a complete set.

*Proceedings of the First Invitational Workshop, Research and Development for Infrastructure Assurance/Information Warfare-Defend,* Jointly sponsored by the Defense Advanced Research Projects Agency (DARPA), Defense Information Systems Agency (DISA), and the National Security Agency (NSA), organized by Institute for Defense Analysis, Alexandria, Virginia, 20-21 March, 1997. This summary report outlines discussions held between government and industry on the topic of intrusion detection for infrastructure protection. I was there and it was a fine conference.

[AL95] J. Alves-Foss, "An Overview of SNIF: A Tool for Surveying Network Information Flow," *Proceedings of the Symposium on Network and Distributed System Security,* San Diego, California, February 16-17, 1995. SNIF is a research tool with some useful network-based probing and processing ideas. The paper is reasonable easy to get through; I suggested it to a group of AT&T network administrators in Europe and a couple of them commented that they thought this looked like an interesting tool. I'm not familiar with its current status.

Edward Amoroso, *Fundamentals of Computer Security Technology*, Prentice-Hall, 1994. This was my first book. I only mention it in this bibliography because Chapter 17 provides a technical overview of audit-based intrusion detection circa 1994 (ancient by today's standards).

Debra Anderson, Teresa Lunt, Harold Javitz, Ann Tamaru, and Alfonso Valdes, *Safeguard Final Report: Detecting Unusual Behavior Using the NIDES Statistical Component*, Technical Report, Computer Science Laboratory, SRI International, Menlo Park, California, SRI Project 2596, Contract No. 910097C under F30602-91-C-0067, Prepared for Trusted Information Systems, December 2, 1993. This group of people, now largely dispersed, is like an all-star team of statistical analysis for intrusion detection. Their lengthy report describes a statistical approach to intrusion processing that includes a novel half-life technique. I found it pretty hard to read; in fact, I needed my old statistics text book to help me get through some of the basics (I will admit to having hating statistics in graduate school).

[AN97] Anonymous, *Maximum Security: A Hacker's Guide to Protecting Your Internet Site and Network*, Sams Net, 1997. The author claims to be a reformed hacker and wishes to maintain an anonymous identity. This is an excellent book with lots of original information on many practical aspects of hacking that are relevant to intrusion detection; the chapter on techniques for anonymity is particularly useful to the intrusion detection system designer. I recently taught a security course to some internal AT&T engineers and this is the book I suggested as the text for the course. Go get yourself one if you are interested in intrusion detection or any other aspect of Internet security. It's one of the few books floating around where the author actually is saying something that is not a rehash of what everyone else is saying.

[BA97] Michael Banks, *Web Psychos, Stalkers, and Pranksters*, Coriolis Group Books, 1997. This is an odd, but interesting book with some useful stuff. Because of the provocative title, I remember looking over my shoulder at the bookstore as I purchased my copy of this book.

Robert Barnard, *Intrusion Detection Systems*, Second Edition, Butterworth-Heinemann, 1988 (ISBN 0-7506-9427-0). This is a very cool book about physical intrusion detection using physical alarms, television surveillance cameras, and interior/exterior sensors. I am astounded at how similar the methodological concerns are for non-computing intrusion detection. Barnard's book should be required reading for those of us trying to do the same thing for Internet-based environments.

[CZ96] Brent Chapman and Elizabeth Zwicky, *Building Internet Firewalls*, O'Reilly Press, 1996. The technologies associated with intrusion detection and firewalls are blurred somewhat. I think this book offers the most accurate glimpse into the plumbing of a firewall and is therefore required reading for serious students of intrusion detection.

David Chaum, A New Paradigm for Individuals in the Information Age, *Proceedings of the IEEE Symposium on Security and Privacy*, Oakland, California, 1984. Intrusion detection researchers are obliged to consider emerging cryptographic protocols for electronic commerce as they provide fundamental barriers to what can be monitored and interpreted. Chaum's work is among the best. One of my favorite things to do is get someone in my office and sketch through Chaum's blinding protocol. People are astounded at how beautiful an idea it really is—and what a headache it can cause for law enforcement.

David Chaum, Interview in Internet Computing, "How Much Do You Trust Big Brother?", *IEEE Internet Computing*, Volume 1, Number 6, November/December, 1997. Chaum offers insights into monitoring, personal privacy, and electronic commerce. I honestly didn't think it was a very good interview, but you might find it useful.

Steven Cheung, Karl Levitt, and Calvin Ko, "Intrusion Detection for Network Infrastructures," *Proceedings of the IEEE Symposium on Security and Privacy*, Oakland, California, May, 1995. These guys are very smart and I thought this paper was pretty good. Karl Levitt, in particular, is one of the steady contributors to computer and network security over the past couple of decades. I don't think he gets enough credit for the fine work he does. I try to read anything he publishes.

[CB94] William Cheswick and Steven Bellovin, *Firewalls and Internet Security*, Addison-Wesley, 1994. This book remains a classic in the field of firewalls and intrusion detection techniques. It is one of my all-time favorite books.

Franklin Clark and Ken Dilberto, *Investigating Computer Crime*, CRC Press, 1996. This book provides practical information related to incident response with law enforcement involvement. It attempts to tell you how to seize equipment in a hacker's bedroom and other stuff like that. The pictures of computer equipment look pretty ancient and some of the discussions will have you rolling your eyes. But I don't know of anything better and this is an important topic. Is anyone interested in writing a more modern version out there?

[CO95] Doug Comer, *Internetworking with TCP/IP: Volume 1 Principles, Protocols, and Architecture*, Prentice-Hall, 1995, Third Edition. If there is a de-facto standard text on TCP/IP, this would be the one.

[CI98] *Common Intrusion Detection Framework*, University of California at Davis, available at http://seclab.cs.ucdavis.edu/cidf/. The CIDF may be the most important academic contribution to intrusion detection in many years. Unfortunately, intrusion detection vendors are currently ignoring it. As a buyer of intrusion detection technology, you will find probably yourself with mixed feelings about the CIDF ("Great idea, but how does it help me now?").

Fred Cohen, "50 Ways to Defeat Your Intrusion Detection System," available at all.net/journal/netsec/9712.html. Fred Cohen always seems to have something interesting to say and this article is no exception. He raises some excellent and entertaining points. I hung this paper over the copy machine for a couple of weeks until someone stole it. I hope whoever stole it, read it carefully.

Neil Cumming, *Security: A Guide to Security System Design and Equipment Selection and Installation*, Butterworth-Heinnemann, 1992 (ISBN 0-7506-9624-9). Here's another book on physical surveillance systems, and it's pretty good. Too many computer and network security analysts turn their noses up at facility and physical security techniques, not realizing how interesting this topic can be.

Jeffrey B. Davis, "Detecting System Intruders," *Sys Admin*, pp. 54-58, December, 1996. Some useful audit processing techniques are described in this brief note. By the way, if you are a UNIX system administrator and you've never seen this magazine, then you're in for a treat. It is filled every month with useful tips written by people who work as system administrators and who would probably never dream of publishing anywhere else. I buy it at Barnes and Noble every month.

[DE86] Dorothy Denning, "An Intrusion-Detection Model," *Proceedings of the IEEE Symposium on Security and Privacy*, Oakland, California, May, 1986. This landmark paper described the foundations of profile-based intrusion processing on a computer system. You might make the case that Dorothy Denning is the most significant researcher in the computer and network security arena *ever*. I will admit to being somewhat in awe whenever I'm around her. She and I testified before the Social Security Administration commissioner recently and I found myself impressed (as usual) by her clarity of thought and ability to make technical issues accessible. If you ever get the chance to see her speak, I suggest you do it.

Peter Denning (editor), *Computers Under Attack: Intruders, Worms, and Viruses*, Addison Wesley, 1990. Although this is somewhat dated, the papers included are classics.

Peter Denning and Dorothy Denning (editors), *Internet Beseiged: Countering Cyberspace Scofflaws*, Addison-Wesley, 1998. Another compendium of Internet security papers.

Whitfield Diffie and Susan Landau, *Privacy on the Line: The Politics of Wiretapping and Encryption*, MIT Press, 1998 (ISBN 0-262-04167-7). Wow. This is an amazing book. It's hard to believe that someone could invent public key cryptography (with some help from Martin Hellman) and write such a literate book (with credit to Landau of course). Most of the information in this book is pretty original stuff. I thought the sections on law enforcement were clear and well-argued. Based on their obvious position on the privacy versus surveillance issue, I have a feeling that they might not care much for intrusion detection technology.

Cheri Dowell and Paul Ramstedt, "The ComputerWatch Data Reduction Tool," *Proceedings of the 13th National Computer Security Conference*, Baltimore, Maryland, 1990. ComputerWatch was an early audit trail analysis tool for the UNIX System V/MLS product. It was a nice piece of work done by Bill Leighton (now a rising executive in AT&T), Paul Ramstedt (one of the technical leads in my group doing intrusion detection), Cheri Dowell (now at Sun Microsystems), and several others who are now either in AT&T Labs or Lucent.

Mansour Esmail, et al., "Evidential Reasoning in Network Intrusion Detection Systems," in *Information Security and Privacy*, Springer-Verlag, First Australian Conference, ACISP '96, Wollongong, Australia, June, 1996. AI-based reasoning is applied to the intrusion detection problem here; the mathematics are challenging. I found the paper while browsing in the AT&T Labs library recently. By the way, I *really* hope that casual, manual browsing in a quiet, *real* library with non-electronic books does not go the way of the eight-track player, drive-in theater, and house-calling doctor. I love the Internet, but I hope we don't get too carried away and destroy our book sanctuaries.

[FE97] Edward Felton, Dirk Balfanz, Drew Dean, and Dan Wallach, "Web Spoofing: An Internet Con Game," *Proceedings of the 20th National Information Systems Security Conference*, October 7-10, 1997, Baltimore, Maryland. I was excited when I read this because it struck me as a clever way to climb inside a browsing session. I've had three graduate students look at this technique closely and we've come to the conclusion that the method will work under the right set of circumstances.

[FO96] Stephanie Forest, Steven Hofmeyr, Anil Somayaji, and Thomas Longstaff, "A Sense of Self for Unix Processes," *Proceedings of the 1996 IEEE Symposium on Security and Privacy*, Oakland, CA, May6-8, 1996. Their anomaly approach focuses on the system call level in Unix processing. This is demonstrated for sendmail and lpr. I look forward to more examples.

David Freedman and Charles Mann, *At Large*, Simon and Schuster, 1997. I could not put this book down once I started reading; it is an astounding account of a hacker who managed to gain access to Internet backbone routers and other interesting things. This is a required text for my graduate intrusion detection workshop at the Stevens Institute. (An excerpt of the book was published in the June 2, 1997 issue of US News and World Report.)

[GS96] Simson Garfinkel and Gene Spafford, *Practical Unix and Internet Security*, O'Reilly and Associates, Second Edition, 1996. If you only buy one book on Unix security, I think this would be a good choice. The second edition adds quite a bit on Internet security and the result is an important technical reference that I find myself using more and more.

Ulf Gustafson, et al., "On the Modeling of Preventive Security Based on a PC Network Intrusion Experiment," in *Information Security and Privacy*, Springer-Verlag, First Australian Conference, ACISP '96, Wollongong, Australia, June, 1996. A simple PC-based intrusion experiment is described in this paper. It seemed pretty interesting.

Katie Hafner and John Markoff, *Cyberpunk: Outlaws and Hackers on the Computer Frontier*, Touchstone Books, 1991. This book chronicles the exploits of three prominent hackers at the time: Kevin Mitnick, Robert Morris Jr., and the West Berliner Pengo. The book is several years old, but remains an excellent source of information on hacking.

Chris Hare, "Monitoring Login Activity," *Sys Admin*, Volume 2, Number 5, September/October, 1993. Simple login activity monitoring is explained in readable terms. You should get this paper and read it.

L. Todd Heberlein and Matt Bishop, "Attack Class: Address Spoofing," *Proceedings of the 19th National Information Systems Security Conference*, Baltimore, Maryland, October, 1996. These researchers from UC Davis describe the address spoofing technique in some detail; this is an example of the type of attack characterization that is required for certain profile definitions. As a general rule, if either of these two researchers publish anything related to network security or intrusion detection, then it will probably be good.

Michael Hill, "Understanding syslog.conf," *Sys Admin*, Volume 5, Number 12, December, 1996. This is description of *syslog* that should probably be looked at by all UNIX administrators. It is not easy reading, however, and the author spends too much time in the article discussing a tool that may not be of much use.

[HO97] John Howard, "An Analysis of Security Incidents on the Internet 1989-1995", Ph.D. thesis, Carnegie-Mellon University, Pittsburgh, Pa, 1997 (available at http://www.infowar.com/.) This thesis has more charts and graphs than any one I've ever looked at. Some interesting and provocative results are in there as well.

[HU95] Larry Hughes, *Actually Useful Internet Security Techniques*, New Riders Press, 1995. I think the title of this book is accurate. When I first looked at it, I thought I was pretty much like many other books. Then I found myself constantly referring to it and I realized that there was some substance in the book. I recommend it for Internet security enthusiasts.

William Hunteman, "Automated Information System (AIS) Alarm System," *Proceedings of the National Information System Security Conference*, Baltimore, Md., 1997. This paper provides an overview of work on-going at Los Alamos Lawrence Livermore, and Sandia in the area of electronic alarm systems for networks.

[HU97] Jill Huntington-Lee, Kornel Terplan, and Jeff Gibson, *HP Open View*, Mc-Graw-Hill, 1997. This is a readable text on an important tool for intrusion detection researchers. The discussions extend beyond HP Open View into more general concepts in network management in an SNMP and RMON environment.

Mario Ibanez, "A Comparison of Firewalls and Intrusion Detection Systems," *SysAdmin*, Volume 6, Number 12, December, 1997. I had some graduate students working on this topic with the intention of writing a paper when Ibanez' short note came out.

The Stevens group was astounded at how close his approach was to theirs. I suggest that you take a peek at this paper as it is useful for Intranet firewall managers.

R. Jagannathan, Teresa Lunt, Fred Gilham, Ann Tamaru, Caveh Jalali, Peter Neumann, Debra Anderson, T. Garvey, and J. Lowrance, *Requirements Specification: Next Generation Intrusion Detection Expert System (NIDES),* Technical report, Computer Science Laboratory, SRI International, Menlo Park, California, September, 1992. This reference and the next several provide more intrusion detection information from SRI currents and alumni.

R. Jagannathan, Ann Tamaru, Fred Gilham, Debra Anderson, Caveh Jalali, C. Dodd, Harold Javitz, Alfonso Valdes, Teresa Lunt, and Peter Neumann, *Next Generation Intrusion Detection Expert System (NIDES) Software Design Specifications,* Technical Report, Computer Science Laboratory, SRI International, Menlo Park, California, March, 1993.

Harold Javitz and Alfonso Valdes, "The SRI Statistical Anomaly Detector," *Proceedings of the IEEE Symposium on Research in Security and Privacy*, Oakland, California, May, 1991.

Harold Javitz and Alfonso Valdes, *The NIDES Statistical Component Description and Justification*, Technical Report, Computer Science Laboratory, SRI International, Menlo Park, California, SRI Project 3131, under Contract No. N00039-92-C-0015, Prepared for Department of the Navy, March 7, 1994.

Harold Javitz, Alfonso Valdes, Teresa Lunt, Ann Tamaru, M. Tyson, and J. Lowrance, *Next Generation Intrusion Detection Expert System (NIDES): Statistical Algorithms Rationale and Rationale for the Proposed Resolver,* Technical report, Computer Science Laboratory, SRI International, Menlo Park, California, March, 1993.

Calvin Ko, Manfred Ruschitzka, and Karl Levitt, "Execution Monitoring of Security-Critical Programs in Distributed Systems: A Specification-based Approach," *Proceedings of the IEEE Symposium on Security and Privacy*, Oakland, California, May, 1997. This paper introduces a specification-based approach to defining profiles for audit trail comparison. I've looked around for others working in this area of specification-based approaches and haven't had much luck. I've been examining techniques for writing egrep-type regular expressions using terminals that are things like IP addresses. Marcus Ranum's N programming language is sort of like this. If anyone knows of work being done in this area, will you please drop me a short pointer at eamoroso@mail.att.net so that I can share the work with others.

[KH97] Andrew Kosoresow and Steven Hormeyr, "Intrusion Detection via System Call Traces," *IEEE Software*, September/October, 1997. This paper describes an interested technique for defining contextual windows of system call patterns and measuring degrees to which these patterns are met in services such as *sendmail.* I consider this work and related research at University of New Mexico to be a major advance in pattern-based detection of hacking. For some reason, there is little mention of this work among researcher in intrusion detection and I think this is a mistake.

Linda Lankewicz and Mark Benard, "Real-Time Anomaly Detection Using a Nonparametric Pattern Recognition Approach," *Proceedings of the Seventh Annual Computer Security Applications Conference*, San Antonio, Texas, December, 1991. A unique approach to detecting anomalies is presented here; the research involves trying to reduce the volume of data about target system behavior by creating patterns and matching them with intrusion detection profiles.

Jonathan Littman, *The Fugitive Game: Online with Kevin Mitnick*, Little, Brown, 1997. While Mitnick was on the run from the Feds, he was confiding in Littman via cell phone. The result is an amazing story.

[LL96] Lawrence Livermore National Laboratory, National Infosec Technical Baseline, *Intrusion Detection and Response*, October, 1996. (Available at http://doe-is.llnl.gov/nitb/docs/nitb.html). This is an excellent survey of intrusion detection technology as of late 1996. Ike Cole of AT&T (formerly and proudly of the US Navy) turned me onto this article and it's worth reading.

Lawrence Livermore National Laboratory, *Report of the Hacker Attack Working Group,* August, 1994 (available at http://www.llnl.gov/ cso/hacker.html). This is a useful technical report on hacker attack methods.

G. Liepins and H. Vaccaro, "Anomaly Detection: Purpose and Framework," *Proceedings of the 12th National Computer Security Conference*, Baltimore, Md., October, 1989. This paper introduces a Department of Energy system called Wisdom and Sense (W&S) that is used to explain their approach to anomaly detection.

G. Liepins, P. Helman, and W. Richards, "Foundations of Intrusion Detection," *Proceedings of the IEEE Symposium on Security and Privacy*, Oakland, California, May, 1992. This is one of the earlier papers on intrusion detection and it has some useful ideas.

T.Y. Lin, "Anomaly Detection – A Soft Computing Approach," *Proceedings of the New Security Paradigms Workshop*, Little Compton, Rhode Island, pg 44-53, August 3-5, 1994. This paper explores the use of fuzzy set theory to model patterns of user behavior.

Jonathan Littman, *The Watchman: The Twisted Life and Crimes of Serial Hacker Kevin Poulsen*, Little, Brown and Co., 1997. Littman writes a wonderful book here that captures the criminal element in the hacking game in a direct manner. I would say that of all the "hacker writers," Littman is my favorite. He's caused me more than any other writers of his genre to sit up late on many, many nights reading his books when I should be getting some shut eye.

Jonathan Littman, *The Fugitive Game: On-Line with Kevin Mitnick*, Little, Brown and Co., 1996. Littman's description of life on the run for Kevin Mitnick provides intrusion detection professionals with deep insight into the thoughts and mind of a complex person.

[LJ97] Ulf Lundqvist and Erland Jonsson, "How to Systematically Classify Intrusions," *Proceedings of the IEEE Symposium on Security and Privacy*, Oakland, California, 1997. This paper describes a taxonomy approach for attacks that should be useful for intrusion detection knowledge bases.

[LU88] Teresa Lunt, "Automated Audit Trail Analysis and Intrusion Detection," *Proceedings of the 11th National Computer Security Conference*, October, 1988. This is a description of an early audit trail analysis system by one of the best-known researchers in this area. She has provided an endless stream of important contributions to intrusion detection over the past of decade or so. She is currently working at DARPA.

[LU89] Teresa Lunt, "Real-Time Intrusion Detection," *Proceedings of COMPCON Spring '89,* March, 1989. Another readable discussion of an intrusion detection system real time capability.

Teresa Lunt and R. Jagannathan, "A Prototype Real-Time Intrusion Detection System," *Proceedings of the 1988 IEEE Symposium on Security and Privacy*, Oakland, California, April, 1988. More on the SRI prototype intrusion detection system circa-late 1980's.

Teresa Lunt, Ann Tamaru, Fred Gilham, R. Jagannathan, Caveh Jalali, Harold Javitz, Alfonso Valdes, Peter Neumann, and T. Garvey, *A Real-Time Intrusion Detection Expert*

*System (IDES),* Final technical report, Computer Science Laboratory, SRI International, Menlo Park, California, February, 1992. This report may be difficult to get as it is not in any general publication.

Belden Menkus, "How an Audit Trail Aids in Maintaining Information Integrity . . . As Illustrated in Retailing," *Computers and Security,* Volume 9, Number 2, April 1990. This paper discusses issues related to missing audit trails, audit trail structure, and audit trail content.

N. MacAuliffe, et al., "Is Your Computer Being Misused? A Survey of Current Intrusion Detection System Technology," *Proceedings of the Sixth Annual Computer Security Applications Conference,* 1990. This is a dated survey, although it does highlight some of the areas in which the technology has not properly advanced in commercial products (e.g., audit trail processing). Someone should do something like this for more modern products.

Abdelaziz Mounji and Baudouin Le Charlier, "Continuous Assessment of a Unix Configuration: Integrating Intrusion Detection and Configuration Analysis," *Proceedings of the Internet Society Symposium on Network and Distributed System Security,* San Diego, California, February 10-11, 1997, pp. 27-35. This paper explores the integration of intrusion detection with configuration analysis in the context of the ASAX research system. I found it hard to read (but that may be more a measure of my limited capacity than anything related to the paper).

[NC87] National Computer Security Center, "A Guide to Understanding Audit in Trusted Systems," NCSC-TG-001, July 28, 1987. This document interprets the Orange Book audit requirements and offers implementation suggestions. Even though it was prepared during the pre-Internet days, it remains helpful.

Peter Neumann, *Computer-Related Risks* (Addison-Wesley, 1995). In computing and network security, like most other disciplines, we have our great contributors. Peter Neumann is probably at the top of the list. This book is a gem—it's filled with incident related information of great use for intrusion detection.

Chris O'Malley, "Information Warriors of the 609th," in *Popular Science Magazine,* pp. 71 – 74, July, 1997. The Air Force Information Warfare Squadron is described in this easy-to-read article with a cool title. Information warfare is becoming a mainstream topic. Pretty soon there will probably be a television show on this, and maybe a video game ("Hacker Warrior Commandos!!!)

[PN97] Philip Porras and Peter Neumann, EMERALD, *Proceedings of the National Information Systems Security Conference,* Baltimore, MD, 1997. This paper provides a thorough and readable overview of the important EMERALD system from SRI International.

[PN98] Thomas Ptacek and Timothy Newsham, "Insertion, Evasion, and Denial of Service: Eluding Network Intrusion Detection," paper available on the Web at http://www.securenetworks.com/papers/ids.html. This provocative article is important reading for anyone interested in intrusion detection .

Nicholas Puketza, Mandy Chung, Ronald Olsson, and Biswanath Mukherjee, "A Software Platform for Testing Intrusion Detection Systems," *IEEE Software,* September/October, 1997. This group from UC Davis describes an excellent platform for playing attacks on a safe test bed for intrusion analysis. This is not a trivial task; I've been involved in many test bed design efforts and the problem of simulating inbound and outbound traffic for staging and test is tough.

[RA97] Marcus Ranum, Kent Landfield, Mike Stolarchuk, Mark Sienkiewicz, Andrew Lambeth, and Eric Wall, "Implementing a General Tool for Network Monitoring," paper available at http://www.nfr.net/ publications/LISA-97.htm. If you are interested in NFR, then this is certainly something you should download from the Internet and read carefully.

Winn Schwartau, *Information Warfare*, Thunder's Mouth Press, 1996 (Second Edition). The new edition adds great material. Don't be frightened by the thickness of this book. Most of it is reference material and sources.

Tsutomu Shimomura, with John Markoff, *Takedown: The Pursuit and Capture of Kevin Mitnick, America's Most Wanted Computer Outlaw – By the Man Who Did It*, Hyperion, 1996. (How's that for a subtitle on a book?) If you are into intrusion detection, I can't imagine how you could not spend some time with this book. I guarantee it will cause you to think.

B.C. Soh and T.S. Dillon, "System Intrusion Processes: A Simulation Model," *Computers and Security*, Volume 16, Number 1, 1997. This paper introduces an attack model and uses it as the basis for some simulations and analysis.

Stuart Staniford-Chen, *Distributed Tracing of Intruders*, M.S. Thesis, University of California at Davis, 1995. This M.S. Thesis is better than most Ph.D. theses. I found the work to be very helpful in my own understanding of the general session thumbprinting concept. I had the privilege of sitting with Staniford-Chen at a recent conference in Texas and I found him to be quite knowledgeable and intelligent. The CIDF, which he helps lead, will someday be considered one of the great research efforts in intrusion detection.

[ST96] Stuart Staniford-Chen, Steven Cheung, R. Crawford, M. Diger, J, Frank, J. Hoagland, Karl Levitt, C. Wee, R. Yip, and D. Zerkle, "GrIDS – A Graph-Based Intrusion Detection System for Large Networks," *Proceedings of the National Information Systems Security Conference*, Baltimore, Maryland, October 22-25, 1996. GrIDS is a system developed at UC Davis that constructs activity graphs for intrusion analysis.

[SH95] Stuart Staniford-Chen and L. Todd Heberlein, "Holding Intruders Accountable on the Internet," *Proceedings of the 1995 IEEE Symposium on Security and Privacy*, Oakland, CA, May 8-10, 1995. This paper introduces the technique known as thumbprinting to detect anomalous activity on an Internet.

[ST87] Clifford Stoll, "What Do You Feed a Trojan Horse?", *Proceedings of the National Computer Security Conference*, Baltimore Md., 1987. This paper is somewhat dry compared with Stoll's personality and other writings. But it has some pragmatic response-related information.

Clifford Stoll, *The Cuckoo's Egg*, Doubleday, 1989. A classic book on catching a hacker written in an entertaining manner.

[SU97] Lee Sutterfield, "Large Scale Intrusion Detection," *Computer Security Journal*, Volume XIII, Number 2, Fall, 1997. Lee is one of the founders of the former WheelGroup (now they are part of Cisco) and his article summarizes some interesting views on intrusion detection infrastructure and processing. I had dinner with Sutterfield and his Cisco colleagues in San Antonio recently and I came to the conclusion that Cisco made a wise choice in purchasing this group.

Paul Syverson, et al. Anonymous Connections and Onion Routing, *Proceedings of the IEEE Symposium on Security and Privacy*, Oakland, California, 1997. This is one of the papers I make my graduate students read in my intrusion detection seminar. I think anonymity is central to intrusion detection avoidance and this paper offers a reasonable means for gateway hiding of identity (as an alternative to firewall-based means).

John Vacca, *Intranet Security*, Charles River Media, 1997. This book has some useful material including a description of some log watching tools for Intranet managers.

WheelGroup Corporation, *NetRanger Mangement System Training Manual*, Version 1.0, April, 1997. The WheelGroup (now Cisco) used to use this document for their proprietary training. It can only be obtained directly from the company. I can personally vouch for the usefulness and quality of their hands-on training course. Their more recent documentation is on CD-ROM and I have a copy on my desk in the office. It looks pretty good.

Bruce Alan Wynn, "Automating Basic System Activity Monitoring," *Sys Admin*, Volume 6, Number 2, February, 1997. Much of the intrusion detection process is consistent with normal network monitoring techniques; this note introduces some useful ideas that are very close to intrusion detection technology.

# Index

## *Order Form*

- Fax Orders: (973) 448 – 1868
- Telephone Orders: (973) 448 – 1866; Have your VISA or Master Card ready
- Internet Orders: http://www.intrusion.net/
- Postal Orders: Intrusion.Net Books, P.O. Box 78, Sparta, New Jersey 07871

☐ Please Send Me _____ Copies of *Intrusion Detection* at $49.95

| | |
|---|---|
| Name | |
| Address | |
| City | |
| State | |
| Zip | |
| Phone | |
| Fax | |
| Email | |

Sales Tax: Please add 6% for books shipped to New Jersey addresses

Shipping: Please add $4.00 for the first book; $2.00 for each additional book

Payment:
☐ Check
☐ Credit Card: ___ VISA ___ Master Card
Card Number: _____
Expiration Date: _____
Name on Card: _____

# *Order Form*

- Fax Orders: (973) 448 – 1868
- Telephone Orders: (973) 448 – 1866; Have your VISA or Master Card ready
- Internet Orders: http://www.intrusion.net/
- Postal Orders: Intrusion.Net Books, P.O. Box 78, Sparta, New Jersey 07871

☐ Please Send Me _____ Copies of *Intrusion Detection* at $49.95

| Name | |
|---|---|
| Address | |
| City | |
| State | |
| Zip | |
| Phone | |
| Fax | |
| Email | |

Sales Tax: Please add 6% for books shipped to New Jersey addresses

Shipping: Please add $4.00 for the first book; $2.00 for each additional book

Payment:
☐ Check
☐ Credit Card: ___ VISA ___ Master Card
Card Number: _____
Expiration Date: _____
Name on Card: _____

# *Order Form*

- Fax Orders: (973) 448 – 1868
- Telephone Orders: (973) 448 – 1866; Have your VISA or Master Card ready
- Internet Orders: http://www.intrusion.net/
- Postal Orders: Intrusion.Net Books, P.O. Box 78, Sparta, New Jersey 07871

☐  Please Send Me _____ Copies of **Intrusion Detection** at $49.95

| Name | |
|---|---|
| Address | |
| City | |
| State | |
| Zip | |
| Phone | |
| Fax | |
| Email | |

Sales Tax: Please add 6% for books shipped to New Jersey addresses

Shipping: Please add $4.00 for the first book; $2.00 for each additional book

Payment:
☐  Check
☐  Credit Card: ___ VISA    ___ Master Card
Card Number: _____
Expiration Date: _____
Name on Card: _____